Praise for Tik Maynard and His Second Book
Starting in the Middle

"This lovely book about starting horses on their journey to realize their potential is also about us and our journey to become our better self. It's about facing our fears. Taking risks. Trying something new. Following our curiosity. And, of course, never giving up."

Art Davidson
Author of the Mountaineering Classic
Minus 148º: First Winter Ascent of Mt. McKinley

"Ever since I met Tik Maynard, his quest to learn has always been amazing to watch. He seeks advice from those he trusts and is completely open to trying any tips you might have for him. He fully engages with the suggestion or technique and gives it a completely honest try, ready to absorb anything the lesson may have to offer. I'm always impressed and inspired at his willingness to try to find better ways."

Glenn Stewart
The Glenn Stewart Horsemanship Academy

Praise for Tik Maynard and His First Book
In the Middle Are the Horsemen

"In 1989 when I was 54 years old I started a Thoroughbred filly for the Queen of England. Upon Her Majesty's insistence that I write a book, I set out to write my autobiography, *The Man Who Listens to Horses*. Tik Maynard's book, like mine, is the tale of a young man committed to understanding horses and life. It is a fantastically written adventure story for horse fanatics and adventure lovers alike.

"My generation began a revolution in horsemanship, and it is Tik's that will continue it. For that I am grateful. A must read."

Monty Roberts
Horseman and *New York Times* Bestselling Author

"It's a shame you have to use the word 'natural' in front of 'horsemanship.' It should all be natural, the way you interact with a horse, the way you converse, teach, and perform together in this incredible partnership. In my day, they called it, 'It' and it was a kind of secret society because people were ridiculed for taking the time to understand the way horses think and learn, rather than just showing the horse who's boss. Today, it is becoming more the way, to train horses using love, language, and leadership; using psychology rather than mechanics no matter what your discipline, from recreational to performance.

"This is not horsemanship versus eventing; it is about laying a proper foundation before specialization. To see Tik Maynard bridging these two worlds in his quest to become a real horseman will inspire generations to come and contribute to making a better world for horses and the people who love them."

Pat Parelli
Bestselling Author, Founder of
Parelli Natural Horsemanship®

"Both a fascinating record of a young man's quest to find his place, and a vivid portrait of an industry and a culture built upon on one of our most ancient and transformative relationships, that between the human and the horse. Acutely observed, vividly told, and not to be missed."

Kathy Page
Author of *Alphabet* and
Paradise & Elsewhere

"People have a hard time being aware. Awareness of their environment, of other people, of what effects their actions have on others, animal or human. Self-awareness is even more rare. This is a book about self-awareness. How does one learn? How does one process the world? Observation is a necessity to be successful in an animal world. How one processes one's own observations is a key to being successful as a human being. Tik Maynard has opened up and shown his ability to be self-aware and observational. This is an insightful book about the journey to acquire knowledge and then use that knowledge to help others, human and horse. It's a joy to read."

David O'Connor
Fédération Équestre Internationale (FEI) Eventing Chair,
Former Chef d'Equipe US Eventing Team, Former President United
States Equestrian Federation (USEF), Olympic Gold Medalist

"Tik Maynard is not only a fantastic writer but a special horseman. His ability to work naturally through a horse's problems and to communicate what he does in a way people can understand is a gift. He has a never-ending want for knowledge about horses, and I hope he continues to share his experiences."

Lauren Bliss Kieffer
US Olympian

"Tik Maynard's writing is engaging and insightful. With each turn of the page I felt like I was right there, rooting with him through the triumphs and challenges of his horsemanship adventure. Loved the gems that came from his experiences and the honesty he shares. Anyone who loves horses and is passionate about becoming better with them will love this book!"

Jonathan Field
Horseman, Author of *The Art of*
Liberty Training for Horses

"About five years ago, I met Tik Maynard for the first time when he attended a clinic I was giving in Maryland. I immediately observed: Tik is a special person who has an equally good understanding for both people and horses. Tik can put himself in his partner's place and listens closely to the horse that has offered Tik his trust.

"Tik possesses the knowledge of both classical riding and natural horsemanship that is necessary to bring them together. Bringing together these two complementary approaches has helped him become a true horseman. He has traveled a rough road. But he never gave up. Over time, he was able to convert every discouragement, every rejection, into something positive. He's tried to learn as much as he can from each of his trainers. That still applies to Tik today and is the basis for this exciting book.

"What can the reader gain from this book? You should never give up and always keep your specific goal in sight—and you must do that in the face of all the adversities that a rider must overcome in the course of his education. In this regard, Tik is a role model for all of his readers."

Christoph Hess
FEI Dressage and Eventing Judge and
Ambassador for Training and Education of the
German National Equestrian Federation (FN)

"As with horses and life, actions speak much louder and mean more than words. I think this statement is true for horses and people: Horses don't care how much you know until they know how much you care. Tik Maynard should be proud to count himself as one of those people. I am happy and humbled to have played a small part in his horsemanship and life's journey."

Bruce Logan
Clinician and Horse Specialist

"Tik Maynard arrived at my barn like an energetic young dressage prospect—with plenty of cadence in his step and a joy that filled the arena. I knew this was going to be fun! With his unparalleled desire to learn everything he possibly could I was hooked. Here was a student who was going to push me, and together we could both become better—student and teacher—understanding our horses more deeply and sharing thoughts and experiences in our blessed lives with our horses. This is who Tik is: engaging, inquisitive, intelligent, and compassionate about his horses and the work he does with them. It takes a great student to become a great teacher, and Tik is both. It was a great joy and pleasure to share time with him."

Betsy Steiner
Dressage Trainer and Coach and Author of
A Gymnastic Riding System Using Mind, Body & Spirit

"Tik Maynard writes like a seasoned novelist but there is no mistaking the authenticity of his story. Whether you're crazy about horses or not, you'll enjoy this ride."

Rick Lamb
Co-Author of *A Revolution in Horsemanship*
and Author of *Human to Horseman*

STARTING
IN THE MIDDLE

Tik Maynard

Illustrations by Erik C. Schmidt

TRAFALGAR SQUARE

First published in 2025 by
Trafalgar Square Books
North Pomfret, Vermont 05053

Some names and identifying details may have been changed to protect the privacy of individuals.

Disclaimer of Liability
The author and publisher shall have neither liability nor responsibility to any person or entity with respect to any loss or damage caused or alleged to be caused directly or indirectly by the information contained in this book. While the book is as accurate as the author can make it, there may be errors, omissions, and inaccuracies.

Trafalgar Square Books encourages the use of approved safety helmets in all equestrian sports and activities.

Trafalgar Square Books certifies that the content in this book was generated by a human expert on the subject, and the content was edited, fact-checked, and proofread by human publishing specialists with a lifetime of equestrian knowledge. TSB does not publish books generated by artificial intelligence (AI).

ISBN: 9781646012480

Library of Congress Cataloging-in-Publication Data is available on file

Cover photograph by Haley Boothe-Zajac
Interior artwork by Erik Schmidt (OffshoreArtwork.com)
Book interior and cover design by RM Didier

Typeface: Minion Pro

Printed in the United States of America
10 9 8 7 6 5 4 3 2 1

Dedication

Sinead, this book is dedicated to you.

Kurt Vonnegut gave the advice, *Write to please just one person. If you open a window and make love to the world, so to speak, your story will get pneumonia.*

As I wrote this book, Brooks turned five, and then six. Violet turned one, and then two. I imagine them in ten years trying to sort their way through relationships and school and sports. Trying to find out what makes them *them.* So I wrote the book with our kids in mind. Not one person, like Kurt said—*two kids.* While this book is about starting horses, I hope it will also offer them guidance they can apply to whatever their passions are. At the very least, they will learn what dreams and adventures their old, old dad had. Something, I'm guessing, not enough kids learn. This book might give them a glimpse into how I see the world (mostly optimistic, sometimes melancholic); how I try to be stronger than I am weak; how I strive to be as authentic as our horses are; how difficult I find it to truly, quietly, listen; how much easier it is to be busy; and how in preparation for Road to the Horse I made a plan to listen to the advice of others, yet in the end return to my own counsel.

It is the greatest privilege of my life to be a part of this family. One day I will not be around anymore, Goldfish and Brooks, so remember, *I love you this much!*

1

I shuffled to the table that stood against the side wall and studied its contents: a pot of black coffee and a stack of white Styrofoam cups still in their plastic packaging; a cardboard box of snacks, including one apple, one orange, two premier protein drinks, one Kiwi Guava Celsius drink, two bags of chips (one classic, one sour cream and onion), five Starburst sweets, one cookie, and eight Jolly Ranchers.

I hadn't eaten yet and told myself I should, but when I reached for the apple, I felt like I was going to puke. Every cell in my body was preoccupied, devoted to something other than eating or digesting: fight or flight. Flight, mostly. This must be what a scared horse feels like, I thought.

Every few minutes we felt the rumble as the crowd above us cheered. We also heard the announcer, but not well enough to make out what he was saying.

I didn't think I would be able to urinate, but I needed to move, to get out of the room. I asked one of The Guards if I could use the facilities, and she escorted me there, then waited at the door. The other Guard stayed with Donal.

Back in the room I sat down, then stood up, then sat down again. I dug in my bag for the books I had brought with me: *The Prophet* by Kahlil Gibran and *Ready Player One* by Ernest Cline. I opened one, then closed it. I opened the other, read the same line three times, then closed it.

After another hour or so the door opened, and The Head appeared. The Head looked at Donal. Donal looked at The Head. The Head nodded. Donal took a breath as he left that I heard clear across the room.

"And then there was one…" The Guard at the back said, peering over her book.

Five minutes later, The Head brought Donal back into the room, having forgotten about a scheduled half-hour intermission.

"A reprieve…" The Guard muttered dramatically.

For thirty minutes Donal paced the room like a tiger in a cage. I stood up. I sat back down. I lay down. I stared at the ceiling. I opened a book again. I closed it again.

Finally, The Head returned for Donal. Donal left with his shoulders square.

"And then there was one…" The Guard said dryly, for the second time.

I was more nervous than I had ever been before.

It was more than nerves.

It was fear.

The fear wasn't just one fear. It was many fears.

I closed my eyes.

2

The first few sentences of a book are like the first few minutes in a round pen with a colt. None of the letters are new; it's how I rearrange them that matters. Partly it's about communication, but more so, it's about motivation—what matters to *him?* I have one chance to make a first impression. I either catch his attention, or I don't.

One of my favorite beginnings is a classic by Ayn Rand:

Who is John Galt?

Another is by Kurt Vonnegut:

Call me Jonah. My parents did, or nearly did. They called me John.

My mother's favorite is by Dick Francis:

Art Matthews shot himself, loudly and messily, in the centre of the parade ring at Dunstable races.

I can't walk by a bookstore without going in. I can't visit a house for a Christmas party without nosily checking out their bookshelves. *Hmmm…Malcolm Gladwell…Barbara Kingsolver…Elizabeth Gilbert…Haven't read that one…Nice!…My type of person.* I can't go to the airport without pausing at the rack of paperbacks. Stephen King, Danielle Steele, Lee Child, Mary Alice Malone…I'm drawn in like a rat to cheese. I crave reading them the way some people feel the urge to pet every dog they see at the park or make a face at every baby in the grocery store.

The first chapter of a book will tell you a lot. It's like a first date. Do they shake your hand? Hug you? Do they ask you questions? Do they look you in the eye? It's the same with horses.

I can't think of a horse that I've met that I didn't like. Each one is a character; each one is unique; quite a few of them are puzzles to be figured out. Are they curious, ready to sniff my hand? Are they bored, with a glazed-over look in their eyes? Are they nervous, flinching when I get close?

What are they telling me?

What's *their* first sentence? *Their* first chapter?

Reading a horse is a specialized skill, like reading a poker player. The difference between playing with cards and playing with horses is that with poker *you* will win or *you* will lose; with horses either you *both* win, or you *both* lose, no matter what you think.

Almost anybody can gain a rudimentary knowledge of Texas Hold 'Em in a few minutes. You might win big in the garage with neighbors on Friday night; you could even win a few hands at a casino. But that doesn't mean you are ready for The World Series of Poker.

I've never been much of a card player, and I have never had the urge to gamble in Vegas. But I do play with horses, and for years I have felt the urge to compete at what is known as "The World Championship of Colt Starting."

Colt "starting" was once called horse "breaking," often as in "break their spirit," sometimes as in "break your neck," but usually as just another word that people don't consider the history or implications of, like "uppity," or "Eskimo," or "avocado." Most folks I know now call it "starting." "Starting horses," as you can imagine, draws in a certain kind of person.

Starting a horse in any amount of time is serious business; starting one in only two hundred and sixty-five minutes, over three days, in front of five judges, thousands of spectators, and dozens of cameras, is a whole different beast. But that's exactly what the competitors do at Road to the Horse, "The World Championship of Colt Starting." The annual competition offers over a hundred thousand dollars in prize money. Fans travel to Kentucky to experience it in person or live stream it at home. It is a high-stakes event that marries entertainment with education, and I've watched it every year for the last decade.

Mostly I've watched it on my television at home, but in 2023, I traveled to the Kentucky Horse Park in Lexington to see it in person.

Seeing Road to the Horse live instead of on TV is like being in a kayak as whales breach the water next to you rather than watching a documentary about them. There is a perspective, and a nearness, and an *alive*ness that is difficult to convey. There is a thunder that you can feel in your stomach as water splashes you on the face, and you smell the salt in the air. There is an awe at the immense *life* and *energy* that no theater, big screen or small, can deliver.

Playing with horses, unlike watching a screen or playing cards, has a massive inherent physical danger to it. I've been kicked, bitten, and bucked off. I've been flipped over on. I've had a serious concussion. My wife Sinead has broken her ankle, her femur, two fingers, her hand (left), her humerus, her collarbone (the right one, twice), her shoulder blade, and six or seven ribs. Being hospitalized is not uncommon for a horse trainer. But the better my ability to read a horse, the better my ability to predict the future, and the safer I am. The more relaxed the horse, the better the relationship I have with him, the less chance I have of getting hurt.

But the danger never disappears completely.

One has to be invited to compete at Road to the Horse, and for over a decade, I had hoped they would choose me as a horse person worthy of the challenge. But after watching the event in person, I was troubled. If I were asked, if I were ever invited, would I be able to do a good job on that public stage?

After I returned home to Florida, I asked Sinead one afternoon what she thought of me entering Road to the Horse. She put down the saddle she was holding. She looked me deep in the eyes. I felt like she was going to offer the inspiration and support I needed.

The corner of her mouth rose as she asked, "Do you even know how to rope?"

"Nope." I laughed sadly. "No, I don't. But I want to do this. I really do."

3

Some men buy an Aston Martin or date younger women when confronted by their midlife crisis. What I did was I watched Road to the Horse 2023, then I entered it (accepted their invitation, to be accurate); then I took nine months to prepare.

When I began the project, in June 2023, my vision was clear: I planned to research all there was to know about the process of starting a horse, then compete in Road to the Horse using what I had learned, then sum it all up in nice little colt-starting-knowledge essays, like a platter of bite-size, delicious cupcakes. Then, I'd collect all these vignettes and arrange them in a book.

But months later, I felt I knew *less* than when I started.

When I began, I would have scored my understanding of starting horses at, maybe, a seven out of ten. The goal was that a year later, after having read dozens of books, interviewed famous people and talented people (not necessarily the same people), started ten or so horses, and competed at Road to the Horse, that I would be at an eight, or maybe an eight point five, or even nine, out of ten. And after achieving this Enlightened State of Zen-Like Colt Starting Mastery, I would write this cupcake-tray of a book.

Fortunately (or unfortunately, depending on your point of view), I am now able to judge the extent of my horse-starting knowledge

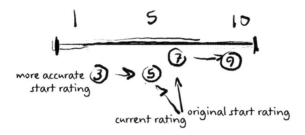

more accurately, and I realize that I probably started at a *three* out of ten, and that now, realistically, I am at more like a *five*.

So, as you can see, I've plummeted from my original starting-point self-rating of seven, to now, a year later, after all that time and work, a rating of five.

In other words, I've gotten worse.

I'm now concerned that each year as I study, I will come to understand that I continue to know less and less. Months and years will pass, and one day I will wake up and realize I'm at a zero. I will be starting horses, but I will know nothing at all.

Perhaps, in order to write a book like this one, it helps to be in that middle ground, somewhere between vanity and wisdom—a time where I feel like I have something to share, before I realize how little I know. I'm forty-two as I write this and there are more and more days I feel *old*. Old and tired. Old and sore. Old and weathered and worn.

There are also, still, many days I feel young! There are moments where I feel like I can accomplish anything! I'm motivated by running, reading, and playing with horses. I'm motivated by work. I *adore* working. My wife does too. We love what we do. My kids, Brooks and Violet, draw me into countless moments that make me feel as though time isn't a factor. Of course, they also offer me sleepless nights and a house that looks like we keep pet baboons— moments where I realize why there might be something to having kids in your twenties instead of in your thirties.

But my biggest motivator, my drug of choice, is *curiosity*. The vast amount to learn about horses stretches out in front of me, like a long winding road. That road is bumpy, twisty, fresh, *invigorating*. And that road stretches out much farther in front of me than behind me.

Dan James wore a crisp button-down shirt and designer jeans. His shirt was pink; his jeans were blue. A knife hung from his belt, and silver spurs jangled on his boots. He smiled in a boyish Tom-Cruise-*Risky-Business* kind of way.

Dan pivoted. His shoulders were back, and his movements were deft. He glanced into the stands. The crowd leaned in.

Fitted to Dan's skull was an obsidian black bespoke hat. It was custom made for Dan by JW Brooks, and even a city slicker would sense its authenticity. A hat from JW Brooks was the Western equivalent of a suit from Savile Row.

A hat like that, JW himself had earlier explained to my father (who was at Road to the Horse with me), cost about four times the price of my plane ticket.

"I'll have to ask my wife," my dad had said.

"There's no way she will say yes," I'd told him.

"I know," my dad had agreed glumly.

JW had then held out a card and said, "My phone number is on the back."

Now, in the arena below us, Dan, with his black hat, carried two white whips. One was a carriage whip, about eight feet long, and the other was a lunge whip, perhaps ten feet.

"G'day, guys. Good morning," Dan said in his Australian accent as a horse trotted around him. The horse's coat was the color of honey. His mane and tail, and the blaze on his face, were creamy white. "The little horse I have here, his name is Wilbur," Dan drawled. "This is his first appearance at an event anywhere. He is just a little three-year-old gelding."

I found a seat and sat down. My father, who had just turned eighty, sat next to me. He still sported a full head of wispy brown hair, which made me a little jealous, and he still rode five or six days a week.

My dad and I didn't see each other very often, as I had moved to the United States, but we still spoke weekly on the phone. We talked about horses…we talked about Vancouver, where he lived, and I had grown up…we talked about how we had both married amazing, strong women.

Dan stepped to his right; Wilbur the honey-colored horse looked at him, big-eyed. Then Dan leaned back, maybe half an inch, maybe not even that, maybe all he did was relax his shoulders, and the horse came and stopped right beside him.

Dan's timing was like the timing of a hawk snatching a pigeon out of midair. It was like a school of mackerel all turning, seemingly, at once. It was like JR Moehringer ending a chapter of one of his memoirs with readers on the edge of their seats.

When Dan removed the halter, the honey-colored horse trotted off. Free.

"It's okay that they leave," said Dan. "It's about teaching them how to come back."

After a break, Matt West, the emcee (the position Road to the Horse calls "The Horseman's Host"), strode onto the main stage of the arena. Matt stood framed by the immense black banner emblazoned with white capital lettering behind him: ROAD TO THE HORSE.

ROAD TO THE HORSE

"Lexington, Kentucky…are you ready for *Round Number One*?" he yelled.

The crowd cried out, "Yes!" and stomped its feet. My father clapped. I whistled.

"Lexington, Kentucky…are you ready for *Round Number One*?" Matt repeated, louder.

We all stood up. The building roared.

"Judges…are you ready?"

The five judges, wearing frowns, holding clipboards, nodded. The atmosphere was tense, electric, as Matt next checked in with the competitors, and each of the four cowboys turned and waved.

"Let's count this down to the beginning of Round One!" shouted Matt. "Let's do it in, TEN, NINE, EIGHT, SEVEN…" We, the crowd, thousands of us, took over: "SIX, FIVE, FOUR, THREE, TWO, ONE!"

I leaned toward my dad so he could hear me over the din. "The best these guys can hope for on the first day is to explain to their horses that they are not predators, that they are partners," I said. "There is a saying: 'Tame them first, train them second.'"

When a horse is "tamed" his wildness is tempered. He feels, perhaps for the first time in his life, that not everyone is out to eat him. Once an animal's fear is blunted, trust can slowly be built. Then, having built trust, we can begin training.

As we watched, my father and I found it immensely satisfying to recite principles of training to each other.

"Pressure motivates, and the release of pressure teaches," I said.

"As much as necessary, as little as possible," he said.

It took so little effort for us to point out when one of the competitors went too fast, too slow, or stumbled. But we were not the ones in the round pens. We were not the ones the steely-eyed judges were watching. We were not the ones with cameras stalking our progress…like lions tracking an antelope, waiting for it to trip, or hesitate, or make a mistake. We were not the ones with elevated heart rates, adrenaline in our veins, sweat on our backs and brows. No, we were father-and-son sports fans; we were classic, beer-drinking, couch-sitting critics.

"What do you think, Dad?" I asked him.

"Would *you* like to do it?" he asked me.

A tingle went down my spine. "I've been trying to get in for ten years," I admitted. "But it's not as simple as just asking. A lot of horsemen are applying for a handful of spots."

"How do you get in?"

"You have to be invited. They are pretty selective." I paused, watching the action in the arena below. "The pressure that these guys are under…I can hardly watch. They must feel it from the cameras, from the crowd, from the announcers. Pressure to not embarrass themselves, pressure to win the prize money. I've never been to a competition like this in my life."

"I think they should invite you!" my father said.

"Me, too!" I laughed.

Fat chance, I thought.

Sinead and I often travel through Boston's Logan International Airport, as we have many clients and friends in the Northeast. We have become all-too-familiar with the tall-ceilinged antechamber that separates check-in from the airline gates—a cloister celebrating the sacredness of security…and sports. Dozens of colorful sports banners hang high above the city's travelers, proclaiming the Boston Red Sox as nine-time "World Series Champions," the Boston Celtics as seventeen-time "World Champions," and the New England Patriots as six-time "World Champions."

These winners of these American sporting leagues were not crowned only Champions of *America*…no! They were celebrated as Champions of the *World! How* can anyone do that? Well, I think, they just *do*. Call yourself the best, and you become the best.

Road to the Horse—owned by *Western Horseman*, owned by Morris Media Network, owned by Morris Communications—has been the self-proclaimed "World Championship of Colt Starting" since 2003. Today they have the best competitors, the most fans, and the largest purse. But when most people read equestrian headlines online or in magazines, it's the Grand Prix events that are highlighted—the very top of competitive horse sport. There isn't much about starting horses, even though every one of those Grand Prix jumpers and dressage horses had to have a start somewhere.

"How often does a well-driller or plumber get to showcase his skill for three days on a world stage?" Jonathan Field, a friend and past Road to the Horse competitor (2012 and 2014) asked me. The best colt starters lay the best foundations for horses to excel in the hands of a human, and every once in a while, someone takes the trade and transforms it into art.

Colt starting *is* an art. Perhaps an endangered art.

The organizers of Road to the Horse try their best to make the event equal—the horses are all three-year-old gelding Quarter

Horses with similar bloodlines, raised at the same ranch—but still, a completely level playing field is not possible.

"Was it a good experience?" I asked Jonathan.

"It left *me* with a positive feeling," he said. "But what's your expectation going in? When I looked at the rules, I didn't go to win. I was proud to win the Jack Brainard Award, and that sticks with me way beyond anything else."

Jack Brainard passed away in 2021 at 100 years old. "Legendary seems too small of a word for a horseman like Jack," said a friend of his. The award given in his name at Road to the Horse, which was created well before his passing, is presented to the trainer that "excels in their power of observation to correctly analyze the best approach, and then apply that method as smoothly as possible for the horse's best interest."

"To hear Jack say, 'If I had a hundred-thousand-dollar colt, I would give him to you to start, and here's why,'" Jonathan said, "*that's* what I was proud of."

In the summer of 2016, I had the idea of creating a website called Horsemanship Nation. It would provide content related to what at that time was called "natural horsemanship" in an inclusive way. "Natural horsemanship" might also be called "horse psychology." It examines how horses think, feel, play, and learn. It also incorporates working with the horse from the ground more than many riding styles, which often descended from the cavalry. I felt that there were lots of interesting people, clinics, events, and competitions focused on the topic, but there was no one place to gather information on everything that was happening in that space. I invited two friends to help me run it, but we only managed a few months before realizing we would either need more time or more money to keep it going. (There still isn't a site that unites the "horsemanship world" in the way I envisioned.)

One of the first interviews I did for Horsemanship Nation was with Tootie Bland, who, along with her husband Stephen, had created Road to the Horse in 2003. That first year the event was called *El Camino del Caballo* and took place in Fort Worth, Texas. Fewer than a thousand people attended.

"We are not advocating starting a colt in three days," Tootie told me in that interview. "But we are saying in the hands of true professionals, *it is possible*. It works. And they prove it…. The prize money? We want to elevate the clinician to 'athlete status.' I know they are not there for the money; they never have been. But it's a nice bonus. And they deserve it."

"Do you want anything to eat?" I asked my dad as I stood up.

"Nothing for me."

"A beer?"

He checked his watch. "Okay," he agreed.

I smiled. "How often do we get to have beers together?"

"Not enough," he said.

I jogged to the bar and got two cold Kentucky Bourbon Barrel Ales, then I went in search of food. I ordered nachos—the kind with liquid queso from a vat. I balanced the cardboard tray of chips and orange drizzle on the beers and hustled back to my seat, just in time to see Jonath "JR" Robles, one of the competitors, take a knee. He bowed his head, crossed himself, then stood up, opened the gate, and stepped into the round pen.

It was Day Three, and the bearded Oregonian had a strong lead. He would have twenty minutes in the round pen, then thirty-five minutes in the main arena to both do the mandatory rail work and to conquer an obstacle course.

The obstacle course is a gigantic ask of both horse and rider, like the final push on an ascent up Everest. Anyone short of oxygen will be prone to errors of judgment. At best those errors are awkward for a moment; at their worst, they are fatal.

Having watched all three days, I expected JR to win. My father expected him to win. If there had been bookies, we would have bet twenty dollars on him. His lead seemed insurmountable.

JR greeted his young horse, saddled him, and mounted. They rolled through the rail work: Walk left, trot left, lope left; walk right, trot right, lope right. Halt, back up, turn each direction. JR then dismounted and picked up each of the horse's feet, led the gelding forty feet forward, and re-mounted.

One judge nodded. Another smiled. JR's points were rolling in.

The first task in the obstacle course was to slalom through six wooden pillars, each one gentrified with textured wallpaper. Flags hung above a few of them. JR rode through, but it was the most hesitant his horse had been all weekend. The turns should have been smooth and tight…and they were not.

I glanced at the clock. He had 20:35 left as he approached the second obstacle. It was a narrow zigzag corridor that the horse

needed to travel through. The sides, the "walls," were poles about eighteen inches off the ground.

JR clucked encouragingly as his legs kept the pressure on. He widened his arms, as if funneling the horse toward the entrance of the zigzag. The gelding's ears were pricked forward, interested, curious, yet…worried. The horse was nervous, just as a boy climbing the ladder to the high diving board for the first time might be. *Wanting to… wanting to…* but thinking, *This is higher than I thought.* The horse was conflicted, and when JR asked again, the horse balked.

At 19:17, the horse reared and turned away.

At 19:02, the horse half jumped over the obstacle, then ran a few feet sideways, like a crab. JR lost his balance over the gelding's neck but caught himself quickly, resettling himself in the saddle. He didn't give up. He re-approached.

At 18:30, JR looked up at the clock on the jumbotron. *Tick, tick, tick.* Time laughed unmercifully.

At 17:46, the horse entered the zigzag. One timid step, then another. The two crept through. We cheered. People were on their feet.

But three minutes to get a "Yes" from a horse is a long time. I wondered how much of his horse he had used up.

"Maybe he should rest a bit," I said to my dad. "Regroup."

"Or maybe he could go for a canter," my dad replied. "Get him thinking *forward* again."

"We really are excellent armchair quarterbacks," I noted, leaning my forearms on my knees.

At 17:20, JR and his horse began the next obstacle: six poles extending from a raised center stand, like an octopus that had lost two legs. The horse walked over them, both left and right. We cheered!

At 16:00, they approached a big blue tarp. The young horse was again hesitant. He tried to leave. JR lost his balance again. The crowd was eerily silent.

At 14:25, the horse kicked out. The beginning of the end. The horse, instead of saying, "I'm not sure…" had just said, "No!" for the first time.

At 13:59, the horse kicked out again. And at 13:45, again.

I leaned back. "I can't watch," I said.

My dad didn't say anything.

The horse kicked again. I squirmed in my chair and dropped my notes. The gelding then brought his front feet off the ground—both of them at the same time.

At 12:50, JR abandoned the tarp and went to the ground poles and three small jumps, designed to be walked over. JR clucked, and purred, "Gooood," to his horse as they completed the obstacle. "Nice job," we could hear him say softly.

The crowd roared.

At 11:33, JR approached the pool noodles in a doorway-like structure that created a "wall" that the horse needed to push through. For many horses, this was the most confusing obstacle.

JR's horse stopped.

"How much time is left?" JR asked the Horseman's Host.

"Eleven minutes and twenty seconds," came the answer over the loudspeakers.

When you attempt something *you* have never done before—trying out for a new sports team, traveling to an unfamiliar country, swimming in the ocean on a dark moonless night—it is scary, and you may be brimming with doubt. You may wonder if you will succeed; you may even wonder if you will survive.

Then, you might attempt something *nobody* has ever even done before. You might try something that you are not even sure is *possible*—like astronauts rocketing to the moon, then walking on it, or Roger Banister running a mile in under four minutes.

But for every celebrated accomplishment there are thousands

of people who have attempted the unknown…and failed. There are also thousands who have thought to start something but have never begun. Fear overwhelmed them, and they never took the first step.

It's impossible, they said to themselves.

That sense of impossible may be what JR's horse felt. His guide on earth, amongst humans and human things, was asking him to go through what looked to him like a "wall."

Can't be done, the horse thought.

At 10:52, JR stopped in front of the pool-noodle wall and let his horse rest. The gelding poked his nose at the noodles, painted silver and gold. One of the noodles wiggled.

"There you go, buddy," said JR.

The crowd was silent. *Maybe?* we thought.

Then, at 9:51, the horse kicked out.

"I'm going to have to come back to this," JR said. "I just want to keep doing right by the horse. I'm sorry."

The crowd applauded.

The next obstacle's goal was to pick up a lariat and swing it. JR widened his hands; his intention was clear, his heart was soft. The horse reared.

JR looked up at the audience. "You know what?" he said. "This horse, mentally, he can't take it anymore. And I'm not going to push him through the rest of the obstacles."

The crowd instantly rose up as one to applaud.

JR looked down at the horse as he said, "I'm sorry." Then he brought his hand to cover his face, and he cried.

The crowd kept applauding. I caught a glimpse of my dad wiping his face. I looked around and saw others were crying as well.

JR dismounted, his shoulders still heaving, and buried his face into the horse's neck.

4

"And to demonstrate what I'm saying," Monty said, "I would like all of you to clap on the count of three."

I was in the crowd with thousands of others who had read *The Man Who Listens to Horses,* written by this man, Monty Roberts, who gave sold-out demonstrations around the world and spoke regularly with The Queen. His memoir had been published in 1996, the year before, and I had devoured it. It had remained on the *New York Times* Bestseller List for fifty-eight weeks.

In the round pen with Monty was a horse that he had met for the first time thirty minutes earlier. The horse was toddling around the edge of the round pen, sniffing, then looking out at the crowd, then gently pawing.

"One…two…" Monty said. "Three!"

On "three," we all clapped once. The horse jumped like he had stepped on a snake. His neck was high, his muscles taut as guitar strings. His eyes bugged. He hit the ground and flew to Monty. He slid in next to the man and lowered his head.

I couldn't believe what I had just witnessed. To me, then, it was more unbelievable than a David Blaine magic show. This "natural horsemanship" guy was seeing so much more in horses than I saw. He did not miss a trick. He knew exactly when to act. He also knew when *not* to act, which is often the most difficult part.

The day of that demo I was fifteen years old. I left, I am embarrassed to say, and went back to doing things with horses the way I had always done things with horses. I was too young, too immature, and too uninterested to take what I had seen in that round pen and use it as a catalyst to continue to learn on my own, with books and videos and clinics, and of course, with *horses* as my teachers. But it *had* planted a seed, and I would have a second chance thirteen years later.

In 2009 I stepped out of an airport in Florida for the first time. The humid Gulf air hit me like a baseball bat. There were palm trees and fully grown adults wearing Mickey Mouse ears. I'd never seen anything like it. I met Olympians Karen and David O'Connor on that trip, and it was at their farm in Ocala, Florida, that I was reintroduced to "natural horsemanship."

David has these amazing lucid eyes, which can cross-examine a student with a single raised eyebrow. Fourteen years after I first met and learned from him, he was settling into his new position behind a desk as "Chief of Sport" for the United States Equestrian Federation, based at the Kentucky Horse Park in Lexington—the same Kentucky Horse Park that now hosts Road to the Horse each year. And so, both of us ended up being there for the first time in 2023. (He only had to walk a half-mile down Cigar Lane to get there.)

I had heard a rumor the Road to the Horse organizers were considering hiring David as a judge for the following year, 2024, so when I saw him, I asked, "How do you like it?"

"Interesting," he said, lucid eyes meeting mine.

Ever the politician, I thought, then pressed: "Do you think you would judge it if they asked you?"

"I'm not sure," he replied. "I think there are some things that need to change." He paused. "We don't want to see horses fail."

David's new role as Chief of Sport had him thinking about

something all of us in the equestrian industry were coming to know as "social license."

"Social license is the ability for the public to accept an endeavor," is how David explained it. "In our case, that's horses, and our playing with horses in the sport world. Does the public trust you to have the best interests of the horse in mind? How does society look at it from outside? It's about *their perception*. If you can't train a horse, and explain what it is you are doing, in the middle of Central Park, then you actually *can't* do it anymore. Because now images are transferred around the world, a lot of times out of context, and it happens in a heartbeat."

"What if I was offered a spot in this?" I asked David, what he had just said very much on my mind. The question of whether colt starting should be a competition was an enormous one. The question of whether I should try such a thing in front of cameras, in an age where questions of social license could end a career, was pretty big too.

"Don't do it," he said simply.

Later, I asked my dad again. "Seriously…. What if I really got invited?"

"I don't think you should do it."

There were so many reasons why I wasn't good enough or experienced enough to compete in the World Championship of Colt Starting. There were so many reasons I should question if it was the right thing to do in the age of social license. But…there was also a tiny voice in my head that kept saying, *You could do this. This is something you could do.*

There was, of course, no proof at all that I *could* actually do it, but when I shut my eyes and sat with myself, it kept prodding me, like a little salesman persistently jabbing me with his fingers:

*You could do it. You **can** do it. And you can do it **your** way.*

But by June of 2023 I had all but convinced myself I *didn't* want to do Road to the Horse. Not ever. I had a lot of reasons.

I was old.

I felt old.

I didn't fall like I used to and I was scared of getting hurt.

It was a dangerous undertaking, and I had a wife, two kids, and a mortgage to consider.

I had a new project I was starting, a book on liberty training, that was going to take any spare time I had.

I was enjoying competing SKM Lux Sonata ("Sam"), an Irish gelding, at the elite level. I didn't want to put him too far on the back burner.

Road to the Horse felt like a dream that was so far out of reach, I might as well try to play professional basketball. *That ship has sailed*, I thought.

And then there were Brooks and Violet (aka "Goldfish"), ages five and one. I wanted to spend time with them. I wanted to be the best dad I could be.

That June we were on the road for several weeks, teaching clinics in New York and Massachusetts and living out of our camper. The campground in Gardiner, New York, was sprawled out across a hill, next to where the Wallkill River met the Shawangunk Kill. Brooks was devastated because the campground's slides were still closed for the season. His eyes went large, then liquid, when we learned the bad news. He looked so soft and vulnerable, and I wanted to give him the world. It was so difficult to see him disappointed.

It is so much easier to say yes than to say no.

I was teaching at a farm nearby when I got a text: *Hey just Tammy from RTTH. Hey if you have a few minutes are u able to call me at your convenience. Thanks!*

During my lunch break, I walked out onto the lawn that sloped steeply downhill, away from the barn. There were paddocks below and woods in the distance. I leaned against a fence, closed my eyes, and took a deep breath. The smell of freshly cut grass filled my senses.

I opened my eyes and made the call.

Tammy Sronce, Director of Operations at Road to the Horse, had an Australian accent and an upbeat tone. It was easy to get chatting with her, but I only had a few minutes before I had to head back to my clinic.

"What's going on?" I asked.

"You're on our short list for next year," Tammy said. "You represent something different, you know? Also, we are thinking about doing an Olympic theme for 2024—with the Olympics in Paris next summer, we thought it would be good. We want to have different countries represented, so could you compete for Canada?"

"Well, that's the only country I *could* compete for."

"So you still have Canadian citizenship?"

"I'm here as a permanent resident. I've got a green card."

"Well, we are interested in having you at Road to the Horse next year. If we were to ask you, would you say yes?"

I looked at the far hills. Thousands and thousands of trees: spruces, pines, and cedars. They formed a green haze. I felt like a diver at the top of the ladder, seized by curiosity to see from how high he could jump.

"Yes," I said slowly. "I would."

"Think about it for a couple days," Tammy replied. "Talk to your family. Like I said, you are on the short list, but we are really interested."

The trees in the distance blurred further as I said goodbye. I took a deep breath. I could feel my heartbeat. I turned around and walked back to teach the rest of the clinic.

Road to the Horse.

My adrenaline was through the roof.

"Guess what?" I said to Sinead when I got home that evening.

"We lost Athena this morning." Tears fell down her cheeks as she spoke the words.

"Oh my god…Sinead…" I went to her, hugged her, but I knew it wasn't the hug she wanted or needed. It was the listening, the caring, the being present. The hug was more for me than for her.

Athena had succumbed that morning to complications associated with foaling. A raven-black event horse, Athena was neither too big nor too small, with a slightly wild look in her eye. I speculated that Sinead saw in Athena an old soul who carried the weight of past traumas similar to her own. The mare had been living in Virginia as she prepared for motherhood, and we had been planning to stop by the farm on the way home to visit her and meet her foal.

Her filly, who we would call "June" after the month she was born, had survived. Now we would be visiting only her.

Eventually, haltingly, I told Sinead about my call from Tammy.

"I know how much you have wanted to do this," Sinead said, eyes still wet. "And I know it didn't just 'happen,' even though it seems like it. You've been following this for ten years."

I had long made a point to introduce myself to people involved with Road to the Horse whenever and wherever I was in the same place as them. Since I lived in the "English" riding world, and Road to the Horse mainly existed in the "Western" riding world, those times were not very often, but still, I had made an effort. I'd looked them in the eyes and shaken their hands. I'd mailed Tammy a book. I'd sent a link to a video of me working with a young horse. I'd made sure they knew who I was.

"You might think that because they get hundreds of applications, they have a long list of who to invite," Dan James had told me, "but the truth is, the list of people that can actually do this is pretty short."

"I'll make you a drink," I said to Sinead. I got up and rummaged around in the cabinets. There was a silence in the camper; we were together but alone with our thoughts. Sinead, I was pretty sure, could think of little else but Athena, and my mind bumbled around between the mare's unexpected death, our kids, money we owed to the IRS, money we owed to credit cards, our mortgage, the fact that I was not seeing my parents or brothers or nieces or nephews as much I wanted to…and now, added to the mix, that this Road to the Horse invitation was the most intimidating news I had ever received.

Sinead and I were both juggling a lot of balls. I had read something recently about the five balls we all need to juggle: career, health, family, friends, integrity. The article said that the career ball is rubber, it bounces. But the other balls are all ceramic. They chip and crack when dropped…and may never be the same again.

But if a ball drops, I thought, *don't just leave it on the ground. Don't give up hope.* In another article that Sinead had sent me, I'd learned about *kintsugi*, the Japanese art of repairing broken pottery in which the artist uses a lacquer mixed with powdered gold to mend the breaks. Each chip then becomes part of the pottery's story, and the cracks, like the wrinkles on my sunburnt face, tell a tale.

Sinead was watching a video of Athena on her phone. "So what do you think?" she asked, without looking up.

I handed her a Tito's and soda. "She was special, but she wasn't easy."

Sinead's eyes left the video and met mine, lighting up a little. I loved her eyes when she was lit up a little—like sunlight on morning dew.

"Are you talking about me or Athena?" she asked.

"I adore you," I said.

She rolled her eyes. "What do you think about Road to the Horse?"

I took a sip of my drink. I swallowed.

"I have so many questions about it," I began. "Am I really going to get in? If I do, I don't even know all the rules. Will I ride in English clothes and saddle, or Western? Who will be my pen wrangler?" I paused. "But the biggest question is, by far, *Can I actually do this? Or am I overfacing myself?*"

The fears swirled in my stomach but had not clearly formed in my mind. They just existed in an overall anxiousness that made me fidgety. I couldn't name them. I looked out the window and saw Brooks and Goldfish with our au pair, Señorita Allisson, walking back, all of them soaking wet, with muddy feet. They'd been in the river.

"You think I should do it?" I asked, still looking out the window.

"Why wouldn't you?"

"Actually," I said, "there are some really big reasons why someone might not accept a spot."

5

I met Glenn Stewart for the first time in the fall of 2022. My hand disappeared into his as I shook it. I'm an even six feet, but he had a few inches and a couple dozen pounds on me. He wore a full horseshoe mustache.

"What are you wanting to accomplish?" he asked me.

I listed off some competitions I wanted to enter, some big results I wanted to achieve, but even as I verbalized them, my list felt shallow as a puddle, and almost as muddy.

Glenn studied me, searching for something more. The creases around his mouth and eyes were passionate and intelligent. "And *why*?" he said. "*Why* do you want to do those things?"

"Well…" I began and stopped. Nobody had ever asked me that before. What *was* my purpose?

"I'll tell you why *I* compete," he said. "I do it to *improve*, not to prove. The last Road to the Horse I competed in, I could have picked an easy horse, but I was looking for one that would test me. What's the reason for me to do this? I like to ask, 'Why?' And so, why would I want an easy horse?"

Glenn had first competed in Road to the Horse in 2012 and had just participated again in 2022, seven months before we met.

I nodded. The benefit to the shift in mindset from *proving* to *improving* was immediately obvious, but at the same time I was thinking, *Glenn, you're an idiot! Why wouldn't you want the easiest damn horse you could get your hands on? If I ever get a chance to do this, I'll pick the easiest-looking horse I can find.*

Just like with kids and dogs, some horses are "easy"—looking to connect, to learn, to figure out the problem and to get along; "tougher" horses are constantly looking to push boundaries. Mentoring any being to the edge of their potential is a daunting task, but it's a little easier with one that already wants to make the trip. Every horse is rewarding to work with; some just require more skill and time.

At the base of the stairs to our barn apartment is a sandbox. It is not a regular-sized kids' sandbox; it's more the size of a squash court. Three palm trees, two about my height and the third one twice as tall, grow in the sandbox. It's like a beach.

One day at the end of June, I turned the hose on for Brooks, then we dug out a path for the water. We scooped sand madly, packing the sides of the stream with the wet sand. Our little river wound around two of the three palm trees, then waterfalled three inches down into a heart-shaped pond.

Brooks, I thought, *you're learning to train.* A river, a horse—it doesn't matter. The flow of the water, the energy of the horse, should be molded, smoothed. We don't fight gravity; we don't go against the laws of nature; no, we learn how nature operates, and we work with her.

There was *life* in that sandbox river…there was *flow.* That's what I want to see in a horse.

- *Throw cold water on the rear end of a mare after she is bred. It will increase her chances of conception.*

- *If a horse rears, break an egg over his head.*

- *Women should never go near a stallion. The female scent will enrage the horse.*

- *Women are too weak to ride.*

There have been a lot of myths surrounding horses. There are also many lenses through which people look at horses:

- *Horses are tough.*

- *Horses are fragile.*

- *Horses go into pressure.*

- *Horses go away from pressure.*

- *Horses have a pecking order—you need to be the boss!*

- *Be the leader.*

- *Be a dominant leader.*

- *Be a passive leader.*

- *Be a benevolent leader.*

- *Be a partner.*

- *Be a friend.*

Oprah had a monthly column titled "What Do I Know for Sure?" in her *O* magazine for fourteen years. Eventually, she compiled the articles into a book—*What I Know for Sure*—that was published in 2014. If I ask myself that question as it pertains to what I do for a living—that is, what do I know about horses, *for sure*?—the answer is, well, not that much. I don't know for sure what they think, or what love means to them. I don't know for sure how much we should let horses struggle through adversity to figure out an answer, versus help them along every step of the way. I know I don't know for sure what the best way to train a horse is. I don't know for sure if we should even be training horses.

I know for sure we have lots of ways we try to communicate with horses. We yell, we whisper, we cry. We call animal communicators who charge us four hundred dollars an hour. We use pressure and release. We use our legs, our seat, our hands, and we cluck, and we cluck, and we cluck. We threaten, we cajole, we beg, and we pray on our knees. There is not much we won't try when it comes to communicating with horses.

I know for sure that a horse can, and will, show stress, anxiety, and fear. I know for sure they can show lethargy, disinterest, and the glazed-over eyes of a whipped dog that has given up hope. I know for sure they can show curiosity.

I know for sure they can think. I know for sure they can problem-solve to a certain extent.

Despite knowing that they can show both stress and relaxation, I don't know for sure if one of these is "good" or "bad." They are both part of what makes a horse a horse, and they are both useful in different situations.

I *do* know for sure which of these I prefer to see in my horses.

Here are two questions:

- *Should starting horses be on a timeline?*
- *Should starting horses be a competition?*

These are the same questions I ask myself every year when I see any competition designed for young horses. For young eventers, young jumpers, and young dressage horses in the English world (usually four-, five-, and six-year-olds), and reiners, cutters, and most racehorses (started at two and competing in the biggest competitions of their lives, derbies and futurities, at three), the prize money and pressure can be enormous.

In 2023 Mage, at fifteen to one odds, galloped up from behind to win the Kentucky Derby. He passed Two Phil's down the stretch and held off the favorite, Angel of Empire. The total purse was three million, and he won almost two million of it.

Mage was three. *Only three years old!*

The Kentucky Derby is an age-restricted race, meaning only horses of a certain age can enter. For this race (and the other two races in the Triple Crown of flat racing—the Preakness Stakes and the Belmont Stakes), that age is three. This means that almost all Thoroughbreds start racing before they have physically matured, and many of them retire before that as well. A Thoroughbred's age is determined by the calendar year, which means horses born closer to the first of the year have an advantage because a foal born on *January* second and one born on *June* second are both officially the same age and eligible for the same races. So, some of the horses running in the Kentucky Derby likely have not even reached their third birthdays yet.

Some young horses survive under this kind of pressure early in their lives. Some thrive. Many crumble.

From a training perspective, at home, I start horses on different timelines, depending on how they progress. The speed of that progression feels good to me, but I recognize there are many who start horses both faster and slower than I do. And while the three days at Road to the Horse is much faster than I would start a horse at home, there are some people who start horses faster.

The Cheyenne Frontier Days is billed as the "World's Largest Outdoor Rodeo and Western Celebration," and "The Wild Horse Race" is one of its feature attractions. Started in the 1800s, this "race" involves saddling an untrained horse and being the first to ride around a track. In reality, it's a bronc-riding show—if the cowboy stays on long enough, and the horse happens to go in the right direction, they'll cross the finish line. Total time elapsed in the relationship between horse and rider is often two minutes or less.

It's possible to start a horse badly, or well, in almost any amount of time—three days, three months, three years. In the case of Road to the Horse, the shorter timeline is meant to showcase sophisticated skill and timing. With the issue of social license in mind, it is the only kind of horse-related event where *all the training* happens, live, in front of a crowd and dozens of cameras. That doesn't happen in the Mustang Makeover, it doesn't happen in the Thoroughbred Makeover, and it certainly doesn't happen in any Grand Prix or World Cup or World Championship competition, where the horses have been prepared at home and the audience only sees the "finished product." And while there are some who argue that the "live audience" environment is an additional stressor for the young horses at Road to the Horse, what I have observed is that the horses' attention appears to be more on the other horses, or on what's happening close to them, or at eye level. Smells, sounds, sights that are close and changing are what horses seem to be interested in, or curious about, or worried about, in that environment. The crowd seems to fade into the background for the horse, much like a highway of busy cars might fade into the background for a horse that has lived in a paddock next to an interstate.

Each year that I have watched Road to the Horse, I have learned more in three days than I usually learn in three months. I have learned from the great moments, where the river waters are smooth, but I have also learned from watching mistakes, where the waters are turbulent. It is unavoidable that we make mistakes. In a public forum, when one trainer makes a mistake, or goes too fast, we can *all* learn from it.

But should such great moments and mistakes happen in the form of a competition?

A colt-starting competition can draw a crowd in a way that a colt-starting clinic does not. There's a hype about it, an energy, an atmosphere. You can hear thousands of people comparing, over a beer, how two trainers saddled a horse, or the wonderfulness of a moment where a horse developed the confidence and curiosity to sniff a tarp or push over a barrel. Road to the Horse and its participants make clear that the competition is a *demonstration format*. It is meant to show what is possible under specific conditions: the right horse, the right trainer, and the right weekend. Training under such a tight timeline with the possibility of a big payout for a "winner" is not something the trainers are advocating for others to be doing at home. It's more akin to a climber attempting a winter ascent of Denali, as my friend Art Davidson did in 1967—a rare event, likely a once-in-a-lifetime event, and one in which we should all be ready to turn for home if the conditions are not just right.

So that brings us back to the question of young horses and pressure. Is the pressure of a timed competition in front of thousands of spectators too much for these horses? Sometimes, yes, it is. And if I could improve *one thing* about the horse world, it would not be people's riding skill, or their access to better veterinary care, it would be our ability to accurately read stress in a horse.

Many people don't *see* tension. Many misread "anxious" as

"excited." Many don't realize what a huge impact stress has on a horse's physical and emotional health, and how much it affects their ability to learn. If we could reduce confusion and tension in all horses by even ten percent, that would be a monumental change. Watching competitors at Road to the Horse helps me better identify and deal with stress in my own horses. When I see one of their horses exhibit tension, when I hear others discussing it in the crowd, and when I witness the ways the trainer finds to ease that anxiety, I learn to better read stress in any horse.

I constantly remind myself that reading a horse is a skill, a craft, an art that needs to be constantly, relentlessly pursued. To not do so is to turn my back on the most important thread that connects us to horses: understanding that they are capable of thoughts and feelings that are as real as our own—perhaps more so.

In my study of horses, in my study of *starting* them, I want to anthropomorphize them less and humanize them more. I want to treat them as horses, and as individuals. I want to treat them fairly. I also want to know, what *is* fair?

6

For five years, I said to myself, *I'll start the book next year.* "The book" was *this* book, and the reason I didn't start was *I was waiting.* What was I waiting for? I was waiting for the moment when I had read enough, studied enough, and saved enough. I was waiting for enough time, and the right time. I was like the kid in Dr. Seuss' book, *Oh, the Places You'll Go*—the boy who got stuck in the "waiting place …just waiting."

Well, Sinead set me straight.

"Enough waiting!"

And then, right when I had decided to *stop waiting* and start writing a book on liberty training, the opportunity to compete at Road to the Horse came along. Perhaps the universe was rewarding me for taking that first step.

So I began writing. I sat in Chelsea's Café, down the road from my kids' school, sipping a coffee. Sinead was at home riding. …and I was sitting there.

Sitting at the computer…

Sitting there for an hour…

And I felt guilty.

Guilty for not riding a horse, or cleaning the barn, or teaching a lesson, or balancing the books.

You know, for all that my parents stressed the importance of using my brain, I still had not managed to escape the feeling that working *physically*, breaking a sweat, was the more important virtue. Working smart, *sure*, that was great. But hard labor! Building, raking, cutting, chopping, digging—with two browned, calloused hands! *That was the thing.* Point out a complainer and my mother's response is still a shake of the head and, "They don't have enough wood to chop."

Writing this book was going to be tougher than I thought.

Come explore a taste of the past and a little piece of the ole West. Kick back and enjoy a campfire-cooked meal or just relax by the fire. Don't forget the s'mores! the online advertisements boasted. But when we pulled into The Circle CG Farm Campground in Bellingham, Massachusetts, it was quiet…not a campfire or kid in sight.

"Still the slow season," I said to Sinead.

Brooks peered out the RV window. "Are there frogs?"

Sinead opened her eyes from where she'd been dozing in the passenger seat. "Dad will take you," she mumbled.

"Dad, who is older, God or Santa?"

I parked the camper. "Mom will tell you."

I unbuckled Brooks and lifted him out of his car seat. "Dad, what's infinity plus infinity?" he asked.

He could climb down on his own now, but I loved lifting him out. "Two infinity?" I guessed, as I lowered him to the parking lot.

"Infinity and BEYOND!" he yelled, and he hit the ground running, headed toward the pond we could see just across a roughly mown patch of campground lawn. I chased after him. As we approached the water's edge, we heard a couple small splashes.

"Frogs!"

"There's one! Slow down…you'll scare him."

The amphibian was a shimmering olive-green, mottled with brown, his body as big as a softball. With his legs extended he would have spilled over the sides of a frisbee. Startled by our arrival, he dove into the water, then resurfaced only three feet away. His almond-shaped eyes glared at us.

"Brazen," I said.

"Can I go in?" Brooks asked.

I looked at the black muddy water. There weren't any steps or docks. There was a sign that said: "No Swimming."

"Don't go past your shorts," I said.

Señorita Allisson joined us after thirty minutes of "froggin,'" and I wandered back to the camper. Sinead made pasta while Chris Stapleton sang on the stereo. Goldfish napped. I made drinks, then sat on a bench outside, thought about Road to the Horse, and scribbled down my self-interrogation.

So you think can do this? What makes you think that?

I've wanted to do this for a long time.

Well, wanting to do this is not the same as being qualified to do this!

That's true.

You're an idiot. I can think of ten people right off the bat that have started more horses than you.

I wrote down the names of those people.

Stop it! What are you afraid of?

A lot of things.

Write those things down. Get them on paper. Maybe that will help.

I wrote down the fears as they occurred to me, quick and raw:

I'll freeze, my mouth will go dry, people will laugh awkwardly. People will ask, what made him think he was good enough? There are people I admire who are morally against the idea of having colt-starting be a competition or a timed-event.

I wrote down the names of some of those people.

Social media.

I was a white middle-aged Canadian, father of two, living in the United States, working with animals, trying my best, and I was still capable of being hurt and intimidated by Facebook. (I couldn't imagine how it affected kids and teenagers. I really couldn't. I guess maybe take what I felt and double it...or triple it.)

So was I nervous?

Yes. Why?

Doing this meant declaring that I believed I was good enough.

Was I?

I sure wasn't at that moment. But I believed I *could* be. I knew I had the curiosity, and I knew I was willing to work, and I knew those things were vital. I just didn't know if they would be enough.

How did I feel about being nervous?

I've often felt nervous. As far back as I can remember, there has been a voice that lives in my body, sometimes in my stomach, sometimes in my chest, sometimes in my brain, that prods me when I am comfortable. The prodding has led me to jump off cliffs into rivers, ski out of bounds, and hitchhike. The little voice pushed me to five-in-the-morning swim practices, in the dark, in the snow. She even signed me up for a public-speaking course, which was more uncomfortable than the swim practices, if that was possible.

One night, when I was about fifteen, while staying at a hotel on a school sports trip, I snuck out of the building, sprinted across the highway, climbed a fence, and made my way through patches of spruce and fir and pine. I stumbled uphill, until eventually I turned around and saw the city lights below. Only then, in the wild dark, looking back at civilization, was that voice quiet for a moment.

The voice doesn't make me brave. She often scares me, and I push her away. Then she screams at me, *Don't live a life half-lived!* I push her farther away, but it's as if I'm battling a northern wind, and she streams around my protective layers and cuts to my soul.

The disquiet of this voice has permeated my existence. I can't remember a time she wasn't there, reminding me to "do something every day that scares you."

To a fault.

But as I get older I push her away more and more. I have less and less need to prove something, and less and less need to compete. Now, it's about finding the middle ground.

Being a parent has given me perspective. I don't just make decisions for myself anymore, I think *How will this affect my kids? What kind of role model do I want to be?*

There is a book I read to my kids called *What Do You Do with a Chance?* by Kobi Yamada with drawings by Mae Besom. Someone gave it to Brooks for his fourth birthday. In the book, a boy notices a winged, flying "Chance," but fails to grab it. And when another

Chance appears he tries to catch it, but falls. He thinks everyone is laughing at him. After that, he ignores Chances. *And the more I ignored them, the less they came around.*

Taking chances is like starting horses—it's dangerous, and nothing is guaranteed, and we are going to make mistakes.

But it's worth a shot.

I saw Brooks returning from the pond. He ran with his hands together as if he was holding something. His shorts were soaked. Allisson was trailing behind, speed walking. My son's face radiated excitement. I watched him break into a gallop.

He has his whole life ahead of him, I thought.

I hoped he could keep this curiosity as he got older. I wanted him to explore the world, to enjoy and appreciate his life. He was only five, and I was already noticing moments when he cared what other kids thought, times when he retreated from a Chance, and that made me sad.

7

"Tammy?"

"Yes."

I breathed in slowly, through my nose. It was June 15, 2023.

"I'm in."

"Great!" she exclaimed. She started reciting details, dates, suggestions.

"Can you email this? I'm not going to remember everything."

As she drawled on, I realized there were other fears I had.

- *How was this going to fit into my life?*
- *Was starting horses going to be my thing? My career? My identity?*
- *Was I going to give up eventing in order to do this?*
- *Was I going to change who I was?*

Sinead was being supportive, but she was being supportive of a lot lately. I didn't want her to think I was flaky, flitting from one thing to the other. (Which I *have* been known to do.) But also, if I was going to do this, I wanted to do a *really* good job with it. I had to take it seriously.

I had listed many of my fears, and I felt there was a ninety-eight-and-three-quarter-percent chance that none of them would kill me.

So I did what anybody in his right mind would do: I decided to be the person I wanted to be.

I decided to be a person who would face his fears.

I decided that saying "Yes" was a chance—a chance to learn more about young horses, more about Quarter Horses, and more about starting horses. Should all that fail, I would learn, at the very least, more about myself. For while I had once thought that Road to the Horse was a test of skill and horsemanship, after watching it live—and seeing all that pressure—I knew it was a test of something else entirely: *character*.

How often in life do we get a chance to test our character under that kind of pressure? Pressure at that level, pressure like that…it's a privilege. But I also knew it would very quickly take over my life. I knew it would never leave my mind. I would need to get some means of control over my mind. How?

Preparation.

I had to prepare like I had never prepared before.

I began my research by reading…which has always been my favorite place to begin. I had a horse-centered bookcase in my office already, and it was constantly expanding. I read a couple "interesting" theories right off the bat:

There are many characteristics and coincidences that make a horse rideable. One of them is the back, strong enough for us to sit on. Another is the mouth, where there is a "gap" between the front biting teeth (the incisors), and the back chewing teeth (the molars), where a bit can sit. Perhaps the "gap" was put there for us by God. An alternative theory is that as the ancestors of horses left the woods and came out to the flatlands, their principal method of survival became flight. Their legs slowly evolved to become longer. And because they ate grass, and had

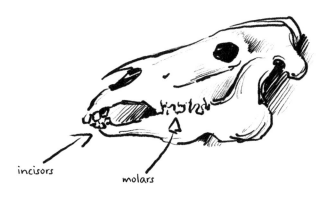

to reach it, their necks and their heads became longer as well.
Thus leaving a gap between the molars and incisors.

Another book offered the theory that there are two main reasons why horses might run scared when under saddle for the first time. The first is because of something they *feel* on their back, in which case they gallop, or buck, looking forward, sometimes down, trying to escape. The second is because of something they *see* on their back. The author argued that the latter can be much more dangerous, because then they are galloping, or bucking, and trying to look back, rather than looking where they are going.

In July, I had a conversation with Nick Rivera about being my pen wrangler. Nick was a quiet Midwesterner with a Big Sky beard. I'd met him in 2018 when he'd started an online platform called The Horseman's University. We'd become friends in 2020 when our loft house above the barn was left not-quite-finished by the contractor, and Nick had flown down to help us out. He'd looked around, shaken his head a few times, and sagely announced, "I've got some good news and some bad news." We'd ended up tearing up the flooring (putting it back down in parallel rows), and taking the doors off their hinges (re-hanging them, level). We (he) had redone most of the electrical, as well as much of the plumbing, and added in some beautiful finishing touches—like sliding barn doors to my office, and a single accent wall that he painted an aqua blue that reminds me of where the sky meets the ocean.

That is to say, Nick is humble and kind, a jack of all trades, and a virtuoso of most.

I was in Florida and Nick was in Wisconsin when I reached him.

"What are you up to?" I asked.

He was on his way to visit friends for the Fourth of July. I could hear his wife Kayla in the background. She was soothing Elodia, their baby girl, who was squeaking and whimpering.

"Want me to call you later?" I asked.

"No, go ahead, we're just driving."

I launched into my ideas for getting ready for Road to the Horse—that I was going to read books, study with different trainers, and take in some extra horses to start at my farm. I was also going to use "competition simulations" to learn the timelines and rules. And I wanted him there to be a part of it all.

Nick listened to everything and then sighed.

"It's a lot," he said. He just couldn't commit to the time I was looking for. His contracting business was booked almost until Christmas. And with their newborn and a mortgage, he just couldn't book more time off.

I wanted him to help me…to be on my "team," so I tried once more.

"I can be there for the competition," he said.

That's not enough, I thought. Nick had never been to Road to the Horse, and I wasn't sure he realized what it was all about. Every moment now I was imagining being in an arena with a colt with thousands of people watching. This was a situation that demanded attention and respect. Respect for the organization, respect for the judges, respect for the crowd, and most of all, respect for the colt and what he was going to go through and experience with me. I felt this respect would initially be shown by how seriously I took the preparation, and I needed a team that "got" that.

"Look, Nick," I said. "You don't have to be there for *all* the things I'm doing to get ready—just some of them. Especially the simulations as we get closer. We need to work together as a team a few times before we show up in Kentucky."

He sighed. "Let me talk to Kayla some more."

I wasn't optimistic after our call. Competing with horses appears to many to be an individual sport (or a "team" when you count the horse), but there are inevitably so many more involved. Coaches, grooms, owners, veterinarians, farriers, wives, husbands, vets...I needed a team, and the first position on the team to be filled was the "pen wrangler." The pen wrangler at Road to the Horse is the caddy, the groom, the editor, the first mate. The pen wrangler must learn the rules and score cards better than the competitor, must understand the layout of the arena, and must know how long the mandatory rest breaks have to be. He would also be in the round pen with me, on hand for the first ride or two—helping me get a little "forward thinking" from my horse, maybe helping me with turning, or backing, or whatever we might need in the moment. Often having a second person on the ground can make things clearer for the horse in the early days of carrying a rider.

Lastly, I would be looking for the pen wrangler to find that delicate balance between being supportive when I got scared, and honest when I got sidetracked or cocky. If I was to be the shoe, the pen wrangler would be the laces.

Who else could I ask to be the laces?

I was going to be the outsider.

I was an event rider, an English rider. I identified more with "animal behavior nerds," liberty trainers, and clicker trainers than with cowboys.

That said, I would love to have been a cowboy, in much the same way a Chihuahua might want to be a St. Bernard.

When not riding or spending time with my kids, I had dorky hobbies like juggling (aka constantly dropping and bruising apples, and searching for them under tables), reading (not just thrillers), and running (wearing short shorts).

And look at how I *looked*—my riding clothes included a helmet and tight pants.

"Western" was a whole genre of movies and books. The cowboy was nonchalant, unperturbed, and full of poise. He was calm under pressure. He didn't care what other people thought; he was strong, yet silent and mysterious. He could ride a horse, rope a cow, smoke a cigarette, and juggle women. He was the definition of cool.

I was none of those things.

I knew authenticity could be cool too, but it was going to take a lot of preparation and vulnerability to chart that course. I considered that maybe buying some designer jeans, growing a mustache, donning a cowboy hat, and putting everything else in the hands of the Almighty would be a lot easier.

"Ferdinand, let's go," I whispered.

Our young Golden Retriever padded after me. It was three in the morning. As I stepped outside onto our deck, the heat hit me like I'd stumbled into a sauna. A film of sweat instantly developed on my stomach and forehead and between my legs. The earthy smell of jungle filled my nostrils. Citra, just north of Ocala, rests in the humid subtropical zone of Florida, and never once has the summer here reminded me of where I grew up.

We lived in the loft above the barn, and I had to descend seventeen steps before I hit sand. The very last step when descending was a different height—maybe off by three-quarters of an inch, just enough to send the distracted, or the elderly, to the emergency room. Enough that at night I had to hold the railing and lower my foot like an octopus arm exploring a crevice.

Feeling in the dark for the last step made me think of how a horse might feel when asked to step off a bank for the first time. When going down a bank, a common "step up" or "step down" obstacle on an eventing course, a thoughtful horse will slow down, look down, lower and lengthen his neck, and then gather his feet in a whispered shuffle to find a takeoff spot. If, while I was on that last step of our deck stairs, somebody rushed me, I would brace and stop. If that person did get me to step off, my shoulders would be tight, and there would be resentment in my gut.

Ferdinand scampered ahead while I walked a short loop of the barns. The horses were still, and all I could hear was the hum of crickets, and far off, the occasional truck on the road to Ocala. I thought about the day ahead and felt a long way from being a kid.

After letting Ferdi pee and checking that the horses were settled, I pulled myself back up the stairs and into bed, and slept another hour.

Mid-mornings in Florida, May through October, were hot. Lunchtimes, clouds would swell up so that they looked pregnant.

Afternoons, those same clouds might threaten us with dry lightning, or they might ooze rain. The best part of the summer rain was that the sand our farm was built on absorbed it, creating great footing for the horses, and the grass—Argentine Bahia—grew forked and tall.

By six Sinead was drinking coffee and Taylor Swift was crooning on the stereo. I emerged once again in the kitchen, ambushed Goldfish, and plopped her in a chair in front of a bowl of yogurt. Sinead wrestled Brooks into shorts and a t-shirt.

After dropping them off at school, I drove to Jake's.

Jake Biernbaum was a cowboy. He was a *horseman*. And a savvy one at that. He lived five miles down the road from me in Citra. Jake knew when to push and when to back off. Over the past few years, he had helped me with young horses, liberty horses, and preparing horses off the track for the Thoroughbred Makeover competition.

Jake stood by his tubular metal round pen, which he had welded himself. Next to him were half a dozen coils of ropes. Each one was a different thickness and color, and boasted different amounts of wear.

"Nylon or polyester?" Jake asked.

I wanted coffee but I picked up a rope. I hadn't roped since messing around at horseman Bruce Logan's place in Texas about a decade before. "What's the difference?" I asked.

"There are lots of kinds of ropes," explained Jake. "This one is poly, thirty-five feet. This one is stiff nylon, forty-five feet. It's pretty new."

"Is this different than roping a cow?"

"A cow will *duck* his head. A horse *throws* his head."

Jake wore shorts and sported a cowboy hat. The hat suited him. I'd noticed that when you wore a certain kind of hat often enough, you could start to look naked without it.

In the United States, a *lasso* and a *lariat* are used fairly interchangeably. *Lasso* is from the Castilian word *lazo*, meaning a snare or a trap. Jake picked up the nylon forty-five-foot rope. He explained the tiny loop that the rope passed through to make a bigger loop that could settle around an animal's neck was called the "honda" (or "hondo"). Generally, the honda was simply a knot, but it could also be an eye splice or metal ring.

"How many throws will I need to know?" I ventured.

"Two," he said. "One overhand and one Houlihan, which is essentially the same throw but when the horse is going in the opposite direction. A backhand, basically."

I wound up and threw. The rope left my hand and flopped—like a dropped chicken or a shot duck—again and again, for thirty minutes.

"Have some *feel*," Jake said gently. "Follow it out. Don't totally let it go. Have a little *feel* in it still, to steer. Watch me."

Watching Jake throw his lariat was like watching a pitcher skip stones on a lake. Watching me throw my lariat was like watching a middle-aged bald guy, heaving overfilled trash bags up into a dumpster. I was neither elegant, nor effective.

I kept practicing.

After watching me miss, and get tangled up, and struggle, and struggle, and struggle, Jake told me: "Realistically, you won't be able to rope the horse on the rail, but you might be able to get him to face up, and then swing a rope over him while he is standing still."

What he meant was I would not be able to get good enough to rope a horse while he was moving, not with the time frame we had (eight months), and not under pressure. At Road to the Horse, I would have to start a horse, and in order to do that, I would have to catch him. Although it was possible to catch a horse many different ways (and it was even slicker if *they* learned to catch *you)*, being able to rope a horse was a nice skill to have.

I nodded.

"If you do get good enough…great. But I'm saying, *realistically*…"

After practice I trudged back to the truck. Jake strode next to me.

"Your grass is long," I observed, changing the subject.

"I left it long this year," Jake replied. "Usually we get a dry spell in August, and if I don't leave it long, it burns."

Before I left, Jake handed me three ropes, each a different color and weight. "Take these," he said firmly. "Practice."

I threw them in the bed of my truck and drove home.

After a few half-hearted attempts during the next couple weeks, I didn't pick a rope up again for months. *Maybe if I had two years...* I thought. I talked myself into the idea that it was better to practice something I had a shot at.

I fell prey to an old emotional trap: it's easier to practice something you're comfortable with than to practice something new.

It was only eight in the evening but the kids and Sinead were all asleep. My brain was not letting up; it was like a pinball machine of thoughts, plans, and ideas. I needed something...something to ease my mind. Not television. Not a drink. My drug of choice on such nights was to take Ferdinand for a walk.

I closed the door gently so as not to make a noise. "*Shhhhh,*" I whispered to Ferdi whose tail was wagging against the railing of the deck like a pneumatic nail gun. I shooed him down the steps and he bolted off ahead of me into the dark.

The rain had just stopped, but it was not cold, not even cool, just a slightly less hot sauna. On my evening walks in the summer, I usually went barefoot and shirtless, but still, it was stifling.

At the end of the driveway, I took a left. I pulled a cigar out of my back pocket. It was light and thin. It was a habit I had picked up a couple years before from my inlaws, and I went through one or two a month. I didn't smoke them all the way through, though; even the small ones could give me a headache. What I liked about them was that when I held one, I walked more slowly. Ambled really. Without the cigar I'd find myself power walking, but *with* the stogy I found myself stopping to look at the stars or to feel the breeze on my bare chest and shoulders.

As I walked I thought about *Lonesome Dove,* which I'd just started reading. I figured I was a little like Call, who walked "though he knew there was no real need. It was just an old habit he had, left over from wilder times: checking, looking for a sign of one kind or another, honing his instincts, as much as anything."

I needed to fill the role of "pen wrangler" for Road to the Horse. It was an important position. I knew myself well enough to know that, when working with a horse, too much coaching, or too little, would mess up my flow. Too much talking, or too little, would mess up my rhythm. I wouldn't be able to handle a cynic, but I certainly didn't want a "yes man" either.

Back at the barn, Ferdinand's walk complete, I threw the half-smoked cigar in the fire pit and climbed the stairs to our apartment above. I read two more pages of *Lonesome Dove* and fell asleep.

By mid-July Nick still had not committed to being my pen wrangler.

"What about one of my brothers?" I said to Sinead. "Hey, Goldfish! What are you doing?"

"I'll get her," Sinead said, hustling over to the door and grabbing our daughter, who was attempting to escape. "If you are going to pick someone just because they are family, you should pick me… and I don't think you should pick me. *Oof.* Can you change her diaper?"

I took Goldfish from her arms. "I think Nick is being careful. He's so thoughtful and doesn't take unnecessary risks."

"He is one of the smartest people I know," Sinead agreed. "But he will regret it if he doesn't take it."

"Hold still," I said to Goldfish, who was squirming like an eel as I dealt with the diaper.

"Thank you," said Sinead.

"Thank *you*," I said.

"For what?" she asked.

"For thanking me," I replied.

And then Brooks raced through the kitchen, begging for us to help him catch lizards. It was getting late, Sinead and I agreed, almost dinner time, and the lizards would still be there tomorrow.

Brooks raced out again. He was going to find the lizards himself. He left the door to the deck open.

"Nick has such a great eye, and is super talented," I went on, "but you more than anyone else know that, in the horse industry, talent is only one of the things you need to have to be a professional. You can be talented *and* kind *and* humble, but you also need something else."

I put some clothes back on Goldfish, then held her upside down, then deposited her on the couch, then tickled her, then placed her back on her own two feet. She immediately began to run, laughing, toward the open door, and the stairs.

Sinead sprinted after her.

"She's a pickle," I said.

Sinead caught her. "If Nick doesn't do this with you, he might regret it," she said again.

"Agreed."

"It might affect his relationship with his wife, with his kid…he might resent them. It might affect his relationship with you."

"Now, let's not go that far…" I laughed.

But we did. We convinced ourselves that Nick owed it to himself to be my pen wrangler at Road to the Horse. And more importantly, we owed it to *him* to convince him that he needed to do it.

"He will regret it if he doesn't," Sinead repeated.

"He will lament it *forever*," I said dramatically.

"Forever!"

But after the kids were asleep, I looked at the request I was making from Nick's point of view. He had a new wife and a new baby. They had just purchased a house, which he was renovating himself in between contracting jobs. He worked about as hard for his money as a human could.

Maybe I was asking too much.

The next day, I pitched the pen wrangler deal to Nick one last time.

He was silent. "Have you ever thought about going into sales?" he asked finally.

"Are you sold?"

"I'll talk to Kayla."

8

Copperline Farm lies at the back of the Bellemont subdivision in Citra, Florida, thirteen miles to the closest coffee shop (fifteen if you want Starbucks). Citra, and the surrounding areas of Sparr, Anthony, and Reddick, are still places one can find peanut crops, live oak trees, raised suspensions, alligator bites, rebel flags, and old-school ideas. (In 2018, the year my son was born, students at the local high school were shown by their agricultural science teacher how to drown a raccoon that had been caught killing chickens. A media furor erupted. The teacher was not charged but did choose early retirement.)

Pinhooking is another old-school concept common in Marion County. There are few things in the horse world that treat horses more like a commodity than pinhooking, which is often buying Thoroughbreds as weanlings, then selling them for more as yearlings (it is also done with yearlings that are resold at age two). Not to say that the pinhookers don't know what they are doing—they mostly do. Just that the idea is based around the idea of buying lots of young horses, waiting till they are older, then selling them. There is little-to-no real training going on, and often little interaction between horse and human. It's like buying cattle. Or oil. Or coffee.

Does it cause horses to suffer? No, not in the short-term, anyway. Horses are pretty content living in a herd, in a big field, and for many young Thoroughbreds, that year waiting to be sold on will be the best part of their lives.

Living above the barn at Copperline Farm is both magical and noisy.

When Brooks was four, he came home from school upset.

"Charlie says I live in a barn," he sobbed.

I picked him up. "We do, kinda."

He buried his face in my shoulder. "I want to live in a *house*."

And not for the first time, or the last time, I had a fleeting urge to give my son everything he wanted.

"Are we traumatizing him by making him live in a barn?" I asked Sinead later.

Sinead didn't dignify my crazy with a response.

The barn we live above is rectangular. Therefore, our loft is rectangular as well. But since the roof slices down steeply, the apartment space upstairs is narrower than the barn space downstairs. The rooms where we hang our coats, where we cook, where we eat, where we read, where we work, are all in a row. It's as if we live in a long, segmented hallway, like Lego pieces laid end to end.

There is only one entrance to our second-story home—that steep stairway to the deck at the eastern end. The western end is my office. Outside the office, a tiny patio juts out. In a fire, if we couldn't get to the front door we could go through the office, I guess, and jump off that little patio to the grass below.

On the east wall of my office are bookshelves; on the west wall are bookshelves. Stood against the south wall is a desk, coffee brown and smooth as river pebbles. For years it was the most expensive thing we owned. A short time before Sinead's father died, he had given us a couple thousand dollars in gift cards for Crate & Barrel, and we had used most of it for that desk. Every time I sat down to write I thought of him. Brooks and Goldfish would have loved him.

He would have adored them.

In preparing for Road to the Horse, I was often at that desk before the kids woke up. I'd turn a lamp on, then quietly make a coffee. I'd pull equine training and behavior and theory books from the shelves on either side of the desk and consider the principles espoused within.

Trainer Pat Parelli's 1993 book *Natural Horse-Man-Ship* listed eight principles:

- *Horsemanship is natural.*
- *Don't make assumptions.*
- *Communication is mutual.*
- *Horses and humans have responsibilities.*
- *The attitude is justice.*
- *Body language is universal.*
- *Horses teach riders and riders teach horses.*
- *Principles, purpose, and time are the tools of teaching.*

Another book, *Equitation Science* by equine cognition and learning expert Andrew McLean and animal behavior and welfare professor Paul McGreevy, looked and felt like a textbook. They had ten principles that "training methods and management" should demonstrate:

- *Regard for human and horse safety.*
- *Regard for the nature of horses.*
- *Regard for horses' mental and sensory abilities.*
- *Regard for current emotional states.*

- *Correct use of habituation/desensitization/calming methods.*
- *Correct use of operant conditioning.*
- *Correct use of classical conditioning.*
- *Correct use of shaping.*
- *Correct use of signals/cues.*
- *Regard for self-carriage.*

Finally, I opened *The Principles of Training* by trainer Warwick Schiller. His principles were:

- *Make the wrong thing hard and the right thing easy.*
- *Don't go to bed angry.*
- *Create a tool before using a tool.*
- *Application of your aids.*
- *Do the opposite.*
- *The Donkey Kong Principle.*
- *Choose where you work and choose where you rest.*
- *They need to know the answer before you ask the question.*
- *Isolate, separate, recombine.*
- *Anticipation is your best friend or your worst enemy.*
- *Change one thing at a time.*
- *Work with the horse you have today.*
- *Relationship before horsemanship.*

I decided to create some principles for myself for Road to the Horse. I thought I might set them down on paper, and my pen wrangler and support team and I would follow them during the competition. I messed around for an hour or so and came up with ten:

1. *Only in the planning do we try to win. Once the planning is done, we forget about it; we never try to win in the execution. The only thing that matters is the process, the execution, these principles. Above all the horse should not know I am trying to win anything at all.*

2. *The goal is to improve, not to prove.* (Thanks, Glenn, for this one.)

3. *Stay nimble-minded; don't get caught direct-line thinking.* (This was where I had seen most mistakes happen.)

4. *As of this moment, be the best-prepared.*

5. *Don't make life any harder than it has to be. Making things easier is not cheating.* (In other words, pick the easiest horse.)

6. *The competition is, above all, about reading the horse.* (I couldn't forget this; it was something I was good at.)

7. *Listen to my gut. Watch the horse's eyes. These are the things that will keep me from getting hurt.*

8. *We are a team.* (The horse, the pen wrangler, and I, plus the three additional team members that I still had to choose.)

9. *Stay above the Copperline. No gossip. No excuses. No wishing other people bad luck. Stay curious.* (This was an idea that originated

COPPERLINE

open
curious
committed to learning

closed
defensive
committed to being right

from a football coach who wrote about keeping an "above the line" culture on his teams. He taught his athletes to stay "above the line" in everything they thought and did, meaning being committed to growth and responsibility, not committed to being right. Since our farm was named Copperline, Sinead and I aimed to stay "above the Copperline" in everything we did.)

10. *More than anything I just want to be able to leave saying I did the right thing, and I tried my best, in that order. Because it's a pretty sweet feeling, actually, win or lose, when that happens.*

I stood on the front steps of a small house about a twenty-five-minute drive from Copperline and knocked. "Hello?" I called.

Loud barking from inside made me step backward. *How many are there? Three? Four?*

I tested the handle. *Unlocked.*

I opened the door a crack to see what I was dealing with.

"Hello?" I called again.

It was a typical Ocala afternoon: eighty-four degrees, ninety percent humidity, muggy, miserable. I had been sweating since I stepped outside that morning. It wasn't like up north where it might cool off a little overnight. I reminded myself that at least we had air conditioning in our apartment. I suspected that it was no coincidence that before air conditioning, Florida had been the least populous southern state, and after WWII, when home A/C units took off, the state's population spiked.

Two dogs trotted toward me, still barking. They were Miniature Long-Haired Dachshunds, each with alert eyes, like a couple of otters. I recognized them, but I couldn't remember their names.

In order to remember names, I often rely on pneumonics, or memory tricks, to help. Someone named Daisy, for example, I would picture with a flower in her hair. I have to make a conscious effort to remember the physical attributes of horses and match them to their names. The stars, snips, socks, for example. Because I not only might not remember a name, I might not realize I know the horse. My wife could meet a bay horse once, then spot it eleven years later in a field of thirty other bay horses. I can't do that. I might not even recognize the horse the next day. In fact, one of my greatest fears when I was a working student, learning from top equestrians all over the world, was that I would be assigned a horse, ride him for two weeks, and then one day go to fetch the horse from the paddock…and get the wrong horse.

My eye for equine movement and soundness isn't great either. I struggle in dressage. And when our veterinarian jogs up our horses, even my students will be nodding along with her prognosis, and I'll be left wondering what it was they all saw. *Was the horse lame on the left front or the right hind?*

My strength with horses relies largely on one particular skill: *recognizing how they feel.* With horses, my mind doesn't emphasize how they felt yesterday, and it takes effort for me to make plans for what I'm going to do with them tomorrow. The question that is easiest for me to answer is simply: *How do they feel right now?*

I've found that some trainers' eyes are drawn more to the horse's physical characteristics—how a horse moves and jumps, for example—and some are drawn to the emotional: Are they scared? Anxious? Curious? Relaxed? Maybe this is similar to the idea that some musicians find it easy to read music, and some never learn. Eric Clapton and Prince are famous for not knowing how to read sheet music. I've heard Taylor Swift is not much good at it either. Jimi Hendrix had *synesthesia*, a condition where he saw music as colors.

Linda Parelli appeared behind her dogs. She wore blue riding pants and a pink shirt that said "Happy Horse, Happy Life." Two sparkling earrings, tiny silver flowers, caught my eye. Her blonde hair, as she so often wore it, was back in a ponytail.

"Come on in," she said with a grin. The two Dachshunds stopped barking.

That summer it had been especially difficult to find babysitters, so every trip off the farm was hard-won. But I managed to get Lucia, from Costa Rica, wife of Abisai, to watch Brooks and Goldfish for an hour, and Sinead's mother, Bernadette ("Nana" to the kids), to watch them after that. Finding babysitters seemed to be the first and largest obstacle in finding time to study colt starting, for all work grinds to a halt when there is no babysitter.

Linda led me to her kitchen. "What can I do for you?" she asked.

I explained that I was looking to learn more about starting horses.

I'd met Linda in October 2013 at a dressage clinic in Maryland and had kept in touch with her ever since. Although colt starting was not her specialty, I admired her ability to read horses and to distill difficult concepts down to their essence.

Linda offered me a seat, but she remained standing. We discussed different methods of starting horses, and I took notes. After twenty or thirty minutes I asked her a question that had been on my mind.

"Who is the best?" I asked. "If I want to learn from the best colt starters in the world, who are they?"

"Well, let me see." Linda got up and got a glass down from above the sink. "I'm not really sure, I don't really keep up with that world. Ronnie Willis for sure…. Water? Probably Jonathan Field."

"Yes, please. I love Jonathan." Ronnie Willis, I knew, had passed away years before.

She handed me a glass of water. "And there is Craig Cameron," she said. "Pat was paired with him in 2012 at Road to the Horse.

I remember he always insisted Craig was the 'real deal.' He was complimentary. And Mike Major. Pat spoke highly of him too."

Linda, née Paterson, was born in Singapore in 1958. Her family moved to Sydney, Australia, when she was twelve. She was in her thirties when she met the founder of Parelli Natural Horsemanship Pat Parelli. Linda had followed the man and his horsemanship to America in the early nineties. At that time Pat was drawing huge crowds to his events. Thousands of people. He would play with a horse and at the same time tell a story, or a joke; he held crowds in the palm of his hand as easily as you or I hold a knife and fork. Sometimes he would enter the arena by running through fog, with spotlights trained on him. He would exit to standing ovations.

Linda and Pat were recently separated, I knew, but her posture in the kitchen was, as usual, independent...elegant. She leaned forward against the counter.

"I was at Road to the Horse this past March for the first time," I said. "Actually, I've applied to be in it." Due to the contract I had signed, I couldn't tell her that I was already *in* it.

"You can learn a lot by watching it," Linda said sweetly. "You can learn a lot by *doing* it. And some of the competitors do a good job… but if you're trying to *win* the thing…*poor* horse."

I was discomfited by her comment, but our conversation turned to what motivates horses, and I shook it off as we discussed the difference between "pleasure" and "happiness"—not only what motivates our horses but how we *want* our horses to be motivated. Do we want them to be motivated by little surges of dopamine, like a kid in a candy shop, or a gambler at the slot machines? Or do we want them to find a calmer, more peaceful place?

"Happiness and pleasure get confused," Linda said. Pleasure, she explained, was short-lived. It was about *taking*. It was about dopamine. Too much could lead to addiction, whether that addiction was related to a substance or a behavior. Happiness was long-lived and was about *giving*. There was no such thing as "too much happiness." Serotonin, a key ingredient to happiness, was about contentment. It was the Zen every creature was looking for, and *that* was what we wanted our horses to find.

Whether it is how to instruct kids, how to train dogs, or how to educate horses, *motivation* is a controversial subject. All sides will point to the science that backs up their view. The problem is, however, that it is not a question that can be answered in labs by scientists. It must be answered by ethicists, philosophers, and every mom, dad, coach, mentor, horse owner, and trainer for themselves, because the heart of it all is not about facts, it is about morality. And morality was not discovered, it was invented.

I checked my watch. The allotted time I had with babysitters at home was about to run out. I thanked Linda for her time.

I stopped at the door. "I have just one more question…" I said, turning to her.

She nodded. I still could not believe her generosity in helping me. I wanted to hug her. I hoped, not for the last time, that I wouldn't let her down.

"I need a good metaphor for starting horses. For example, *'Starting a horse is to riding a mature horse as blank is to blank.'*"

"That reminds me of something Ronnie Willis used to say," Linda replied.

"What did he say?"

"The start isn't just something. It's *everything*."

"That's a great quote." It was more fun to start a horse right than to work with one that was traumatized or that had learned unhelpful habits; it was easier for me; it was less stressful for them.

The dogs followed me out the door. "What are their names again?"

"Moxie and Lulu."

Moxie and Lulu, I repeated to myself.

But I'd forgotten their names by the time I started the car.

JR Robles was in Arizona at a reining competition. I had gotten his number from Tammy at the Road to the Horse office. He answered on the fourth ring, his voice husky and quick.

"How's it going?" I asked.

"Hectic."

Par for the course for a person with horses.

I was at home, sitting on the leather sectional couch Sinead had found on Facebook Marketplace. My laptop was perched on my knees. Directly behind me hung a large mounted print of two cows, maybe four feet by five. One cow was chocolate brown with a mottled creamy face, the other was black with a fluffy dirty-white forelock. Their heads were bigger than mine. Their eyes were searching.

"What's your advice for me?" I'd told him I'd accepted the Road to the Horse invitation, which had now been officially announced, and he'd said he was happy to share a few insights.

"The politics, the interviews, the photoshoots, all the behind-the-scenes stuff…" JR warned. "The whole thing…it's a…lot. Having a good team to keep you organized is big." JR's voice was deep. The voice of a singer, I thought. Baritone, maybe. "It was eye-opening, that's for sure," he said.

"Is there anything you could have done differently?"

"The way it ended, I couldn't have dreamed of it a different way," he said thoughtfully. "I would have loved to have won, but the way it ended was perfect. I wouldn't switch it. The colt that I drew. I got everything out of him that I was going to get out of him—some can go through a three-day colt-starting format, and some just can't…"

Goldfish suddenly bolted through the room. She had her pacifier in her hand. Bernadette, who was looking after her for a couple hours, came through the room a second later. Goldfish looked her nana directly in the eye then shouted, "No!" and darted out of the room. Bernadette started after her with a glance my way.

"Sorry," she whispered.

"Study the horses," JR went on. "Watch them unload. Watch *how* they unload. Study them, but it's also luck of the draw."

"What about in the round pen?" I asked.

"Have a stopwatch. Have a plan. My pen wrangler was great. We did a fantastic job of over-communicating. We had a timeline, but it was fluid."

"There's *nothing* you would have changed?" I pushed.

"Round Two in Kentucky I put more pressure on myself," he admitted. "I caught myself looking outside of my round pen. I recommend *not* doing that. My pen wrangler did a good job of snapping me back into what I was doing. Make sure you use your pen wrangler, you get points for it."

I made a note of that, then asked, "Bit or no bit?"

"I would recommend *not* going to a snaffle. You do so much in the halter getting them ready, and then if you switch it, you are almost resetting everything. Have either a rope halter, or a firm loping hackamore, or a bosal."

"Thank you for this advice, JR. Anything else you think I should really know?"

"I made a mistake after Round Two," he replied, taking a moment. "I read some comments on social media where someone said the horse I drew must have been green-broke and everybody else actually had wild horses. They said no way could I be doing what I was doing if my horse wasn't already broke. My advice? Stay off that stuff after each round. It will get in your head if you allow it." He paused again and cleared his throat, then said: "Here is one thing I told myself: Enjoy it and be in the moment. That's my *best* advice."

I wondered how present I would be. Would I be looking outside my round pen at what the others were doing?

"What are you up to?" I asked.

"Just building a barn."

"And?"

"And I'm in," Nick said.

YES!

I could have hugged him.

I updated him on the logistics. The times, the hotels, what was covered, and what wasn't. I knew it would be a big time, energy, and money commitment for him. Especially with a new baby.

"Who else is on the team?" he asked.

"Juliette and Sinead so far. We have room for one more."

"What's the role of each of us?"

"Sinead has the role of…well…"

"Wife?"

"Too many beautiful things to name."

"Uncategorizable."

"Beyond description," I agreed. "For Juliette, I think I will write 'Equine Behaviorist and Logistical Support.'"

"What do you think your biggest weakness is?"

I answered without hesitation: "Knowing Quarter Horses.

Knowing their bloodlines; their strengths and weaknesses. Knowing their conformation, tendencies, and behaviors. Just generally knowing my way around them."

"I can help with that."

"I know you can. Hey, Nick?"

"Yeah?"

"Tell Kayla I say, 'Thanks.'"

I could hear his grin through the phone. "I will," he said.

9

Once the Road to the Horse 2024 competitors were announced officially, and it became more widely known that I was participating, the question I was asked the most was: "What's your plan?"

While I may not have had all the answers, I did have a plan:

- *Talk to people*—learn from past participants, judges, and spectators.

- *Watch, or re-watch, the previous years' competitions.* Some of these videos were easy to find online; others were harder and involved investing in old DVDs.

- *Assemble a team that will help and support me.* So far I had Nick, Juliette, and Sinead. We had room for one more.

I had spoken with a lot of people I respected already. The best way I could sum up the advice I had gathered so far was:

- *Don't go to win.*

- *But…win the horse's confidence.*

- *Don't be in a hurry.*

As far as the idea of not going to win, that was a tricky one. The trick would be to follow my principle of *looking to win in the planning stages, but not in the execution*. I never wanted to let my horse feel that expectation. To the horse, I wanted to appear completely in the moment, not thinking ahead, not going any faster than he was ready for.

One past competitor told me he didn't learn the rules or change any of what he usually did with a horse, he just "went in and did his thing."

Geez, I thought. *You're insane.*

I wanted to know the rules. I wanted to know them inside and out. I wanted to know what the arena was going to look like, how much time I would have, how it would feel to be on the clock, how many judges there were going to be, how they were going to score, what the obstacles would be, what the mandatory display of skills would be (what Road to the Horse called "rail work"). I wanted to know *as much as possible*! And instead of being constricted by that, I felt like it would give me the freedom to not worry about it. The better I knew it, the less I could think about it, and the more I could just do my thing. Since I had signed up for Road to the Horse, I was accepting their parameters. *So*, I thought, *I might as well know 'em.*

And just because I accepted the rules didn't mean I had to push the horse to win. In any equestrian discipline, we can choose when and how to back off to protect the horse's well-being. And at Road to the Horse, JR had showed us that in 2023. He hadn't been vilified for it; actually, he'd been celebrated.

I needed to remember that.

I stood in our kitchen one stormy morning, late in August. My laptop, a silver MacBook Air, was perched on the long dining table made of four planks of rough-cut hardwood. As I talked to Martha and Becca from my publisher, Trafalgar Square Books, I walked laps around the table. Ferdi lay with his snout on his paws, his eyes following me on every loop.

I read a list of thirteen names I had written down. The individuals named were spread out all over the world, although most of them lived in the United States. Many of them had competed in Road to the Horse before.

These were the people I wanted to train with.

"Okay," I heard on the other end of the line.

"Then I will talk to people who are thinking about horses maybe a little differently. Whether it's from a scientific point of view…or positive reinforcement point of view…or a more empathetic point of view. I even found someone that doesn't believe we should be riding horses at all, much less starting them." I read that list to them.

"So, they are all women?" Martha said.

"That hadn't occurred to me until just now…but, well… yes."

"And all the people you plan to be actually starting horses with are men?"

I stopped pacing and flipped the laptop around so it faced me. I glanced at my first list.

"That also hadn't occurred to me until just now…but, again, yes."

There was a silence on the line.

"I'll see what I can do to diversify my lists," I mumbled.

Before we ended the call, Martha said something that struck me: "The people that start a lot of horses, and that we have never heard of, *they* are the real horsemen. They are the ones with no ego. They are just in it for the horses."

There was some truth to what she said, but I wondered if I could find those people. Finding the people I had never heard of would be, by definition, more difficult.

I looked at Ferdinand. His doleful eyes were still following me. I went over and crouched beside him. I rubbed him behind the ears.

I was reminded of another question I had been thinking about.

Did being a "good horseman" encompass being a "good human"?

No, was my first thought. I had seen plenty of people who were skillful with horses but sucked with people.

I then wondered, as I thought about the trainers I knew, where the line was between a pride in their work, and a vanity about it.

The more I thought about it, the more I thought, yes, a "good horseman" should encompass being a "good human." Yes, you needed to be polite, curious, and honest, and maybe even, occasionally, joyful or funny.

And so, on that day, as my dog was my witness, I mentally adjusted my definition for what a "good horseman" is.

Only a few days after I was invited to compete at Road to the Horse, I tore my groin for the third time.

It was Jenny that bucked. But it wasn't her fault. I don't believe it's helpful to lay blame on a horse. Credit, maybe, but not blame.

I should have seen it coming. I should have slowed down.

Jenny was actually doing more than bucking; it was a real bronc ride. She thrust her muzzle low and dropped her withers. As she did that, I swung my lower legs forward and pushed my feet hard into the stirrups. I slid my seat back. I gripped the reins and tried to get her head up. Later my fingers would be raw and pink; it would hurt to wash or even to close my hands for a week.

Some people call rope burns "learn burns." Not wearing gloves when I ride or do groundwork makes it more personal. It keeps me present. I remember my mistakes. And I don't want to forget the mistakes I make with horses. I owe it to them. And if a burn on my hand will burn that mistake into my memory, and my soul, keep 'em coming.

I should have slowed down. I should have been more present.

Jenny was on her fourth bronc when I started thinking, *This might not get better...she might not come out of this.* Simultaneously, I was thinking about my groin, trying to gauge how much it was tearing.

On the eleventh or twelfth buck, I came off over her right shoulder. As I hit the ground, I was aware of where I was in relation to her—out of the corner of my eye, I saw her turn left, away from me. My main concern was which way she would kick in the few seconds after I landed.

She kicked in the other direction, then continued to buck. The bucks gradually turned into porpoise-ing, and then into a gallop as she ran down the driveway. I crawled to the nearby fence and leaned back against it. I didn't say anything. I didn't reach for my phone. I just watched Jenny as she turned between two paddocks and slowed down slightly.

Then Sinead rounded the corner of the barn, having spied the loose horse. She ran on the balls of her feet, her head high, her eyes scanning. She was quick and graceful and worried. When she saw me against the fence, her shoulders relaxed slightly.

He's conscious, I saw her thinking. *He's okay.*

A couple hours later we were both riding in the arena when she caught my attention. I brought my horse back to a walk.

"How are you feeling?"

"Tired," I said. "Hurt." I paused, studying the space between my horse's ears. "*Old*. Like this was something I used to be good at. That it's hard to let go of something I used to be known for."

I didn't mention Road to the Horse. But riding a buck, and getting up from a buck, were skills that might be needed. Would almost *certainly* be needed.

It would be easy to look at me and think, *This guy isn't good enough. Why did they invite him?*

"You're not hurt," Sinead said, riding her horse up alongside me. "I've seen you hurt."

I nodded. I felt pretty darn sore, but I knew what she meant.

"Maybe your pride is hurt," she said.

"It is," I agreed.

But my main concern was being ready to compete. My groin had been nagging me since January. Then I had hurt it a second time. This was the third time. The falling didn't hurt nearly as much as the gripping to stay on when the bucking started.

The injury was also not allowing me to run, which affected my fitness, and my mood.

"I want so bad for this injury to get better."

"I've started meditating," Sinead said. "You should try it."

"Yeah…" I nodded.

That first mistake, and the second, and the third, all happened because I didn't listen to that little niggle in my stomach, in my gut. I believe that very few accidents are truly accidental. Looking back, I feel that every injury I have ever had could have been prevented. Just because *I* failed to predict what was about to happen does not mean it was unpredictable.

I was distracted. I was rushing. I was tired.

I remembered a group session with mental performance consultant Dr. Jenny Susser, where she'd asked each of us what we wanted help with.

"I'm afraid of cross-country," said a novice rider.

"I get so anxious before dressage," noted a teenager.

"I get nervous at shows," whispered an introvert.

Dr. Susser listened, and asked questions, and helped each rider in the group feel hopeful. Then it was my turn:

"Well, often, being at shows is where I feel the most present. For me, the problem is at home. I feel pulled in so many directions. The fences that need to be nailed back up. The mower that needs to go into the shop. The text message that says someone needs to reschedule. Am I going to be done in time to get the kids from school?"

Dr. Susser studied me for a moment. "You're just being intellectually lazy," she said. "Next question."

Well, that set me on my back foot. But she was absolutely right. No one was going be present *for me*. There was no point in doing two things at once. I had to plan my day better, and I had to focus.

Sinead's horse and mine ambled beside each other. They were both bays. We headed down the driveway to give both horses a chance to cool down.

"I'm riding too defensively," I said. "It feels like if they buck or rear I won't be able to hold on. Every time I grip with my thighs, a wave of pain ripples through me, right up into my ears. And if I *don't* tighten my legs, I flop around, like a fish on a dock, making him more likely to rear and me more likely to fall off. And just knowing that makes me ride tentatively: my heart rate is up, I'm quick to pull on the reins, and I'm not giving him a forward, confident ride."

Sinead laughed. "Welcome to the club. Now you know how the other half feels."

I tore my groin for the *first* time on New Year's Day, 2023.

The gelding held his head high, the muscles in his neck were taut as chopsticks, and his ears were pricked.

As soon as my seat hit the saddle, he took off.

He didn't buck or rear, but he cantered flat out in the round pen. Each lap he was a little more off balance; each lap he seemed to go faster. Three laps, four laps, five laps. Dirt flew.

Then he tripped.

I lost both my stirrups.

With no stirrups on which to balance, I wrapped my legs around him tighter in order to stay on, which, of course, only caused him to speed up more.

Nine laps, ten laps, eleven laps.

His eyes were wide.

Adrenaline was pumping.

Eighteen laps, nineteen laps, twenty laps. He wasn't slowing down.

Was I going to have to bail off the side? My heart rate was through the roof. I couldn't find a moment to get my stirrups. I held on.

Thirty-two laps, thirty-three laps, thirty-four laps.

I tried pulling the rope attached to his halter. There were no reins and no bit. When I pulled his neck tightened and he braced against me, like a Husky, bracing into the wind, pulling a sled with all his might.

Forty-seven laps, forty-eight laps…

Finally he trotted. I slid off and let my feet fall to the earth.

I stood there. I held the reins. His body was tight and still, his eyes unblinking. My own body felt hazy and disconnected, like I imagined a deer might feel after being hit by a car. I stepped toward the gate, and there was a flash of lightning that began two inches above my knee and tore straight up my body. It ripped into my stomach, then pierced my chest, before splitting into three fragments—two that raced into my arms, electrifying them, and one that climbed into my neck and brain. My jaw went tight, and my knees buckled, and I winced in pain. I caught myself from falling with a hand on the fence.

I handed the gelding off to someone—I can't remember who. I took tiny steps as I grunted back to the house. I stopped every few steps to catch my breath. By avoiding any forward movement or stretch with the right thigh I could prevent more jolts of searing pain.

I held on to the railing as I climbed the stairs to the door of our apartment. I led with the left foot, the right foot always just catching up.

A few weeks later I was on Fenwick, a chestnut gelding. A Thoroughbred. As we passed the shed, my parents, who were visiting, opened the door of the apartment and stepped out onto the deck.

Fenwick, surprised by their sudden appearance, reared. He went straight up.

My brain, with four decades of neural wiring, knew exactly how to respond to this precise situation. I had been in the same position hundreds, maybe thousands of times, before. My hands softened and went forward. My chest also went forward so I stayed in balance, more or less upright compared to the ground, nine feet below. My eyes, clear, looked ahead—not at the ground or Fenwick's neck, and not off into the distance, but at a spot about head-height, maybe fifty feet away, so I had a focal point. My lower legs went slightly forward. My ankles flexed, and my heels dropped. It all happened simultaneously and smoothly.

Most of what we must do when a horse bucks or rears is the exact opposite of human instinct, which is to assume the fetal position.

I reacted just how I knew I should, just how I'd been trained, except for one piece of the puzzle: I needed to wrap my legs around the horse's body, just enough for me to stay on, but not enough to concern him. Like a wet t-shirt that sticks but doesn't squeeze. Like glue.

My legs closed.

My groin tore for the second time. I screamed.

My legs came off. I flopped on Fenwick's back, which scared him. He reared again, and I was faced with the two options: Close my legs and feel a sickening jolt of pain, or don't close my legs and thump onto his back, my legs flopping against his sides as the spike of pain hits me anyway.

He reared again. I tried Option A. He reared again. I tried Option B.

Another scream erupted from my soul, through my lips.

On the seventh rear, I flopped off. I hit the ground, and the pain went all the way through me. I had no control of it. Another scream was inevitable.

The final scream had actually been years in the making.

I'd heard wild animals scream the way I did that day, but the only time I'd heard a human scream like that was when my brother-in-law came down from getting a rebound while we were playing basketball and just kept going down. He collapsed. He pointed at his leg. His right kneecap was five inches higher than where it should have been. When we picked him up, he screamed. It came from deep inside him. Like it wasn't from him. It was an inner beast trying to escape. Something he had no control over.

That's how I felt that day. The pain came from a primal place.

I felt naked and raw and outraged.

I lay on the ground sobbing and shaking.

There is a saying: *The master is not the one never knocked off balance, he is the one who regains balance with the most grace.*

I was definitely not in balance, I had not *regained* balance, and I certainly lacked grace.

I was okay. I wasn't dead. But it felt worse than that: I was embarrassed.

"You've been trying to ride, and your groin just isn't healed," my mother said, sitting next to me a few hours later.

"You need to rest," my father told me. "No work until it's better."

Upset, I resorted to yelling. "I have to!" I cried. "I have to work!"

"Why?" my mother asked.

The two of them looked at me. I felt trapped in a corner.

"We have to pay the mortgage! We have to pay the staff! Do you even know how much money goes out every week? I can't take one day off, much less a week or a month!"

The way they looked at me.

I couldn't understand it.

I couldn't process it.

I realized later what it was. My parents just wanted me to be safe. They didn't care what I won, or what I did, or if we had to take a second mortgage or sell the horses. They didn't care if we lost the farm. They just loved me.

And riding horses, starting colts, winning competitions, buying a farm—nobody put any of that on me but me.

In March of 2022, I was at Red Hills, in Tallahassee, Florida, for their last event. (They have discontinued their horse trials, like so many locations around the world.)

First up in an eventing competition, the triathlon of horse sports, is the dressage phase. I had to ride a series of precise movements that displayed a number of desirable qualities, including rhythm, straightness, and suppleness.

All three horses I rode—Bean, Sam, and Galileo—were tense.

"Well, that wasn't great," I said quietly to Cat afterward. Cat, who was grooming for me that weekend, was there to help me care for the horses. She was bundled up in a jacket and scarf.

"It wasn't great, was it," she responded.

"No." I went to walk the cross-country course—the second phase of competition.

The course was twisty, like a roller coaster. The jumps were big—bigger than we were ready for. And they were technical—more technical than we had prepared for.

I had a pit in my stomach.

Usually, I am prepared. I *prepare*.

I am also usually confident on most horses, in most situations. But I had lost my mojo. All three of the horses I was riding at Red Hills had arrived in my training barn with baggage, and while I had succeeded in getting them going, emotions could run high.

I was distracted as I walked from the cross-country course back to the barn. Years before I had promised myself that if I was ever lucky enough to be in a position to compete horses at a high level, I would savor every moment. I was breaking that promise.

Cat was brushing Sam as I walked into the barn.

"Why do you look like that?" she asked.

"My confidence has got to be down at least fifty percent," I mumbled.

Cat laughed. "So now you're like a normal person."

"Maybe more than fifty percent," I said. I wasn't bound to showing horses, but I felt claustrophobic.

I don't know if I want to keep doing this.

I helped clean the horses' stalls, but it didn't help.

"I'm going for a run," I announced. "I need to clear my head."

I tore off through the woods. Trees flashed by. There was a hill. I sped up. I was looking for that familiar pain in my legs; instead, I ached in my heart. No sunlight was getting in. I ran faster.

I was holding it together...*barely.* There were all the usual stresses in my life, but there was something else as well, a straw that was breaking my back.

Is it just this show? Just this month? Or do I need to change my life?

I was holding it together...*just barely.*

My horses were not enjoying their job, and that made *me* not enjoy my job.

What does a horse that enjoys his job look like? I didn't know. But I sure knew what a horse that was *not* enjoying his job looked like. It looked like tail swishing, mouth open, and ears pinned. It looked like eyes rolling back or staring. It looked like pawing or biting. It looked like stress.

For years, I had looked around at what other people who I thought were successful were doing, and what they were doing was this: *they were winning.* So "winning" had become a major part of my definition of success.

I had positioned myself exactly where I thought I wanted to be, and in doing so, had lost what I enjoyed. The reason I enjoyed horses was the same reason I enjoyed writing—the thoughtfulness. The appreciation for subtlety.

It's just one bad day, I told myself as I ran. *And sometimes we need to struggle for things we want. Not everything comes easy.*

And then... *I can't keep going like this. I don't love it enough.*

I emerged from the trail and ran into a clearing. I stopped

running. I lay down on the grass and leaves. I held my life in front of me and I studied it.

I had been competing in sports for three decades: basketball, track, cross-country, rugby, swimming, fencing, modern pentathlon, show jumping, eventing. I had experienced many highs, and even more lows.

I was exhausted.

I felt like an aged, bruised apple.

But there was no smooth off-ramp for me. I had just turned forty, which was a big turning point. I had a son, and at that time, a daughter on the way. This was *not* the time for a career change.

That evening I fell asleep thinking about about camping, and cuddling watching movies, and reading books to the kids by firelight. I thought about running and hiking and leisurely writing at coffee shops. I thought about quitting and making money, so we weren't short every month. I thought of buying horses for Sinead. I thought about watching the kids grow up.

I got all three horses through cross-country at Red Hills, and then show jumping—the third phase—the next day. But on the drive home I just kept thinking, *Is it worth it?*

It wasn't.

Something needed to change. I didn't know *what* needed to change or *when*. And then there was the biggest one of all: *How*?

How was I going to change my life?

I told Sinead I was not happy.

"What are you waiting for?"

"What do you mean?"

"Why don't we figure out what to change?"

God, does she ever not understand. I began to list all the reasons things couldn't possibly change—money, time, kids, family—all the usual suspects.

"It's not those things. You're afraid."

I was silent. I *was* afraid.

What was I so afraid of?

It is the characteristic excellence of the strong man, wrote Dietrich Bonhoeffer, *that he can bring momentous issues to the fore and make a decision about them. The weak are always forced to decide between alternatives they have not chosen themselves.*

"What are you waiting for?" Sinead asked again.

I looked at her. I was empty.

"Tell me, what is it you plan to do with your one *wild* and *precious* life?"

I knew she was quoting Mary Oliver, and she knew I knew, and yet instead of laughing at the cliche, I felt like I had just been hit in the stomach. I couldn't breathe. I realized I had been treading water for the past few years. Waiting for the right moment in which to begin.

10

One of the features of horseman Monty Roberts' Join-Up Method was that he could do it in thirty minutes or less.

That was the first time I had heard of a time frame for training horses.

Making the starting of horses a timed event is a bit like making kindergarten a competition. Imagine if the teacher of the most successful kids won a hundred grand.

When I worked for David O'Connor in 2009, he one day walked out of the round pen and handed a stick to me as he wiped his forehead.

"Looks good," I said. "It looks so slow. You've been in there a while."

"I don't understand trying to get this done quickly," he responded. "In fact, what I love most about it is getting lost in it…not having any idea how much time is passing."

I've gotten to the point where I don't enjoy riding every horse. I'm pickier. But I haven't yet found a horse I don't enjoy working with from the ground. On the ground I feel safer, calmer. My timing is better, and I'm more creative with the exercises I come up with.

I get lost in it.

When you're lost in enjoyment, in creativity, is there a place for a clock? I believe there is. Both things can exist, within reason.

Both Socrates and Oscar Wilde are reported to have said, "Everything in moderation, including moderation."

I pulled off County Road 225 onto the shoulder. To my right was a grass field that held cattle. One of the cows gazed dolefully at me, then flicked a fly away with her tail. It was just after nine in the morning. I had just finished a jump lesson and was hot and sticky, but I had waited weeks for this call and I wasn't about to delay it.

We tried FaceTime but the connection wasn't strong enough. We tried with audio only, and the call went through. On the screen a still photo appeared: A horse lying down. Relaxed neck, ear tilted, soft eyes. Next to the horse was a curly-haired woman I knew was Stacy Westfall. Stacy had competed at Road to the Horse, and won, in 2006.

"Road to the Horse," I stated dramatically.

"Well…what are you worried about?"

Where to start?

"The culture of the whole thing…it feels like a reach. The Western saddle…the ropes…Quarter Horses. All of it."

"Look," Stacy said practically. "The only way you lose is if you offend the horse or the crowd. What does winning look like to *you*?"

I was silent.

"Be authentic," Stacy said. "Be your authentic self!"

"Did you struggle with the idea that starting horses shouldn't be a competition?"

"Are you running into that?"

"Yes, with a few people close to me."

"My first day at Road to the Horse everyone was saddling and riding, and I just had a halter on my colt. That night I bought the horse. Statistically, mathematically, I was way behind. Everybody else was doing *all* the things. And I went in there the next day because I wanted to know the answer."

"The answer?"

"Road to the Horse asks two different questions: The first is, would you start a horse in a time frame, which *happens* to be a competition? The second is that competition is an opportunity for you to act a certain way under pressure. How do *you* act?"

I looked at the cows. My head was spinning. Wasn't it Kipling who asked, *Could I keep my head while all around me people were losing theirs? Could I trust myself while others doubted me, yet make allowance for their doubts as well? Could I dream, and yet not have dreams be my master?*

"Road to the Horse is a game," Stacy told me. "It's about getting in the right head space. Showing, teaching, starting horses—those are the building blocks. *You have those skills.* You might have to re-arrange them into an order you are not familiar with, but you *are* familiar with the pieces. This will be a *great, deep* exploration for you—before, during, and after. It's an amazing growth opportunity."

She had to go, she had another call. I thanked her for her time, nodded to the cows, then pulled off the grass back onto 225.

I was so far out of my comfort zone it was affecting how I ate, how I slept, how I drank. I felt raw and vulnerable, like I was preparing to stand naked in front of a mob. It took an enormous amount of energy. I coped by not letting the energy wane.

It's a game, Stacy had said. Well, that was right up my alley. I loved games. Loved to play. And if I could make it fun for me, maybe I could make it fun for the colt as well.

She kept talking, so I took my pants off.

"I moved here to ride and work," she said. "My husband is still in New York. But the horse life here is so much better."

"Ocala is addictive like that," I said, folding my pants. "If you're into horses it's a great place to be." I looked around the room. Bare. There was a single table. I laid my pants on the floor and glanced at my watch.

Rachel, slightly older than I was, kept up a steady stream of chatter as I went over to the table and sat on it.

"Long Island. That's where I was for years," Rachel went on. "Now we alternate trips to see each other. Lie on your back."

I stretched out and shut my eyes. *This is going to hurt.* But I felt a massive pressure to get healthy. Starting a horse while you're injured is like pretty much anything else that you do while you're injured—not much fun.

Confucius said, *A healthy man wants a thousand things. A sick man only wants one.*

The groin injury was rough. If I slipped sideways even an inch and had to catch my balance, I would wince from the pain. This was affecting my colt starting in particular because of how much I liked to play with my horses. I wanted to run and jump alongside them, swing onto their back and lie on them. I wanted to touch them and feel their sweat mix with my sweat. I also needed to be able to get out of their space quickly if needed—to retreat in an instant.

I'd met a lot of cowboys who were never going to run unless something was chasing them. They looked down on wasted energy. And if I lived in rattlesnake country, smoked cigarettes, and didn't have access to physiotherapy, I might feel the same way.

I opened my eyes. I saw Rachel walking toward me. I shut my eyes again.

I'm going to start working out more, I told myself, *get limber*, *become more flexible, feel better about myself, and trim extra weight. I'll eat healthier, and work on my vertical leap.*

I imagined preparing for Road to the Horse like a ninja.

Rachel put both hands on my thigh. I flinched. She began to work. The pain this week felt different—duller and grittier, like grains of sand caught in a telephoto lens as it slides.

"What is that?" I asked, knowing she felt it too.

"That's new. That's an adhesion. There is scar tissue being created, and the pieces that are supposed to be sliding smoothly are not. It's normal as you heal. Your body is trying to protect itself by building scar tissue to keep it still."

What Rachel did hurt, but it was a *good* hurt.

When she was done with my leg, I asked if she could also do my back. My lower back hurt constantly, and so did my shoulders.

Rachel reached for something that looked like brass knuckles, a kind of silver blade. She held it with two hands.

"Turn over," she said.

My jaw clenched as she ran the instrument over the muscles next to my spine.

Finally, it was over. I picked my pants up off the floor.

"I saw a sign outside a church on the way here," I said. "And Adam said, '*I'll wear the plants in this family....*'"

Rachel half smiled. "Take a look at this." She handed me a pamphlet entitled *How to Talk to Your Cat About Abstinence* by The American Association of Patriots. The cover featured a closeup of a cat looking timidly away from the camera. Around the cat's neck was a collar with a heart-shaped pendent that said, *I am worth waiting for.*

I flipped through it. "This can't be real."

She grinned. "Best four dollars I ever spent. When are you back?"

"I'll be back next week. We need to prioritize this."

I wanted to feel healthy so bad I could taste it.

"How was she? Goldfish! Goldfish, I'm warning you! That snake belongs to Brooks."

It was a stuffed snake—like a teddy bear, not a deer head.

"How was who?" Sinead asked, eyes on the car in front of us.

I passed Goldfish some goldfish-shaped crackers to distract her in her car seat. "Janet Jones. How was she on the podcast?"

"Interesting!" Sinead said. She pulled off East Silver Springs Boulevard into the Montessori parking lot. Two teachers came over to greet our kids.

"Can you pick me up early?" Brooks asked as he got out of the car and gathered his lunchbox. His lunchbox had a cartoon of a soccer ball with a face.

"I can't today," I said. "But tomorrow is the weekend, and we can make rivers in the sandbox."

Goldfish, holding her teacher's hand, marched off, eyes up, chest first. Brooks, four years older, was more timid. He followed reluctantly.

"There they go," I said to Sinead. "Goldfish never looks back, does she? What was your main takeaway?

"They are so cute."

"They are *so* cute."

Sinead pulled out of the parking lot. She drove efficiently, eyes bright, reminding me of Goldfish. But we were only going a few blocks.

"They are so different."

"They are *so* different."

Sinead turned into a spot in front of The Gathering Cafe.

"That fear should never be punished," Sinead said, circling back to my question about neuroscientist and horsewoman Janet Jones, who Sinead had interviewed on her podcast *In Stride* that morning. "We are here to be horses' guides, their mentors. We are here to lead these horses as they walk in a new land."

I liked that.

If I was dropped into a strange country, and I didn't speak the language, had no understanding of the culture, and was lost, what kind of guide would I want?

Our orders at the café counter were fairly simple: two lattes, one pump of hazelnut in each. *Just one pump, please.*

"Could we have for-here mugs?" I added.

"Janet also spoke about…well…you know when someone like her looks at a competition horse from a psychological perspective, it is so interesting. She is seeing something different than the rest of us. The horse might be in shoulder-in, but instead of watching the angle of the horse's body, she is saying, *Watch the eye, see the tension, and then…there! See it change. See the eye! There is more relaxation and understanding.* It's like she is seeing it from a different perspective, one that is exciting and interesting to her, with no judgment."

I put down my coffee. I took Janet's book out of my bag, along with my computer. *Horse Brain, Human Brain: The Neuroscience of Horsemanship.* The book was paperback, thick, with a pink and purple cover. I was re-reading it. I looked at the part I had just underlined:

> *Horses are not just smart; they are learning machines. They scout for cues everywhere and soak up information. Once acquired, new knowledge sticks to a horse's brain like superglue. If there's a problem with equine learning, it's that horses learn too quickly—and forget too poorly—to accommodate human error.*

Sinead drank her coffee. She flipped her laptop open. I paged randomly though the book.

"Ahh. I love this part," I said. "She talks about the difference between instincts, emotions, and feelings, and gives a nice definition of each." I sipped my latte. *Just enough hazelnut.* "I love it when people look deeper at words. It's so common for someone to talk about a horse not respecting them, without having any idea what they are talking about. What does 'respect' even mean? And what does 'respect' mean to a horse? What does it *look* like? Or *feel* like? Are we both using the same definition?" I made some notes and said out loud again, "I love this."

Sinead looked at me over her laptop. "That's what Janet was like with the horses. She said things like, 'There is this *animal*, a whole different species, and we are communicating with them. It's fascinating! Inter-species communication, who would have thought? And that they are willing to participate? It's so cool!'"

"It *is* so freaking cool. It's easy to take it for granted."

When I was able to meet Janet in person a few weeks later, she would tell me, "Humans are smarter than horses in some ways, and horses are smarter than people in some ways. *Teach.* Don't *expect.*"

She also would tell me she was not a fan of training animals with treats, and she was not a fan of colt-starting competitions.

"I've *got* to work on this," Sinead said, her eyes leaving mine and moving back to the computer. I knew she was preparing for a session with "transformational life coach" Natalie Hummel. In the first of four episodes produced by Ride IQ, Natalie prompted a group of eventers to talk about their goals, and what might stand in the way of their success. She asked each of them: "What would you reach for, if fear wasn't a factor?"

Natalie had bright brown eyes, little dimples, and constellations of freckles. She lived in Costa Rica half the year.

In one of my first interactions with her, she had come to Copperline to do a group session with us and our staff. Seven of us gathered at the long kitchen table. The smell of hot coffee, made in a French press, filled the room.

I remember one moment in particular, when one of our barn staff described a feeling that others were accomplishing their goals, and she wasn't. She didn't mean day-to-day goals; she meant they were getting to go to horse shows and jump and compete. "How can I be a team player, and be happy for others, when I'm stuck doing the grunt work?" she asked. "I'm trying to be selfless, but it isn't working."

Natalie smiled at her, brown eyes warm. "That resentment you're feeling, that jealousy, don't fight that. *Listen to it.* That is information. It tells you that there is something you want. It's so *special* to want something. Now you just need to figure out the steps to follow in order to achieve it."

Now that Sinead had pushed me to keep searching for what I wanted to do, I embraced Natalie's point even more. If I felt even a hint of jealousy, I examined it. *Hmmm… That must be something I want.* Then I asked myself, *Do I really want it, or is it just a passing fancy*? If it was just a passing fancy, studying it made it easier to let it go. If it was something I *really* wanted, it helped me start to figure out what I needed to do to get there.

It was a blessing to have a passion, and to be living in a place where I was allowed to work toward achieving it.

The coffee in front of me was getting cold. I left Sinead working, and I went back to the counter. I asked for an espresso.

As I made my way back to our table, I thought about everything we had on our plates.

I sat down. "Do you think we are going to make it?" I asked Sinead. "What we are reaching for seems so overwhelming. It's going to take so much work…effort…time…money…luck…so many things have to line up."

"It's just us, Tik. Now. In the present. We have to make this work. Not 'after we win.' Not if 'this' happens, or 'that.' *Now*."

"I married a smart woman."

She put her coffee down. "You did. Now get back to work."

I grinned.

I went back to preparing.

11

"This is so cruel," Debbie said.

A group of seven of us were watching the 2018 Road to the Horse on DVD. The competitors were Vicki Wilson, Dan James, and Nick Dowers.

"I hope you never do this," Debbie said.

I braced, let me tell you, I braced right up. My shoulders tightened; my jaw set like quick-drying cement. My heart rate shot up. *Easy*, I told myself. *Easy*. I relaxed my shoulders. I took a deep breath.

"Well, Debbie…actually, I would like to."

"It's so cruel!"

"Debbie, we're only five minutes in. They are still trying to catch their horses."

Debbie sat on the edge of the couch, her feet square on the floor, her hands on her knees. She admitted it was the timeline that she didn't like.

I could understand that.

There are many kinds of competitions. Some emphasize speed of training, and some emphasize depth of training, and if I had to guess, I would say a competition like Road to the Horse falls roughly in the middle. It is not set up like a Spanish bullfight, in which the human and the animal are adversaries. One wins, the other loses.

The idea is that if the animal wins, the person wins. If the person wins, the animal has also won.

When you think training a horse is a zero-sum game....when you think marriage is a zero-sum game...well, you have a long road in front of you, most likely involving lawyers and therapists.

Every horseman, if he knows his profession, makes many choices, every day, every second, on how to proceed. He can start and stop, he can go faster or slower, he can change plans, exactly as much as he wishes. There are constraints in the Road to the Horse arena, but no more than the random assortment of constraints that are imposed on us at home: kids needing to be picked up from school, a storm rolling in, the need for money to put new footing in.

In order to find the way forward, we can't go too fast, and we can't go too slow. Too fast, and there is stress. Too slow, and there is no progression. Too *too* slow and there is boredom.

The only way to find that middle ground, that sweet spot, is to have made the mistake of going too fast or going too slow. Or to have seen someone else do it.

I have heard people say horses should be one hundred percent relaxed in everything they do. I don't believe that. For horses, and for us, there is a small amount of stress in playing, in learning, in expanding our comfort zones, in building new relationships, and in exploration. The trick is to keep it small. Small enough that we can stay thoughtful.

When we watch colt starting done as an art, it looks easy, just as any art done well appears effortless. Granted, trying to keep that same art, that same degree of smoothness and timing, is more difficult in three weeks than three months, more difficult again in three days than three weeks, and more difficult again in front of a crowd, with the clock ticking down, and with prize money on the line.

But it's not impossible.

While hurricanes in Florida generally arrive from the Atlantic, traveling east to west, smaller storms arrive in Ocala from the same direction that Shawna Karrasch did: from the west. Shawna beat the storm to Ocala by a few minutes. The black clouds were so low and uniform, they created a dark ceiling to the landscape.

We both ducked as I hustled her from her car to the tack room. There was little talk about the weather, however, as both of us were already chatting about training horses. Shawna was not in riding boots; instead she wore colorful new Nike runners.

Although Shawna rode in the very ordinary hunter divisions in New Mexico, she trains horses in what, for most, is still a somewhat unusual way. She uses a "clicker"—a small, handheld metal noise maker that makes a sound to "mark behavior when a button is depressed—and she uses positive reinforcement in the form of food rewards. The two techniques are related and are often used together, but they are not the same thing.

Whenever I see somebody do something with horses that I don't know how to do, I get all riled up. Curiosity spreads like a grass fire in my brain. So before she arrived at Copperline, I had spoken with Shawna a few times on the phone, and I was already experimenting with a clicker. (The most dramatic success I'd had so far was not with my horses, however, but with Ferdinand.)

The clouds suddenly exploded. Rain pelted down like falling nails on our metal roof. Shawna sat down across from me in the tack room and explained how her career began. I strained to hear.

Although she was around horses as a kid, Shawna had begun her career using positive reinforcement to train sea mammals at Sea

World in California. Then in 1992 she'd watched the Del Mar Show Jumping Grand Prix. "There were probably thirty horses in it. And maybe two horses looked happy," she remembered. "The rest were over-threshold."

What she meant was that most of the horses were anxious (or nervous, concerned, scared, or in pain) to a degree that made her uncomfortable.

"I began to question why the horse world was not using positive reinforcement. Everyone I asked, everywhere I looked, the answer was, 'No. You can't do that. Horses are not trained that way. Horses are not smart enough.' But I had trained hundreds of animals with positive reinforcement. I wanted to give it a try."

The premise of *positive reinforcement* is that desirable behavior is rewarded, often with food. Historically horses are mostly trained with *negative reinforcement*, the *removal of pressure* when the horse finds the right answer. "Pressure motivates, the release of pressure teaches," is a common saying. (*Negative* and *positive punishment* are also occasionally used. While *reinforcement* is used to indicate you want *more* of something—for example, to trot—*punishment* is used to show you want *less* of a behavior, like kicking out.)

Through a series of coincidences, Shawna had met jumper rider Beezie Madden and her husband John. They had one of the best jumpers in the world, Judgement, but the stallion was having trouble with water jumps. Not only did Shawna help Judgement, but the Maddens adopted many of Shawna's ideas for other problems. Later, John told her, "If you can turn this big of a 'No!' into this big of a 'Yes!' there is a place for you in the horse world."

The rain stopped abruptly, as it often does in our part of Florida. We peeked out the door and saw the clouds gliding off toward the Atlantic. The tack room was intensely quiet after the storm.

"I was abused as a child," Shawna said. She said it simply and softly, in a way that showed both forgiveness and a need to never have that happen again. "I knew very early in my life that I never wanted to force my way onto another living creature."

That is the first argument for using positive reinforcement: we are not *making* horses do anything. They are *choosing* to do it. For food, usually, at first, and perhaps later, for other less tangible rewards: For the sake of knowing and practicing a skill they understand and are good at. For the harmony of being in sync with another being. For the joy of play. For the satisfaction of solving a puzzle. For the reward of using their bodies in an athletic way.

While the first argument is philosophical—*Do we want to make animals do things?*—the second argument for using positive reinforcement is more basic: *it works.*

For the last couple decades, that is where Shawna has been: teaching positive reinforcement in the horse world. As we'd been talking in the tack room, a puddle had formed just outside the doorway, and now we had to jump over it as we left to visit Remarkable, a long-legged chestnut Thoroughbred that was very special to me.

Consider two components of training horses: *communication* (Do they *understand*?) and *motivation* (Do they *want* to do it?). Communication is important, but so is motivation. Does the horse canter to *get away* from my leg or to *go toward* food?

For motivating horses, generally speaking, we use negative reinforcement. In other words, we motivate through the *application of pressure* and the *release of pressure*. Even something as simple as leading a horse with a lead rope is generally trained with negative reinforcement: pressure is applied on the halter when the horse resists, and slack is offered in the rope when he follows.

As I've mentioned, we also commonly use punishment. Think about it this way: Punishment is yelling, "No! Stop!" Reinforcement is saying, "Yes! More!"

To make matters more confusing, there are *positive* and *negative* versions of both punishment and reinforcement. This can get complicated, especially when it comes to labeling types of training "good" or "bad."

The word "negative" has an emotional connotation. People tend to think "negative" is bad and "positive" is good. But in animal behavior terms, hitting a dog to stop him from licking your hand is *positive punishment*. (You *added* the hit.) Instead, "negative" and "positive" should be thought of in mathematical terms: subtraction and addition. Taking away the dog's toy for barking (*subtracting something*) is *negative punishment*.

Shawna carried a clicker in her left hand. On her right hip there was a white plastic container a little bigger than a coffee mug. She called it her "side bucket." The container was brimming with sweet feed (a mixture of grains and molasses). We stopped at Remarkable's stall.

Hello, my old friend, I thought. His eyes were large and trusting.

Shawna paused at his doorway, just watching him.

"Shawna, what's the biggest change you have made in your training since your book came out?" I asked. Her book *You Can Train Your Horse to Do Anything!* had been published eighteen years before.

She kept watching Remarkable. He turned away from us and went back to eating hay. "I'm reading the horse's emotions more. When I was at Sea World, we didn't talk about *fun* much, but it was a big part of what we did. If the animals didn't pop up out of the water ready to work, we would probably call the vet."

I nodded. I could picture that in my mind. With horses we want them to *want* to work. If they don't, it could be due to physical pain, but it could also be about how they're feeling. Like Shawna, I believed we could teach "try," and we could mold attitude. We can't change an animal, but we can bring out the best in him.

"With sea mammals, there is no negative reinforcement," Shawna continued. "They do it all for the food and the fun."

Remarkable looked at Shawna with those big, wet, doe-brown eyes. He had a wonderful face and a magnificent expression.

Shawna held out a handful of grain. He shuffled over to the door. She "clicked" her clicker as she fed him, the sound audible to all. Shawna seemed mildly surprised at Remarkable's pluggish, gentlemanly pace in eating. He preferred to look around, take his time. "Since he isn't muggy, we reward connection," she explained.

Remarkable came a step closer. Shawna clicked and fed a second time. He looked at her; she clicked and fed again. He took the food delicately each time. He chewed and chewed. He lowered his head after swallowing. Shawna clicked and fed; clicked and fed. She wasn't shy about giving hand, after hand, after hand, of grain. "And giving grain is easier and cheaper than giving 'treats,'" she explained.

At the start of her form of training, it is just about relating the clicker to the food. Some people call this "loading the clicker," and it is the foundation of all the work that follows.

But in a subtle way Shawna was already teaching behavior as well. She would click when Remarkable connected with her. With a more aggressive horse, one that pushed into her space, or nipped, she would do the opposite—clicking when the horse looked or leaned away.

After only five or six minutes, Shawna said she was done. She emptied the last of the grain into Remarkable's feed bin. "I always do that," she explained. "Sometimes they get so connected that they want to follow me out, or they worry about the session ending. This way they are happy to stay in the stall, and running out of food is not associated with me leaving."

"So once you load the clicker, what's next?"

"What we just started was *bridge conditioning*. It's really classic or Pavlovian conditioning. It is the 'bridge' between the click and the treat. The horse learns the clicker has the value of the *primary reinforcer*, which is the food. After that, the second step is usually 'target training.' Then leading. And then anything. Riding even. I have a horse that competes in the hunters that is trained through clicker training."

"Do you stop and give your horse treats as you ride?"

"I do at the start. But in the end there should be no difference if you watched a round that my horse did or somebody else's horse. There should be no difference in how they look. The final result is the same. It is just how we got there that is different."

Fajita was no bigger than a wheelbarrow. He had coal black, suspicious eyes that didn't quite hide his curiosity and *joie de vivre*. He had come just a few months earlier from Hope Equine Rescue, and he was still wary, skittish as a feral dog.

I opened the door to his stall; he hid in the far corner.

I took a step toward him and he froze, head high, neck tight. I backed out.

"I've worked with him with the clicker a few times, but he still flinches each time I click," I explained to Shawna. "I'm not sure how to get him more comfortable."

Shawna stepped past me and sat down just inside the stall doorway. She poured grain into his rubber feed pan, pulled the feed pan to about two feet from her, then leaned back against the wall and waited.

And waited.

Fajita took a step closer. His eyes were wide inky caves. A minute later he took another step. Shawna shifted her weight and Fajita sprang back, head high again, neck tense again. After a few minutes, he inched his way forward once more.

Eventually, Fajita reached the bucket. After a few bites, he pulled the bucket toward him with his muzzle. "When I think that is going to happen, I tie a little string to the bucket so I can pull it back to me," Shawna whispered.

For some reason, I thought to myself, *This is how you tame a squirrel.*

After a few more bites Shawna tucked the clicker into her shirt sleeve, and then when she clicked, the sound was muffled. Fajita didn't flinch. He kept eating.

I smiled. *Genius.*

Once he was done eating, Shawna poured some more grain in his bucket and then eased out of the stall. The session lasted about twelve minutes. Shawna left the horses when they were at their most interested and motivated. It was like meeting someone special at a cocktail party—leave them before they are bored with you. Sneak out while you are still intriguing.

Riordan, on the other hand, was about as shy as Ferdinand had been when he was a puppy. That meant when Shawna entered his stall, he got right in her space.

Jace, our barn manager, came over to watch. "Any ideas on what to do at feeding time?" he asked. "He gets aggressive. We have to get in and out of the stall pretty quickly."

Shawna nodded and asked Jace to get his lunch. Then she went right into the stall and started feeding him. "He wants the food, so I'm going to give it to him. I don't want him to be frustrated, I don't want him to think I'm holding out on him."

This was counter to my instinct of only rewarding the "right" thing. Instead, Shawna was treating the *cause* (he was frustrated and anxious about food). But after his first couple bites she began training—she started to click and feed him only when he got out of her space. Her point was Riordan was frustrated because he wanted food. So she gave him food. *A lot* of food, and quickly. And then, when he was chewing and not worried about food, she was able to start teaching him.

After working with two more horses, two of them for less than ten minutes, and one of them for just under fifteen minutes, Shawna said, "That's it."

"Short and sweet," I said.

"Exactly. They should be excited about tomorrow."

"Nobody invented this. The way they learn is the way they learn," Shawna told me the following morning.

We had Remarkable out in our jump field. We were practicing leading. But Remarkable seemed happier to just hang out and eat grass. This was the downside to positive reinforcement: I had to be able to offer something better than what he had already.

Remarkable did come to me then, and Shawna grinned. She explained the attitude that she wanted to see in horses: "With positive reinforcement the horses are better in the arena—it's almost like they are in love! Everything is *happier, nicer, rosier*. It affects how they deal with everything." Everything a horse gave her was information. "If they don't want to come near me—it's information. If they run me over—it's information. The more information I have, the better I can train them."

Possibly the most important idea Shawna emphasized was that *we should not skip a teaching step*. Everything must be broken down and taught. There is no *making* things happen. No expecting things to happen. Or hoping for them. It is up to us to *teach* them.

The idea of breaking things down can be and should be implemented, whether I am using positive or negative reinforcement. The reason teaching each step is important is that "clarity is our best friend in training."

As Remarkable followed me around, I asked Shawna, "What is the biggest mistake you see people make when using food during training?"

"They get an over-excited, over-aroused horse," she replied. "They teach their horse it is all about *doing* something. The horses start to feel like every time you show up, it's like Disneyland. 'So much is happening! Everything is busy!' It should not be all busy."

I nodded. I could picture that.

"Instead," she said, "we should be teaching relaxation. We should teach manners."

I thought, *This is just good training. Most of what you are showing me has nothing to do with the food at the end, it is simply good training.* It was about reading the horse. It was about starting wherever the horse needed to start. It was about working on connection. It was about treating the cause of a problem and not just the symptoms.

"More than anything," I said to Shawna, "I love how you are able to break this all down. And that idea that 'everything is information'— you don't get upset."

"It makes sense," she said.

Remarkable looked at me. I clicked and fed.

"It makes sense."

12

"I got so much hate mail."

"I can imagine," I said.

I had just read Ren Hurst's books *Riding on the Power of Others* and *The Wisdom of Wildness*. They were difficult to read. They felt like personal attacks on my source of joy and livelihood. If she was a climate activist, I was Shell. If she was a gun-control advocate, I was Smith & Wesson. For Ren, training and riding horses was always an abuse of power. "All use of a dependent animal in one's care is abuse," she said.

But if I was going to compete at Road to the Horse, I wanted to go in, eyes wide open. I wanted to explore different ethical positions, not just as related to the event itself, but as related to horses in general.

At home, the kids were making a mockery of neatness, and so I snuck out and called Ren from Bernadette's farm, which she had just taken to calling "Innisfree." Bernadette is my mother-in-law. Her farm is next door to ours.

Ren, I was surprised to learn, had a lovely timbre and warmth to her voice. Throughout our conversation, which lasted about an hour, she was nonconfrontational, but she also wasn't trying to make anybody else feel better about her point of view.

"Have you thought about the words you use?" I asked her. "Take a word as simple as 'training,' and it's pretty non-emotional. But we can take that word and change it; we can take that action and emotionally charge it. We can charge it in a romantic way, like I've seen some trainers do, by saying, 'I'll *guide* him through the dressage test.' Or, 'I'm *mentoring* him in his responses in the round pen.' Or, 'I'll *encourage* him at the base of the jump.' But you seem to do the opposite with words like *abuse, control, manipulate, coerce, reduce.*" I paused and took a breath. "It seems to me that just as some people use words to make something that might be bad sound better, you're using words to make something sound worse than it is. Are you worried that your message, the way you present it, is going to alienate people?"

"My purpose is not to shift society one percent," she replied.

Ren wasn't interested in appealing to the masses. She was confronting something about herself, and about the world, that was not easy to do. She was speaking her truth. A big, bold, no-room-for-gray-area truth.

"It all depends on what your overall goal is," she said. "If you want our species to maintain these abuses of power that will lead to our collapse, then look away. If you want to be on the side of history that is mature, then a deep dive is the only way to go."

I asked Ren about her definitions for the words "trauma" and "domestication." It seemed like the way she used the words in what she said and what she wrote were different than how I would define them.

She acknowledged that while her definitions might be different, she had a clear idea of what they meant to *her*.

I asked her about pets.

Ideally, she told me, we would not have dogs or cats or horses as pets. She felt we used them as crutches, instead of solving our own problems and confronting our own inadequacies.

"So," I asked, "what is the place of animals in our lives?"

Her answer was one I appreciated: *Wild creatures. Not domesticated ones.*

"I've been in communication with ravens," she said. "I've had them just come and sit next to me. I have approached wild horses and just used my regulation to earn their trust. And I just feel their surging power that is free from domestication. But most horses are emotionally immature. Even a feral Mustang. To see a truly wild horse, you would have to go to Mongolia or something like that. Their energy is palpable. It is so much more fulfilling."

I, too, thought we should be learning more from wild animals.

So many of our decisions related to animals are emotional. Look at what's for sale in the local grocery store: Pigs but not dogs or cats. Cattle but not horses. Which animals we decide to eat, or not eat, are decisions based on emotions, not on the sentience of the species, or their ability to suffer, grieve, or enjoy a sunny day.

Why not eat more insects?

"Can you explain the phrase 'all use is abuse'?" I pushed.

"When animals are captive," Ren said, "they can't give us accurate feedback. It is so easy to manage them if we have energetic awareness. But captive dependents cannot consent. Just like children can't consent. When we use anyone we have power over, that is misusing them. And that is abuse. We take advantage of their captivity. Is that what you want to do?"

I mentioned to her the name of someone who I respected for starting wild horses in a slow, gentle way.

"To tame the wild is to take advantage of that wild. You have to look for the 'No' and honor it instead of taking someone's 'No' and turning it into your 'Yes.' What traumatized women lack in overt dominance, they make up for in subversive manipulation. Really, it's more honest to hit them than to manipulate them.

Women have taken over the [horse] industry, and it's become more manipulative."

"But you have horses at your place," I said. "What are you doing with your horses?"

"I just take care of them because I had them before I changed. I am not making money off these captive dependents. I am here to write and support and teach and help."

"It's like you're *trying* to antagonize people."

"Softening my approach *would* make it easier to access," Ren replied. "I realize I trigger a lot of people, and then they turn and walk away. I can weed out the individuals who are not ready for the next step."

"And what *is* the next step?"

"A radical acceptance of themselves. I don't want to move humanity *one* percent. That's a therapist's job—a therapist can meet someone where they're at and soften the blow. I'm not interested in that. I want to help people who are ready to dive in *one hundred* percent." And then, "I'm willing to die for this, though, so I don't have a lot of fear. This is why witches were burned. True authentic love is very confronting."

I was silent, thinking. In search of common ground, I asked, "Who are some of your literary heroes?"

"Octavia Butler. Paulo Coehlo. Toni Morrison," Ren replied immediately. "I love parables and how people infuse wisdom and truth into a story."

I thought about my bookshelves in my office. I had a few by Paulo Coehlo. *It's the possibility of having a dream come true that makes life interesting*, he wrote. I'd read *Beloved* by Toni Morrison: *Me and you, we got more yesterday than anybody. We need some kind of tomorrow.* I made a mental note to add Octavia Butler to my reading list.

I could see why Ren would get hate mail, why there would be nasty comments about her on social media. What the world can do to someone like her...someone willing to be different...someone willing to die to be different...

I thought for a moment of Road to the Horse. I thought of one of my main concerns: *Please don't let me do something super embarrassing in front of ten thousand people.*

Being embarrassed should be the least of my worries.

When we were presented with how Ren lived her life, it either made us feel uncomfortable, or it didn't.

My truth is not a condemnation of yours, wrote Cheryl Strayed.

Ren was willing to die for her cause. I found myself asking myself what causes I would be willing to die for. She kept asking why, and she kept going deeper, even when she knew she might end up all by herself. When it's you against the world, there is bravery there. When you are scraping a living together true to your values, there's a bravery there as well. Sharing a message the rest of us don't want to hear can't be easy. I knew then Ren was as brave as any person I had ever met.

"How can I help?" I asked her.

"Be *you.* Do *you.*"

"No, I want to do more."

"Well, we always need hay. It's twenty dollars a bale right now."

I sent her a hundred bucks on Venmo. Five more bales of hay.

13

"What if horses were given a choice?" Elsa Sinclair asks in the trailer for her documentary film *Taming Wild*. "Would they carry us?"

Her voice is slow and clear. Soft. Grass shimmers. Then we see the legs of a trotting horse. The shots are backlit, and the images have an angelic dreamy quality to them. The screen cuts to Elsa. "I wanted to know the answer to that question," she says. Hay bales fill the background behind her. "I came up with this idea for a project. I was going to take a wild Mustang that knows nothing about people. I was going to be the one and only trainer. I was going to use no tools at all—no halters or bridles or ropes or sticks or whips or spurs or any of the things that people use to train a horse. I was just going to use my body language." The screen changes again, and we see Elsa on a horse. No bridle, no saddle. "And I'm not going to bribe her with anything either. We are going to spend a year. We are going to spend a year to develop a language. To develop a way of being with horses that is more collaborative, and less about force. Because I want to know: *Would she let me ride her?* If it's just a collaborative partnership and she has a choice, would she *let* me get on and ride?"

Sinead and I sometimes hosted clinics with trainers we admired. It was one of my favorite ways to spend a day. It gave me an excuse to sit by the round pen, in the shade, with pen and paper. Inevitably, visiting trainers gave me new ideas. Almost always they did something better, or different, than the way I did things, and that got me excited.

After watching her documentary, I knew Elsa had to come.

Elsa began her day with a talk, which I usually prefer to just jumping right into working with a horse. She had set up an easel and poster-size flip pad under a large live oak. On the first page "Freedom Based Training" was written, which was the name she had given to her approach to horses. About a dozen of us sat, coffees in hand, ready to learn.

She took a quiet breath and began.

"You can *choose* what kind of relationship you want with your horse," she said. "Most of us follow certain unwritten rules. Go to school. Get a job. Partner up. Pay the mortgage. Have kids…then grandkids. Get old. Die.

"We apply the same mentality to horses. We send them to school. They live in pens. We buy them a halter and give them food rewards. They must become 'functioning members of society.' They learn. They learn they are *not* truly free…just like we learn we are not truly free. In other words: We need to earn our dinner. They need to earn theirs. Everything is based on that.

"But what if it doesn't have to be like that?

"The more time we spend training 'in freedom,' the deeper the bond. Freedom Based Training is slow and meditative. It asks us to have fortitude, persistence, patience. It is difficult emotionally. It takes more time to see progress, but the rewards outweigh the costs."

Both in person and on camera Elsa speaks tenderly and eloquently, like a cross between a monk and a professor. Like I imagine Kahlil Gibran would have.

In her documentary, Elsa takes a year to train Myrnah, a Mus-

tang she adopted. What they accomplish in a year many professionals could do in a month. At least, they could do it in a month if we
are just checking boxes: sit on his back, *check*…walk, *check*…trot,
check…canter, *check*.

Imagine two humans checking boxes in *their* relationship: first
date, *check*…third base, *check*…house with a thirty-year fixed-rate
mortgage, *check*. Kids, *check*.

Are any of those checked boxes a reflection of how deep and
satisfying that relationship is?

Elsa pays attention to definitions, and nuances, and the gray areas that determine the tone and ripeness of a relationship. Some of
these definitions are simple. "*Feel* is knowing *what* action to take.
Timing is knowing *when* to take that action." Other definitions require more explanation: "The two parts to a *partnership* are *leadership* and *friendship*. The more balanced we are between leadership
and friendship, the more enjoyable the relationship will be."

Elsa explained that there are different kinds of leaders and
friends.

Dominant leaders fight for a leadership position. They have no
problem creating discomfort to get a "Yes" answer, sometimes at any
cost. *Assertive* leaders *ask* their followers to move their bodies and
get a "Yes" answer. *Passive* leaders are smart about *where* to be, *when*
to be, *why* to be. Others watch this kind of leader and take note.

Characteristics of a good leader may include: investigating
danger; taking actions that create trust and respect in the long run,
regardless of how they feel in the short term, or in the moment;
pushing boundaries and teaching the ability to become comfortable
in a greater number of situations; building a sense of safety by
moving with rhythm and confidence.

"Horses are drawn to confidence. It's the strongest magnetism
there is."

Friendship is helping our horses become comfortable. A friend will scratch that itch in that hard-to-reach spot. A friend will run away with you when you're scared. A friend is closer when you want closeness, and farther away want you want space. *Good* friends are adaptable to what one might want in a friend on different days, in different situations, and in different moods.

Elsa believes there are times to be a leader and times to be a friend.

Elsa asked for two horses to be let loose in the round pen. We led Remarkable, my chestnut Thoroughbred, and Larry, a dark bay, in. They were both retired and had been living out together for a few months. They got along well. (Just because horses are herd animals and like having other horses around doesn't mean they like *every* other horse.)

We watched the geldings. Elsa told us to ask ourselves who the leader and follower was in any given moment. She pointed out detail after detail that I was missing. "Notice the ears," she said. "See how he stopped his feet moving just *after* the other horse stopped his feet moving?"

Elsa entered the round pen, waited a few minutes, observed them, then began to interact with them.

"They are tolerating me being in their space," Elsa said, as she matched steps with Larry, and then backed away to the far side of the round pen.

Learning, she explained, happens in stages. The first stage is *tolerance*. It is where every new skill starts. The second stage is *acceptance*. It has a neutral feeling, neither good nor bad. The third stage is the ideal—*enjoyment*. This is when the horse seeks us out and chooses to be with us more and more. Sometimes horses go through the stages in minutes; sometimes it takes weeks or months.

When the process happened slowly, Elsa said she might ask herself: "Can I find another way? Can I break it down more? Can I find the path forward in smaller steps? The concept of *advance and retreat* can be applied here. Go into the exercise, then out of it. Take a break. Then try again with more tact and better timing."

A lady next to me was fidgeting. She raised her hand. Then she interrupted Elsa. "What about when a horse doesn't even stay?" she pressed. "He isn't even tolerating it?"

"In that case," Elsa replied, "the first stage of learning for that horse would actually be *in*tolerance."

Elsa walked over to where we all sat to explain more. I noticed she had chosen a lovely moment to give Remarkable and Larry a break.

"When we have a halter or bridle on the horse," she said, "we have the capacity to hold the horse in a place even when he is upset, and then we can push him through to the 'other side.' The 'other side' might be *tolerance* or *acceptance*. The same is true when we use food. Because horses need food, they might stay even though they are upset."

In reading about the training of other animals that are commonly trained with food, I had learned that it was not uncommon to withhold food from the animal for a certain amount of time beforehand. This prompted the question: was the animal going *toward* food or *away* from hunger?

An ethical trainer was not going to starve animals; however, an animal must have some level of hunger in order to see food as a reward, which left the door open to a large amount of gray area in terms of: *How hungry was okay*? Some trainers solved the moral dilemma by offering free-choice food of something less palatable while training with a more palatable food. Others offered free-choice access to the same food they used for training. In this case, food obviously was not the only motivator—it had to be combined with the horse participating in the training for another reason that appealed to him. (Play? Curiosity? Harmony? A sense of mental or physical achievement?)

"In Freedom Based Training, if a horse is in the stage of intolerance, we don't stay there," Elsa continued. "We don't push through with a rope or halter or food. Instead, we use some version of advance and retreat. We introduce things *soooo* slowly. The timing of the retreat becomes so important. If we only retreat when the horse is frustrated or upset, we *teach* him to become upset. We must retreat *before* we hit resistance, *before* he is upset. We must train our timing!"

Oh, to read a horse that well! I thought. I smiled as I took notes. *To be that in the moment! To have that kind of timing! To go at the exact speed of that particular horse, on that particular day! Wow! That is not easy.*

"She is so bloody good," I whispered to Sinead, who was sitting next to me.

"She notices just the tiniest things, nonstop," Sinead said without taking her eyes off Elsa.

"If I could read a horse *half* this well," I said. Then, "I'm surprised we don't have more people here today."

"People don't get what she does. It feels too slow for them."

I shook my head. I sat and watched Elsa play with horses and teach people for another six hours. I made note after note about her timing. I wrote about her ability to read a horse. About her presence and intuition.

She is a master! I wrote.

On the second day, Elsa went into our round pen with an overweight, high-headed, mustard-colored gelding.

"Tolerance with enough advance and retreat will grow into acceptance. When the horse is in acceptance, and he can do it, then do it until there is enjoyment, then retreat. The last thing that happened is the lasting impression. End on the strongest 'Yes' answer you can find," she said. "Ask yourself this: What percentage of the time do you get 'Yes' answers from your horse, and what percentage of the time do you get 'No' answers?"

She stood in the middle of the round pen, and the horse walked away from her. Elsa repositioned where she stood. She began her subtle dance in which she slowly became interesting, calming, and warm to the horse.

"What do tolerance, acceptance, and enjoyment look like?" she asked us. "We look for positive body signs, but there is also an intuitive sense. Watch the ears, eyes, tail, facial expressions. Watch the body and how it moves. Watch the rhythm! Be aware that there are many degrees of each stage—it's not black or white. Watch the nuance. *Always* aim for *better*."

Elsa continued her dance with the mustard-colored horse, who was starting to relax more and more. As he sniffed and nosed the top of a barrel, Elsa joined him and explored it as well. Elsa touched it, tapped it, then retreated. She was showing that she was interested in what the gelding was interested in.

It reminded me of the saying, *It's more interesting to be interested than to be interesting.*

"Check *your* rhythm," Elsa said. "Check *their* rhythm. The emotional and physical are linked. How often do they stand square? Stability is comfort. Look at the level of the head. Where are the eyes focused?"

All Elsa was doing was walking here and there in the round pen with a horse that was also walking here and there. But she was explaining everything she saw, and it was like listening to an old tracker talk about what he saw in the sand. For the tracker, a whole book could be written about a single paw print. The audience, fourteen women and two men, was silent and attentive.

"What lowers stress?" Elsa asked—then answered her own question: "Leadership and movement."

She picked that moment to leave the mustard horse. It was a good moment again, wise and well-timed. She came over to the group watching.

"So often we try to give horses friendship when they crave leadership (and safety), or we try to be a leader when all they want is a friend."

I didn't know if I would ever have the patience of Elsa. But I began to notice smaller and smaller details. And the more aware I became of details, the faster everything went.

14

"High involvement, low attachment."

It was on a Sunday afternoon in the fall that Sinead said these words to me for the first time. We were in the house. I was making a cheese-and-tomato sandwich. Toasted, with mayo, salt, and pepper.

"Exactly," I replied, spreading mayo and having no idea what she was talking about. "Just what I was pondering!"

"*High involvement*," Sinead explained, "means keep moving. It means action. Full steam ahead. Have a vision. Work hard, train hard. It means sweat, and miles, being smart, and having a clarity of purpose. It means listening to your *ikigai*."

"How do you spell that?"

"I'm not sure," she said.

"T-H-A-T."

She ignored me.

Sunday afternoon was family-time-kid-time. Sinead wore tight jeans and a white t-shirt that said, "Eternal Optimist," which was cute. "*Ikigai* is the Japanese concept of having a purpose in life—a place where profession, passion, mission, and vocation intersect," she explained.

"I love that." I took a bite of my sandwich and thought about it. "Can your *ikigai* change?"

"Not only *can* it change, it *should* change. Your *ikigai* when you are fifteen will probably be different than when you're fifty. Sometimes it's tough to leave your old *ikigai* behind in order to make room for your new one."

"I'm not sure what my *ikigai* is."

"The voice of the *ikigai* is quiet. It leads, it does not command," Sinead quoted.

"Speaking of quiet, I've been thinking about how, with coaches, that when a specific instruction is given as a command—'Eyes up!'—the advice is obvious and more likely to be followed. But when there are passing suggestions—'Maybe you should get here earlier next time...'—or even something that is more like a hint in the right direction—'There is a good book I just read...'—those are easy to miss, but they can be more valuable."

"The loudest voice is not the most important. It requires stillness and awareness to pick up on the hints. You have something right here..." She touched her lip.

I wiped a crumb away from mine. "And low...?"

"Low attachment," she completed my prompt to return to her original statement. "Attachment is clinging to how things *should* be, or how they *should* happen. We compare our experiences to other people's."

Immediately I thought of horses.

When I stepped into a round pen with a horse I didn't know, the horse doing what I wanted was not guaranteed. It was not even *likely*. But every second he gave me information, and I could choose what to do with that information.

When working with horses, getting rid of the word *should* was about the number one thing I would recommend. "The horse *should* load by now." "The pony *should* be better at the show." "The gelding *shouldn't* be nervous." If the horse does do these things, great; if he doesn't, that's just "where he is," that's just information to gather.

"Low attachment comes fairly easily to me with horses," I re-marked, "but not as easily with dogs…or kids, for that matter." Then I admitted, "Actually, that's not totally true. If it's my own horse, or if I'm competing, that 'should' word occasionally creeps into my brain."

"It's good, right?" Sinead asked about her catch phrase.

"I think it's going to change my life," I said, half-joking.

Natalie was in Costa Rica.

I called her as I drove to pick up the kids from school. It was a twenty-five-minute drive.

"Tik!" she shouted.

"I have some random questions I'm trying to sort out."

She laughed, knowing that meant I was looking for her help. "Yes?"

"Natalie, I have this big thing coming up in my life. A big dream."

"Yes," she repeated.

"I look ahead at myself in ten years. That person should be my hero, right? Did that person work hard? Was he kind? Did he sur-render to his fears?"

"Yes," she prompted.

"I want to follow this dream, but the fear…the *fear*…is that normal?"

"That's normal," she said, slowly and warmly.

Her reassurance helped. It helped a *lot*. I took a breath.

I drove south on NE Jacksonville Road. I drove through Sparr, then passed Jumbolair Estates. The air conditioning was on full.

"Do you think we should stop riding horses?" I asked.

"I don't think people will stop riding," Natalie replied. "But the way a lot of us are with horses is really entitled. We think they owe us something because we feed them and take care of them."

"Have you heard about *ikigai*?"

"Yes..." she said. "So...the only problem I have with *ikigai* is when people put purpose outside themselves—for example, to say, 'Horses are my purpose.' Your purpose is to be whole, worthy, present, and complete in every moment. What you put that onto, that's your purpose *in that moment*. Then you can go through life gracefully."

I turned right onto NE 25th Ave. "I might need a minute to wrap my head around that."

"Think about an apple tree. It is not going around saying, 'I'm going to be the *best* apple tree,' or, 'I want to be a *peach* tree.' The apple tree is just an apple tree. *It just is.* And it blossoms beautifully. When life wants to move, we can have resistance if we hang onto something."

That was me. All the time.

"I hang onto things," I told her. "Why do I have so much trouble with that?"

"The ego wants to identify with something."

I was silent. Then I ventured, "How do you know when to see something through, and how do you know when to quit?"

"You will know when identity is not a part of it."

That was about the truest and toughest thing I had ever heard.

"I don't know if I can do that."

"Life is graceful. Life also celebrates grittiness."

"This is changing the subject again, but do you think a majority of athletes are motivated by unhealthy things?"

She laughed, throaty, as if caught off guard. "Yes, for sure. So many athletes, CEOs, successful people—they aren't happy. They have a god-like complex. They have something to prove, or this big thing behind them that they are running away from. What they have really is a deep-seated feeling of unworthiness."

"All of them?"

"No, not all of them."

"You think, like ninety percent of successful people?"

"That sounds about right. I'm thinking about the ten percent. I'm thinking of Kobe Bryant right now. He's dead, so we don't know for sure. But I think he really started to understand what motivated him on a deeper level."

I waited for traffic to thin, then turned left. The street was quiet and lined with old oaks. I was having trouble with the idea of entirely dismissing the ego, something I saw as necessary and even good.

"Have you ever read *Anthem* by Ayn Rand?"

"Didn't she write *Atlas Shrugged*?"

"Exactly. She argues for the importance of the ego. Rand values individualism and reason above all else. That book is called *Anthem* because it is an ode to the ego."

"I'm not saying don't have an ego, I'm saying have a *healthy* ego."

I pulled up outside Montessori Preparatory. I parked in the shade. "I gotta go in and get the kids," I said.

"Go get those kids," she said. "Give them a hug."

I was on my hands and knees in the office, looking for a book.

The books were haphazardly organized into three areas: fiction, nonfiction, and a third section for horse books and training books. The task I had set for myself was to re-read *The Black Stallion*, originally published in 1941. I had first read the novel when I was not much older than my son was. Then I had read most of the rest of the twenty-or-so books that Walter Farley had written between 1945 and 1989.

This time, I wanted to investigate the main character Alec's approach to colt starting.

I found the book, a hardcover, ratty and dog-eared. There were some good quotes in it, my favorite being, *The Black was a creature of contradictions, both wild and gentle, fierce and noble,* which reminded me of the saying "within every wild horse is a tame horse, within every tame horse is a wild horse." But there was not, unfortunately, much to learn about colt starting.

If I was writing a book about colt starting, what would I write?

If I was on a desert island with a wild stallion, what would I do?

My first step would be establishing just one "word," one simple thing he could understand.

Language, in other words. *Communication.*

Like when 1st Lieutenant John J. Dunbar (played by Kevin Costner) communicates in Lakota for the first time in *Dances with Wolves.*

Like when Helen Keller's fingers were formed into the sign for "water," while her hand was held under water running from a tap.

All it takes is one word. *One word!* One word for the eyes to begin to glow with understanding. Once the eyes are lit, the most important part is done. The first step is the most difficult. After that it's just word after word. One after the other. One foot in front of the other.

Being able to communicate is one of the most pleasurable things we are able to experience. It's right up there with watching the sunset, tending to a bonfire, reading a book, jumping into a mountain lake, watching children play. These things are not something we need to reward ourselves for doing, they are rewards in themselves.

I had created a list of what I wanted the next eight months to look like. I got Nick, Juliette, and Sinead—my Road to the Horse support crew—together on a Zoom call. Sinead and I had met Juliette in June of 2020, and since that time she had worked for us in varying capacities: working student, groom, syndicate liaison, and clinic organizer. Her twin passions were horse behavior and dressage. She was a five-foot-two brunette (with a touch of unnatural blonde) with an endearing curiosity and wit. I'd asked her to run logistics for the team.

"You guys hear that Marion County just outlawed the big round hay bales?" I began.

"What?" Juliette gasped.

"Yeah, not enough horses have been getting a square meal."

Juliette tilted her head. Nick scratched his beard. Sinead shook her head.

"Try to be professional," my wife whispered.

I was not totally comfortable leading this group. It would have been easier to be in the supporting role. But it was something I wanted, and something I had signed up for, so "comfortable" was not in the cards.

"The main thing today is to discuss the schedule for the months ahead," I said. "I want to be ruthless about time. I want to get better about saying no to things that do not take steps in the right direction. I also want to talk about the roles each of you play on this team, and find out how you feel you can help."

One of my biggest concerns was that, out of the four of us, I was the only one who had actually *been* to Road to the Horse. I felt the need to convey what it was like. If I wasn't ready, it wasn't just going to be embarrassing for five minutes, it was going to be rough going for *four hours*, in front of five judges and a crowd of thousands of people, not to mention the filming that was recorded, streamed, and accessible *forever*.

"My goal is to do four learning clinics or trips, and four competition simulations," I told them. "That may not be realistic in terms of time and money, but that is our starting point, and we can adjust as needed. With eight months to go, that's about one weekend a month. I don't expect you all to come to all of them, but you are welcome to."

They all nodded.

"Sinead, I'd like you to go through dates with me and help me prioritize commitments for the next eight months. Nick, I need you to know the rules better than I do, and look at dates as well. Juliette, can you please create a spreadsheet of people I should interview, or visit, or host here? I'll forward you what I've got so far. There are thirty-nine people on it right now, so there's a lot of outreach and scheduling to do."

I felt like their expressions said they felt that I was making a pretty big deal, pretty early on, about not a big deal.

But I was a little worried, moderately scared, and extremely driven. In retrospect, it wasn't a horrible combination.

15

Vancouver is a city of coffee and sushi, flanked by water and mountains. Southlands is a small area, about a square mile, within the city limits of Vancouver, that is zoned agriculturally. It is crammed in between two golf courses and the Fraser River. When I was growing up, no one in Southlands golfed. We had horses.

Southlands was a place of contradictions: There were hundreds of horses but few open fields for them to graze. We lived in the city but were raised as if we lived in a village. People loved where they came from but sold their land and moved. Every year another farmhouse was torn down and a "castle" sprang up to take its place. Families moved into the massive structures "to be closer to nature," then complained about the open ditches, the horse manure on the trails and paths, and how we let the grass grow long on the sides of the road in the spring when ducklings were hatching.

I grew up in Southlands. My parents grew up there as well. In the 1960s my mother adopted a wood duck that she raised there.

"As I was driving through the forest," she told me, "I noticed a tiny bird beside the road. I could see it was a duckling, so I stopped and waited, but no mother appeared. Finally, I scooped it up, nestled it under my sweatshirt, and continued to camp.

"It still had a tiny egg tooth on the top tip of its bill, so I knew it was less than a day old…I called my duckling Albert, after the naturalist Albert Hochbaum (even though the duckling was a female). Albert, of course, became imprinted on me, and over my next eight years she accompanied me everywhere…. She was friendly to others and loving to me. I learned to tell her emotions (yes, ducks have emotions) by the way she raised or flattened the tiny feathers on her face, head, and neck. I really loved her."

I'd also raised a few baby ducks, although they were Muscovies or White Pekins, never wild. My brothers, Telf and Jordan, had their fair share of ducks, too. The ducklings nestled in our pockets, nuzzled into our necks. They followed us through the drizzling rain, over the grass, up the slippery steps, and into the house. They sat on our laps as we ate breakfast or settled down on our stomachs as we lay by the fire.

Every night we would herd the family flock of ducks and chickens into a raccoon-and-coyote-proof pen. When I completed the chore by myself, I could do it in a few minutes. But, when I had a friend from school assist me, it could take twenty minutes or more, with ducks waddling off in the wrong direction, and chicken feathers flying as they scooted away.

Those were my first lessons in how important lines of pressure are, how going slow is often faster than going fast, and how essential it is to read animals. (Sinead suggests I read animals better than I do people. "Read the room, Tik," she often reminds me sternly, when I come in chattering on, only to realize a few minutes later that I interrupted a conversation about something serious.)

On the second floor of the house I grew up in, at the back, was a room with every wall covered by books. One section was devoted to ethology, the study of animal behavior.

Like my mother's beloved Albert, I had experienced *imprint training* with a few of my pet ducks. My mother had also recommended a book called *King Solomon's Ring* by Konrad Lorenz. The author was best known for his work with geese, and in particular, the study of *imprinting*. Imprinting is the special bond, in some species, between a newborn and its caregiver. The "ring" of King Solomon referred to the legendary *Seal of Solomon*, which granted the ability to speak to animals.

I'd also found the book *Imprint Training of the Newborn Foal* by Dr. Robert M. Miller. On the cover was a painting of a man in a yellow shirt, sitting, with a foal resting his head in the man's lap, as the mare stood guard, watching. I remember thinking, *A horse would not imprint on us, would he?* Definitely not like the ducks I had raised!

Thinking about duck starting versus colt starting again made me call my friend and fellow Canadian horseman Jonathan Field.

"I call it 'early learning' instead of 'imprinting,'" he said. "The things horses learn at that stage are more lasting. But be careful because if they learn the *right* thing, it's stronger, but if they learn the *wrong* thing, that's stronger too."

Dr. Miller wrote:

Scientific studies have shown that the imprinting and bonding period occurs right after birth and lasts only for an hour or two. After that, the presence of strangers elicits a fear reaction in the foal. It is obvious that this pattern of responses is useful to help the foal to survive in the wild where predators constitute the greatest danger. During the first hour of life, the foal's vision seems to be the primary sense involved in attaching to, and wanting to follow, large moving objects.

I sent a message to Dr. Miller via the contact page on his website, inquiring if I could speak with him. The next day I received a reply from his son Mark: "My dad is almost ninety-seven years old," he

said. Mark wasn't sure if his dad was well enough for a conversation, but said he would let me know.

I put my computer away. I put my books away. I thought about my own dad…eighty-one. I contemplated the cycle of birth, life, and death.

Brooks burst into the office.

"Will you play with me, Dad?"

"What do you want to play?"

"Bugs."

"Bugs?"

"Let's collect bugs."

"How about we play inside? It's hot outside. The bugs are probably resting."

"Can we play 'Strong Man'?" Brooks asked, which I knew meant me lying on my back, and a four-year-old jumping on my chest and groin, and hitting my head.

"Yup," I agreed. "I *love* 'Strong Man.'"

After a minute or two of the beating, I curled into the fetal position, like a pill bug, and pleaded for a break. Brooks sat cross-legged next to me and tapped my head. *Tap, tap, tap. Tap. Tap, tap, tap.* Then the tapping slowed and became more deliberate, like the tapping of a carpenter searching for the stud behind the drywall.

"Brooks?"

Tap. Tap. Tap.

"Yes, Daddy?" Brooks said seriously.

"What are you doing?"

Tap.

"I'm tapping where your hair is."

"Oh. Thanks."

The tapping became harder as Brooks gained confidence. I buried my face in a pillow. Then the tapping switched to my neck and shoulders.

"Dad," he said, tapping my back. "You actually have *lots* of hair."

"Brooks?"

"Yes?" He giggled.

"You're a pickle."

I never did talk to Dr. Miller. He passed away before I got a chance.

16

The truck barreled around the curve straight toward me. I slammed my foot on the brake. The seat belt dug into my chest. In a split second my brain went through various possibilities—*they* were out of control, *they* were cutting the corner—until I hit on the correct scenario: *I* was driving on the right side of the road, in other words the *wrong* side of the road. I should have been driving on the left.

This was Ireland, after all.

I flung the wheel to the left, veered across the narrow lane, and came dangerously close to tumbling down a cliff and ending my life. (Sinead later said I was being dramatic, but she hadn't been there.) The narrow road twisted like rope through the hills of Connemara. I glanced to the left and glimpsed the cold blue lough Corrib. *Loughs* are Irish lakes, and there were hundreds of them in this area. I looked up again; I accelerated around the next bend.

Thirty minutes later, I arrived at the house of Emer.

The first thing of note in Emer's house was Emer's father Joe. He had white hair, rosy cheeks, and eyes that twinkled. He wore a pressed button-up shirt that had thin red-and-blue stripes. He was sunk deep into a recliner in a small room that was crowded with furniture. I shook his hand, and he invited me to sit opposite him. I did. A fireplace, unlit and silent, rested beside us.

"Coffee or tea?" Emer called from the kitchen. The ceiling in the house was low, and there were walls here and there, like in a maze. In America, someone would inevitably renovate such a house, pointing to the walls and saying, "Let's open this up!" But the effect was quaint, and I imagined with the fire going in the winter, it would have been cozy.

Joe was a breeder of Connemara ponies—smallish sturdy horses native to Ireland and known for their athleticism and hardiness. His father had also bred Connemaras, and his father's father had too.

"Think of them. How they lived! No, how they *survived*," Joe said. His accent was as rich and Irish as the clover outside was lush and green. I could understand about three-quarters of what he said. "The pony was a real asset to the family. But they had to buy it and they had to feed it. It couldn't need a lot of maintenance. It had to survive on little. The pony was tough and worked hard for a living."

Joe leaned back. Emer brought in coffee and a plate of chocolate-covered digestives and placed them in front of me. She brought nothing for herself, and nothing for her dad. Presumably it was all for me. I reached for one.

The ponies, Joe explained, arose out of a need, and out of geography. Like skis for the Swedes, or dykes for the Dutch. The need, like for many breeds of horses, was work. They carried stones out of the fields to clear land and create walls. They carried peat from bogs. They also transported seaweed from the coast.

"And what did they do with the seaweed?" I asked. It was difficult to imagine this man, or his forefathers, using it to make sushi rolls.

"Look at the hills." Joe gestured to the small window.

The hills. Old, dull, brown, gray. A few areas of green grass, good enough for a lawn. Ancient stones scattered as if tossed like marbles by a giant. Sheep grazed—fluffy mammals that looked from a distance like slow-moving marshmallows.

And the *sky!* The sky was as eye-filling as any I had ever seen.

"Where the fields are green, it is from seaweed to enrich the soil," Joe said.

The Connemara pony was bred to be a workhorse.

"So they didn't ride them?" I asked.

"Well, the kids did," Joe admitted, giving a small grin. "And they raced them."

"Raced them?"

"M' dad would have done a bit of that. Raced 'em on the beach. It would have been the only little bit of enjoyment a man might have had. That and a stout. A woman might not have had any enjoyment at all. Think about it. We had no money, and the neighbors had no money. The only little treat you had was pony racing on the beach."

"Did you start the horses yourself?"

"That would have been m' dad."

"How did he start them?"

"Crude methods," he said bluntly.

I tried the coffee. I felt its heat on my lips. It was still too hot to drink. I put it down carefully. I took another digestive instead.

"They wouldn't pamper the pony. At eighteen months they would start them lightly."

"What does that mean, 'lightly'?"

"They would get them used to the halter. Lead them at the walk and trot. Then they would get them used to the long traces."

Traces were long lines, or ropes, that trainers used to drive the horses with, similar to if the horse was pulling a cart, but the person would simply walk behind, holding a rope in each hand. At its most basic, equivalent to the classical training technique of *long-reining* or *long-lining*.

There was a pause. "And Emer," I asked, for really, *she* was the one I had come to see. "How do *you* start horses?"

"The most important thing is the mouth of the pony," Joe continued, not really meaning to interrupt, I thought, just excited to share. "At three, we use a breaking bit, with a little 'bit butter' on the bit and in the corners of the mouth. It creates saliva and a soft mouth. At first, we will just leave the pony in the stall. The mouth is so important. Anybody can sit on a pony; the head carriage says everything about how he has been broken."

I picked up another digestive. I thought about what he said about the mouth and head carriage. How could I save it, respect it? *Maybe at Road to the Horse I will start the horse with no bit.* I knew some trainers had used a bit during the competition, and others hadn't. There was no "Road to the Horse Rule" that said what kind of saddle or bridle or halter should be used, although all equipment *did* have to be checked by the judges.

"When we first start longeing our ponies, we don't use a bit," Emer said.

She had the same strong jaw as her dad. She wore a purple t-shirt. Her brown hair was parted in the middle. I guessed she was about my age, early forties. Maybe younger. She stood, seemingly undecided about replenishing the plate of digestives.

"What's the breaking bit you use?"

"It has three little keys on it. They play with it." She paused. "And then we begin long-reining," Emer went on. "We go out on the road."

The traces! I thought. "A couple times?" I asked.

"Maybe five times a week for five or six weeks."

"So a lot," I said, taking the last digestive. There'd been four in all.

"It depends on the horse. Sometimes it's just for ten minutes. It depends on his temperament. We build up his courage slowly. He's got to face the roads, people walking dogs, cyclists."

"And then you get on him?" I asked between bites.

"The backing process is in the stable, in the aisleway. We stand on a hay bale and lean over him," Emer described. "Then we see what his reactions are; some are grand with certain things. Others are not. Then we have a saddle on him, and we lean over that."

"How many horses do you start?"

"Six or seven a year. Half of those are ours, half we are starting for other people."

"How is it with other people's horses?" I asked, now drinking the coffee, letting it almost-but-not-quite burn my lips.

"A mixed bag. Sometimes it's just a tune-up. What people don't understand is it's not 'on' and 'off' like a light switch. Horses are like dogs—it's the owners that need training," Emer said, finally sitting down. The furniture was squeezed into the small room, and my knees were inches from hers, and from Joe's.

I nodded.

"People are very, very stupid," Joe said. His accent gave "stupid" a pleasant ring. I grinned, I leaned back, I made a note.

"When you are riding, where do you start?"

"Sitting astride. Having a second person lead the pony in and out of the stable. Then the arena," said Emer. "But the arena can be an open invitation for horses to let off steam. I like to get them on the road. In the arena they might liven up and buck; on the road they are not as confident…and their mind is occupied. Soon we will load them up and take them to the beach."

"Omey Beach. Or Ballyconneely. Or Aillebrack," Joe said.

I had just been to Ballyconneely beach with Brooks, Goldfish, Sinead, and Bernadette. Brooks had immediately stripped off his shoes and taken off. He'd had tide pools in mind.

"Want to follow me on the rocks?" he'd shouted.

"More than anything," I'd replied sincerely.

"It's my birthday!" he'd yelled.

"*Yesterday* was your birthday," I'd told him. "We went to Cong, remember?"

He'd shrugged and exclaimed, "Follow me!" as he ran onto the barnacle-covered rocks. Closer to the water, our feet slipped on oar-weed, spiral wrack, and sea lettuce.

"The Connemara is changing, though," Joe said.

"How?"

"Let's say Emer has a show in Roundstone, where I grew up. She has to van the ponies fourteen miles from Clifton to get there. She competes, then ships back home. Maybe puts rugs on them at night." He paused. "When *I* was young," he continued, "I'd *ride* the fourteen miles. Race on the beach. Maybe enter a second race. Then *ride* fourteen miles home."

The horses, he implied, were getting "softer." We were helping the individual, but not the breed.

It was getting late, and I wanted to see the barn and the horses. I said goodbye to Joe, and Emer led the way out of the house, and then a few steps down the path to the barn.

I opened the windows. Wind flew through the car as I drove back to where we were staying on Lough Corrib. I grabbed my notes as they tried to tear free out the window. I saw the sheep on the hills and smelled the seaweed from the coast. I stayed clearly on the left side of the road.

With all the science and all the books and all the studies, I could still sure enjoy having a chocolate-covered digestive and listening to the wisdom of an old Irish farmer who grew up around horses, whose dad grew up around horses, and whose grandfather grew up around horses.

I slowed down as I passed a little pub. In the window was a poster with a turtle looking over his shoulder and grinning. On his back sat a glass, black as night. Large red letters called out: *Have a GUINNESS when you're TIRED.*

It would have been nice to stop for a drink, to sit at the bar and write down my thoughts, but there were two little kids about to go to sleep back at the house we had rented for the week.

I drove on.

It wasn't until I read *Next of Kin* by pioneer chimpanzee communicator Roger Fouts that I decided to teach Brooks sign language.

We watched videos on an app called "Signing Time." Before he was two, he knew thirty or forty words in sign.

- *Water.*
- *Milk.*
- *Mom.*
- *Dad.*

open hand, then
closed hand = milk

three fingers
to lips = water

touching index finger and thumb
repeatedly to mouth = bird

I learned maybe seventy or eighty words.

- *Bird.*
- *Brother.*
- *Sister.*
- *Happy.*
- *Sad.*

Washoe the chimp worked with Fouts and his team and became the first chimp to learn American Sign Language (ASL)—or at least the first chimp to learn as much as she did, which was around three hundred and fifty words.

That's a lot!

Washoe also learned to combine words, so if she didn't know the word for "thermos," she might sign "metal, cup, drink." She would often slow down her rate of signing for novice signers, which must have been humbling.

When researchers first began to teach Washoe language, they used a simple technique, similar to clicker training. When Washoe tried a sign, she was rewarded with food or tickles, her two favorite things. Training progressed, slow and steady. Then, one day, two researchers who were fluent in ASL signed "toothbrush" to each other. The next day Washoe, lo and behold, knew the sign for "toothbrush"! What they realized was that for chimps, just like for humans, learning to communicate just for the sake of *understanding* could, in itself, be motivating.

Washoe also loved painting. When given a big white blank canvas, when given cups of paint—ocean blues, fire-engine reds, sunflower yellows—when left alone, she would paint for ages. She would take her time; be creative; create works of art.

But when researchers rewarded her with food or tickles for painting, she would just splash something on the canvas quickly, thoughtlessly, so she would be rewarded.

For some of us, being creative, and communicating, are rewards in themselves.

Most animals don't gallop away without a destination when faced with stress or fear. A fox will head for his den. A bird will take to the sky. A mouse will run to the wall, then along it, looking for cover. A chameleon will camouflage. Some animals may initially flee, but will then turn and fight. Others will freeze, feign death, bare their teeth, or rattle their tail.

Horses, for the most part, and more than any other animal I know, *move when they are stressed*. In particular, they move to open spaces.

In order to lead a horse, in order to ride a horse, in order to walk, trot, canter, jump, and trailer load, all we have to do is find a horse that is stressed and steer that stress in the preferred or desired direction. Simple. We can even create the stress in the horse so we can do this. It's not so difficult to do—horses are easily stressed.

I'm going to go out on a limb and say that the number one cause of stress in horses is confusion. *They just don't understand.* There can be pain, and turnout issues, and feeding issues, yes, but by and large, the biggest source of stress in domestic horses that I see is *confusion*.

I thought again about what Janet Jones had said to me: "How would it feel to be in a country where you don't speak the language, don't understand the culture, don't know where you're going, and don't know why two strange men just loaded up your only friend in a white van?"

Learning clicker training, where I only rewarded what I *wanted* and ignored what I *didn't* want, was valuable because it meant "steering stress around" was no longer an option. For clicker training to work, the horse had to truly understand what I was asking for. I also had to learn to break things down into tiny steps. I, too, had to have a better understanding—in my case, a much deeper grasp on how animals learn.

But clicker training also missed something. It missed allowing the horse to go forward out of innate heart and desire. It was like never letting Washoe paint for painting's sake—always just painting for treats.

Horses can gallop out of exuberance, or out of fear or stress, or for all kinds of reasons in between. Using a horse's ability to *want to move* could be the best thing, or the worst thing.

17

Sinead was out of town for the weekend. I read *The Little Blue Truck* to Goldfish, then *The Pout-Pout Fish* to Brooks.

After they were both asleep, I found Road to the Horse 2011, featuring Pat Parelli, Clinton Anderson, Chris Cox. I pressed play.

Chris Cox read his horse in an almost mystical way. It reminded me of "A Surf Legend's Long Ride," an article I'd read in *The New Yorker* by William Finnegan about Jock Sutherland, an aging surfer:

> *It's a rising swell, and the sets are starting to produce a lovely peak right next to the channel. The crowd has moved over there, but Jock instead points toward the horizon: "Let's go, Bill." I see nothing, but I follow. He's paddling fast, moving way out, away from the crowd. Eventually, a wave appears—easily the biggest of the day, standing up far outside. It's physically impossible, I believe, that Jock could have known that wave was coming. But he gets there in plenty of time, right to the heart of the peak, and spins. Everybody else in the water is caught inside by at least forty yards. People are shouting in dismay and disbelief. It's a demonstration of basically incomprehensible mastery....*

Jock's ability to read the ocean surpassed the other greats of his era. He saw subtle signs that were invisible to the rest of us. And because of that, he was able to predict what was coming next. He was able to predict the future.

On television Chris came across as smart and ambitious, with an inner fire, a presence. There was a ferocity, a sort of raw animal instinct in his movements. Like the way a fox hunted.

Chris had competed and won Road to the Horse a record four times. Each year he seemed to enter the pen with a plan, but then he would forget it, and change. He never went faster than the horse could handle. One horse he might start with a stick, another with a flag, a third with nothing in his hands. He would use his body language sometimes like mime, but more often like an athlete. He could be seen sprinting, vaulting, sweating.

Over the years, I had tried to find someone to introduce me to Chris. I wanted to go study with him. One humid evening toward the end of August I decided to just call the number on his website. The lady who answered was extremely polite. She said I needed to sign up for a clinic, just like everybody else. That sounded fine to me, but when I checked the clinic locations and dates most were in Texas, and all were on weekends when I was already committed. Nothing seemed to work.

Instead, I ordered videos from his website called *Colt Starting: Building Confidence Through Knowledge*. I knew I could learn a lot from watching.

What if we could distill horse training down to four ingredients, the way Samin Nosrat did with the four ingredients of all good cooking? *Salt. Fat. Acid. Heat.* The four building blocks of all good horse training, as it were.

Observation would be the first block. The foundation. The most important.

A few years ago I looked into what it takes to train dolphins. At reputable aquariums, trainers have to go through years of education before they are allowed to train sea mammals. A lot of that program is observation. The students learn *about* orcas. They study sea lions and spinner dolphins. They have tests on their habits, their tendencies, what they eat, and how they interact. Students watch dolphin training, but at first, they aren't allowed to train. They learn through observation. That's it. They just watch.

Compare that to the three most commonly trained animals: dogs, horses, and humans. No license is needed for any of them. No certificate. It's easier to get one of these animals than it is to get a cell phone plan. I can speak to that incompetence. When I was presented with a tiny, slimy, baby boy, in 2018, I'd hesitated before taking him from the nurse.

"I've never held a baby before," I'd said.

"I haven't either," Sinead had said, before taking Brooks, and carefully cradling him. She'd smiled at me. "It's not that hard."

Jane Goodall didn't go to Nairobi in 1960 to *train* chimps. She went there to study them. To watch them. To be a student of who they are.

To be a good observer in horse training, I was learning, we must observe three things.

The first is *the horse*. We have to watch him with no judgment. What do we see? Perhaps the left ear flicks lazily back. Or he yawns. Or kicks. Or rolls.

In the Nature documentary series *Cloud: Wild Stallion of the Rockies*, a Mustang stallion approaches a foal from a rival herd that was born a few hours earlier and has not been able to stand yet. The stallion sniffs the foal, inspects him, then picks him up and shakes him, before finishing him off by trampling him to death.

There is no "good" and "bad" with horses, no human morality. Horses *are*. They play, they fight, they scratch each other, they run, they eat. These things all happen for various reasons, but the reasons are not based on a human-invented set of morals. The most wonderful thing, and occasionally the most frustrating thing, about horses is that they are living in the *now*. For horses, it's about how they feel in *this* moment.

When we study horses, we learn patterns. We begin to see that when *this* happens, then *this* happens next. And just because we fail to predict something does not mean it was unpredictable.

The second thing we need to observe is *the surroundings*. Try to sense everything our horses sense. Smell. Taste. Touch. Hear—and don't just hear, *LISTEN!* See—and don't just see, *WATCH!* We need to use other senses as well, more subtle ones. Ones to do with space and balance and energy and self-awareness.

And we must remember that people don't perceive things the same way as each other, much less the same way as horses.

In *Musicophilia,* neurologist Oliver Sacks explores *synesthesia,* the combining or mixing up of the senses. People with synesthesia might smell sounds. They might taste words. Textures might cause emotions. Time might have a physical characteristic to it. Pain might cause them to see color.

The struggle for a horseman is to constantly—relentlessly—see things from the horse's perspective. And his senses might affect him differently than mine affect me. When my gelding suddenly raises his head in alarm and I don't *see* any danger, and I don't *hear* any danger, what I might be missing is that he can hear differently than I can, and he can see differently than I can. And maybe it's not something he even saw or heard, maybe he *smelled* something, for he can smell differently than I can.

The third thing we must observe is *ourselves*. This is the most difficult. This is anger, frustration, fear. This is where we are upset that it's not going as well as yesterday. Or we become hopeful, too hopeful, for how it will go tomorrow, and we push too hard. This is confusion. Inadequacy. Shame. Vulnerability. Love. We are humans, we are so often ruled by emotions. We do crazy things out of love.

Sometimes, in the training process, a horse bucks off his rider.

Usually that is not a big deal, but if a horse *learns* to do it, if he thinks it is the answer, it can become habit, and if the horse is athletic, smart, and has the ideal combination of being both very confident in himself, and a little afraid of the rider, it can become a *Very Big Deal*. A horse can learn to buck the way a cornered wolf learns to bare his teeth. He might even have a signature move. A move as practiced and slick as a boxer's jab-cross-hook-slip-hook combination. He might drop his head between his front legs, plant his feet, drop his right shoulder, buck and twist. It might arrive with little warning, and as long as he has zero losses on his record, the horse has faith in his system.

Robot jockeys are not a new idea.

Since 2004, robot jockeys have been used in camel racing as a replacement for human jockeys (partially due to the repeated human rights abuses suffered by the small children that were usually employed). The jockeys are R2D2-like creatures that sit on the camel's back, control the reins, and carry a whip. They can detect the camel's speed and heart rate. They are managed by remote control by a human following in a vehicle.

But technology has come a long way since 2004.

In 2016, in Singapore and Pittsburgh, self-driving taxis were first trialed.

ChatGPT, launched in 2022, can write, in seconds, an outline for a book on starting horses. (I've tried it. It was pretty good. But my contract with my publisher stipulates that I did not rely on any form of artificial intelligence in the creation of what you are reading now.)

The Cetacean Translation Initiative (CETI) is a group of marine biologists, robotic specialists, AI gurus, linguistics pros, cryptography experts, and data scientists determined to learn the language of whales. They are currently studying sperm whales off the island of Dominica. CETI's goal is to be able to exchange ideas and experiences with whales by 2026.

While the robot jockeys are fairly crude machines operated by remote control, and most AI advancements are more to do with knowledge than physical skill, that is already changing. In Mountain View, California, there is a team that has created a self-learning robot that plays ping pong. "Imagine a tireless playing partner that adjusts as you improve," wrote James Somers in a November, 2024 article called "Getting a Grip" in *The New Yorker* about robots learning to use their hands as smoothly and efficiently as we can use ours—maybe even better.

Will a robot jockey one day be able to help teach a horse that bucks not to buck?

Will AI one day be able to start a horse?

If the number one thing that causes tension in training is confusion, it seems possible that a computer that can measure tension in the horse and respond to it instantly could help a horse understand more quickly than a human.

If AI has no emotions, experiences no fear, and is constantly learning from its mistakes, could it start horses better than we can?

The idea makes me sweat. I feel the indignation the journalist has for ChatGPT, the raw anger a coal miner has when his job is made obsolete. It is the philosophical revulsion a business owner who has gotten ahead through intelligence and hard work might have for communism.

The blue whale and the bison are endangered. The coal miner and camel jockey are too. Are the novelist and colt starter threatened as well?

Communication is the second building block. It's what allows us to explain what we are thinking and what we want. And it allows horses to tell us how they are feeling, and that they understand, or that they don't.

For communication to work it has to be *understood*. We need to develop a language with our horses. I don't expect a colt to know something right off the bat; I have to teach him first. What I'm teaching are what we call "cues," or "aids," or "words." I don't just "say" a word once and expect a colt to know it. Just like when I learn Spanish on Duolingo, the language learning app, a word is broken down, taught, then repeated before I can go out into the real world and use it in a sentence. Duolingo has me read it, write it, hear it, say it, and say it again over many days, in many contexts, before the word becomes a part of my expected vocabulary.

Motivation is the third building block. Everything happens for a reason. Some people say, "My horse spooked for no reason," or "He bucked out of nowhere," but everything has a reason. There is a motivation for everything any of us do.

Temple Grandin, known for her work studying autism and animal behavior, wrote an article that listed the four "drives" of cattle and horses as: *fear, aggression, learned responses,* and *instincts.* The most common motivators that horse trainers refer to are *safety* and *comfort* and *food*.

When a horse doesn't feel safe, he isn't worried about anything else. The opposite of *safety* is Temple Grandin's drive *fear*. This is a number one motivator for horses.

Comfort is number two. Comfort and discomfort are on a spectrum. Something can be mildly uncomfortable, like when it's a little too hot at the beach, or you're trying to brush your teeth with your non-dominant hand. Or you can be *really* uncomfortable, like having a whole swarm of mosquitoes attacking at dusk. Using the contrast between comfort and discomfort is how most people train horses, most of the time. The greater the artist, the less the discomfort and the greater the comfort.

Food is the last big motivator, and the most controversial.

There are also other smaller, more subtle ways to motivate a horse. Curiosity…harmony…play…

Play is the fourth building block in horse training. It's my favorite. Play can come in many forms. Washoe the chimp painting murals with ocean blues and sunflower yellows—that's *play*. Steph Curry hitting a game-winning shot from ten feet outside the three-point line and smiling before the ball even hits the net—that's also play. Play can be the unruly wrestling of puppies. It can be the organized lifts, cuts, and turns of Lionel Messi in Miami, or it can be the concentrated play of a riddle.

It can be swordplay. Wordplay. Horseplay.

It can be foreplay.

But does "play" mean there is no adversity? No stress? No adrenaline? No danger? Is play *always* fun? Solving a riddle or completing a puzzle are problems to be solved, and that comes with varying degrees of stress.

Harmony might also be a sort of play. Harmony is when both horse and rider want to do the same thing at the same time. It looks like a school of fish, or a flock of birds. It looks like a herd of Thoroughbreds in Ocala, moving together, stopping together, raising their heads together.

It looks like dancing.

Initially, horses may be moving *away* from pressure. But the drive to move in harmony with another being is an instinct for them. For us to move *with them* feels good. For them to move *with us* feels good. It feels good to move together.

But if I had to name the most important ingredient in the building block of play?

It's when you are caught up totally in the moment. When you are in the zone, the unthinking place, the place where time slows down. *You are in the present.* And most horses have *never* met a person, in their entire lives, who was entirely, with every cell in their body, *present.*

18

Like most mornings, Sinead was in the kitchen first. Then Goldfish. Then Brooks and I crawled in together, wrapped in blankets and moaning.

Goldfish bobbed her head to the sound of George Ezra crooning. One arm fed herself, and the other arm danced up and down.

I yawned, but I started to weave to the music. Then Brooks started jumping. Even Sinead couldn't help herself. She tapped her foot. She wore pajama bottoms and one of my old tee shirts. Her eyes were more awake than mine. That song had been on every morning for the past week. George had provided the soundtrack to that year of our life.

"You smell good," I said to Sinead, kissing her cheek.

"This is it," she said. "This is our life. Right now."

After I dropped Brooks and Goldfish at school, I drove to Silver Springs State Park. I laced up my running shoes, double-knotting them, then set out on the winding single-track trails through the forest.

In my twenties I ran to improve my times, and to win. In my thirties I still liked to run and occasionally race in a "5k" in order to stay motivated, but my days of improving my times were behind me. My main goal had turned to staying in good enough shape that I could keep up with my brother, the once or twice a year we got to run together. Now, in my forties, I just hoped to keep it up long enough that I could one day run with Brooks or Goldfish on these trails, or on the paths near Whistler, or on Salt Spring Island, or on the Sunshine Coast.

As I ran through a stand of tall pines, light flickered through the needles and freckled the path in front of me. There were dozens of thoughts circulating through my mind: bills that had to be paid, time off for staff that had to be organized, school forms that had to be filled out, deciding whether to use an English saddle or Western saddle at Road to the Horse, new passport applications that had to be remembered. The list went on and on, and I couldn't let them go that morning. They just kept circulating.

Training horses is different than running: more brains than muscles.

With horses, as opposed to running, I was still improving. Still on the upswing. I imagined how good someone could get with horses in a lifetime. I guessed I had accomplished not even ten percent of the harmony that could be achieved with a horse; not even ten percent of the skills I could master.

If, one day, I couldn't compete horses, would I be happy just training them, just doing groundwork?

That was an easy one to answer!

If I couldn't train horses, would I find equal joy in just being with them?

That one was more difficult.

I carried these questions, all my thoughts, with me, all the way back to the car, sweaty and drained. But still stressed. Not a good run.

Most runs I'd get to where my mind could "let go," and I'd begin daydreaming. *Those* were good runs.

I'd daydream about a vacation where Brooks and Goldfish and their cousins could get to know each other and play together; about building a proper riding arena, and where we would put it; about Road to the Horse; about books I wanted to write; about the Unitarian Church in Vancouver; about lying on the rocks of Wise Island in late August, the sun beating down on my back, then rolling like an otter into the salty, deep, black, frigid, kelp-forest, swimming down, then turning and looking up at the sun filtering through the sea-weed, dappling everything below it.

On some runs, occasionally, I'd stop daydreaming. Then I was an animal, my legs knocking out a rhythm beneath me, like a lion trotting across the Savannah. My arms swinging freely at my sides. The rain or wind or sun biting my back and shoulders. My mind would become still, only seeing what was immediately in front of me. My mind wouldn't talk to me, it would just direct my feet: *Step there. Step there. Step there. Don't step there. Step there. Step there.*

That? That was a *great* run.

In my twenties I would run three and a half miles under seventeen minutes. In my forties, instead of fast times I had:

- Back pain.
- Groin pain.
- Stomach pain.
- A receding gumline.
- A receding hairline.

I'd never again run like I could in my twenties. But still, some fitness might help me at Road to the Horse. It certainly wouldn't hurt. And for my mental health, even a "not-good" run was better than no run.

The first stumbling block was her distraction.

I "got big" to get her attention. I hated that. I just wanted it to be smooth. Over the years, the better I got, the less "big" I had to get. I wondered if I could ever be quiet all the time. I doubted it. Not with *all* horses, *all* the time. Jonathan Field had once told me, "If you want to have the ability to work with every horse, in every situation, you have to have the ability to be as soft as a mare with her foal, and as firm as one stallion can be with another."

It was September in Mequon, Wisconsin. It was my first attempt at a simulation of the Road to the Horse time parameters: an hour and forty-five minutes on Friday, with fifteen minutes of mandatory rest breaks. The same on Saturday. Then Sunday, twenty minutes in the round pen, and thirty-five minutes in the open arena.

The horse was a four-year-old Quarter Horse mare named Leah. She was the color of fresh butter.

Leah's owners said the mare was "lightly started," which in this case meant she was halter broke and had carried a rider at the walk a few times. My goal was to go at her pace, while getting used to what the time restrictions of Road to the Horse felt like. I wasn't going to push it.

The property did not have a round pen, so I had to choose between a small paddock with a run-in shed, a large indoor arena, or a tiny indoor arena usually reserved for a therapeutic riding program. The tiny indoor and the large indoor were connected by a small viewing room that stood between them.

The small indoor was rectangular, with ground that was harder than I would have liked, but it was the best space overall. I recruited some volunteers, and we used some jumps to section off one end of the space so that I was left with a square, about forty feet by forty feet, in which to work. It wasn't round, but it would do.

There are pros and cons to the training tool horse people call a "round pen." The main reason I wished to replicate a round pen as closely as possible in this instance was to mirror the space I would be working in at Road to the Horse in March.

I wanted to begin by just giving Leah a rub, but she was distracted, so I went ahead with groundwork. *Back up, go left, go right*—that kind of thing.

The owner of the barn, Kathy Happ, and the owner of the horse and a couple of visiting trainers watched most of the Friday session. They came and went, as they did chores or took a phone call. Even with just three people watching, I felt like I was on the spot. *Just three people!* That was all it took for the pressure to hit me, for me to start second-guessing myself. *How will I ever make it in the coliseum in Kentucky?*

The time allotment itself was surprisingly easy to adjust to. It didn't seem too short, or too long. But I never got to attempting any obstacles with Leah on our simulated "Day One." There was just so much other stuff to work on.

The second day I rode her, and she bucked. Ever since getting bucked off Fenwick, I had been avoiding situations where a buck could happen. Partially because my groin was still not healed, but mostly because I was scared.

I sat it. The worst part of horses starting to buck is not knowing how much they might throw at me. Once I felt it once, I knew I could sit it, which gave me a little confidence.

I wrote two things in my notes before bed:

- *Sometimes it would feel like twenty minutes had passed and it was only five minutes. Other times it was the opposite. I need to practice feeling that time.*

- *Don't start anything in the last twenty minutes. Finish on a good note, even if it's early.*

On the third day, Nick drove out from the Madison suburbs to watch. I gave him a hug and he sat down to watch. Nick was silently observing, his beard, black and deep, fluffed onto his chest like a little pillow. I could not imagine how he did not get food stuck in it constantly.

The rail work went well. So did the obstacles—until we got to the tarp. The day before, I had spread it out so that it was about three feet wide by eight feet long. But now I had it open the whole way, so it was a large square, about eight feet by eight feet.

The mare had been smooth and forward, but now her feet stopped. She glanced left. Then she looked right. I kept suggesting. Then I started asking. Her feet drifted left and right, without getting any closer to the tarp.

I had seen this before at previous Road to the Horse competitions. It was as if everything had been going so well up to that point, I couldn't *imagine* it not working out. I was caught in the same trap I'd seen other trainers fall into, unable to turn away, but flummoxed about how to continue. My gut feeling was to leave it. *No,* I resolved. *We can do this, this will work.*

But as soon as I got stubborn, as soon as I got gritty, it was over. Leah wasn't having it. The more I dug my heels in, the farther apart we got.

We teach kids that arguments can be solved with talking, instead of yelling or fighting. As adults we lose our tempers—about work, or

sports, or politics, or who made the bed—and we tell ourselves it's more important, or it's different, than what our children might be arguing about.

It's not.

Later, Nick asked "You want my input?"

"Of course."

"At the tarp, the mare was distracted. She was looking to the back of the arena where another horse was walking, going in and out of her view."

Geez, I thought. *How could I have missed that? Observe the horse! Observe the surroundings! Watch the eye!*

With a mature, competing horse, I watch the body: how the horse jumps, how he moves. But with a green horse, or an emotional horse, *watch the eye!* It was the eye that was the biggest tell to what the horse was thinking and how he was feeling. Mounted, I can't (easily) see the eye. I have to feel the horse's tension, feel his heartbeat, feel his adrenaline. I must be aware of his even rhythm—or his abruptness. I must notice moments when the horse relaxes, or even moments when he *starts to think about* relaxing.

If I had noticed the other horse at the back of the arena that Nick had, I could have done a couple things. I could have moved away from the tarp, reconnected with Leah, and then come back to it. I could have simply asked her to cross the tarp from the opposite direction so that she would be going *toward* the horse she was curious about.

Or I could have just left the tarp sooner, which had been my gut feeling anyway.

"Your key is talk to the wranglers. Ask them about each horse. Were they doctored as a young horse? Were they lassoed and then injected, so now they are rope shy?"

I was speaking with Vicki Wilson, two-time winner of Road to the Horse (2017 and 2018). I sat at my desk, computer open, looking at her face, somewhere on the other side of the world.

"Watch them when they come off the truck," Vicki said. "Watch them when they go out into the arena. Don't take the ones that creep off the truck; take the ones that come confidently! You don't want the one at the back—you don't want a follower as such, it makes the job harder on the Sunday. You don't want the one that gets picked on. The leader is tougher, but brave." The first day, she explained, should be about curiosity. Create bravery through curiosity. "You want them to stay in a thinking part of their brain."

Vicki's mahogany-colored hair covered her shoulders. Her skin was bronzed from the New Zealand wind and sun. Because of the way she moved, tough and catlike, and the way she spoke, like she was used to thinking on her feet, she gave the appearance of a pure athlete. Beneath the surface there was a tenaciousness...what I might sometimes call *doggedness*. She had chosen horses, but it felt like she would have been equally successful as a snowboarder, middle-distance runner, or solo-circumnavigating the world in a sailboat.

"Three days is big for a horse, but it's possible," Vicki continued. "Quarter Horses are exceptional for delivering under pressure...just don't let it drive you to get results." And then, "Just be ready to think outside the box. You will not know enough. But you can be open to what the horse is telling you he needs. Your toolbox will expand. When it doesn't go to plan, keep asking, 'How do we solve it for the horse?' Curiosity is the future. We start it on day one. And that's what we need down the road."

I thanked Vicki and allowed myself to begin to grasp that *I would not know enough,* I just wouldn't—and that was okay, if the horse and I were still curious in the end.

19

The gentleman on the screen in front of me reminded me of a Roald Dahl character. Sparkling rosy cheeks. A slightly gaunt face. His last name was Smiley. He sported a tan sweater and reading glasses.

"When people send a horse to you for starting, is the first question, 'How long will it take?'" I asked.

"That is certainly true in Ireland," Eric Smiley replied. "They will expect six weeks. Canter and jump a few fences and be ready to go to a little show. With some horses it happens. As you know, though, with some horses, it can take six months.

"Ireland is in a hurry. It's a 'sell' nation. If a horse is not doing something by five, it is assumed there is something wrong with him. You can't do that! You need to take time with them. You need to understand them as individuals. You create more problems for yourself if you rush. The strange thing is Ireland is a producer of wonderful horses, and amazingly naturally talented riders, but they spoil and ruin as many horses as they produce. Go look at the performance sales in Ireland—amazing four-year-olds. But it will probably take two years for those horse to recover from being started. Very few people take Irish horses slowly."

I thought of Sam, the horse I was competing that year. He was born and raised in Ireland. I wondered what his upbringing had been like.

I also wondered what Eric would say if I told him I was going to be starting a horse in three days…in a competition, no less.

"In every country," Eric continued, "we have fewer people who are connected with animals than we used to have. We have less natural feel than we used to have. That reflects in how we do things with horses."

Eric had been an event rider for Ireland at the international level for years. It was only when he stopped competing that he began breeding and producing all his own horses. He started them at age three or four. Until then they lived in fields—the yearlings in one, the two-year-olds in another.

"It makes them comfortable," Eric said. "I start by leading them around the pens, so they have someone in there with them. The companionship of the herd system is critical to their comfort and their state of mind.

"Then with the three-year-olds, most of that is in the barn. I'll lead them around. They will get led both ways, and with their friends right next door, just on the other side of the partition. They are always chatting with their friends. People miss that part. They take horses to a round pen or an arena, away from their friends, which is very alien to them."

I shifted my weight in my chair in front of my computer. "Did you go through any formal training to learn to start horses?" I asked.

"I'm a Fellow of British Horse Society," he said. "I don't always follow a lot of their systems, which *are* logical and thought through, but what I do is often more natural and easier for the horse. For example, I try *not* to give the young horse secure footing when I do something with them. Then they are less inclined to do something to get hurt."

It seemed like a strange concept, and he must have noticed my surprise on my face, as he continued to explain, animated on his side of the Atlantic.

"When horses are insecure in their footing, they are more conscious of that, and they are less likely to do something against you," he said. "The passageway in our barn is concrete, and they tend to slip on concrete, so they are quite comfortable with me doing things with them there. When it goes well, then they learn I'm not a danger."

The idea of having slippery footing *on purpose* seemed counterintuitive to what I knew about working with horses, but I remembered I had read something similar in a training manual years ago: the author recommended teaching horses to stand for tacking up by situating them in an area that was made up of round smooth river rocks, about the size of baseballs—not the easiest footing for a horse to dance around on.

(Later, when I spoke to Sinead about doing a first ride on concrete she said, "Ninety-eight percent of the time that might work." I agreed with her, and we had a little laugh about what that likely meant for the remaining two percent.)

"Too many people try to 'get the bucks out of a horse,'" Eric went on. "That only creates a thought process where horses learn to associate tack and equipment with a buck. I never try to put myself in a situation where they react against tack, because if they are comfortable with it, why should they not be comfortable with me?"

"And the first ride?" I prompted.

"I'll sit on them, let them chat with their friends while in the passage. Then we walk to the other horses in the barn. And they are quite comfortable doing that because they are curious. Trying to 'give them a mouth' too soon before they become comfortable with a bit is an irrevocable mistake."

Eric was referring, I'm pretty sure, to teaching horses, or attempting to teach them, to have "an educated, soft mouth" at an early age. Instead, he seemed to advocate for just letting them get used to the feel of the bit in their mouths without trying to steer or stop with it. Just letting them *carry* the bit.

I liked the theory.

"If I let them wander, they just chat with their friends," he reiterated. Eric spoke clearly and simply. Bright curtains fluttered in the breeze behind him.

"Do you think of starting horses as a separate discipline?" I asked. "Its own specialty? A different skill set than riding 'made' horses?"

"Yes," he acknowledged quickly. "Very few people at a high level start their own horses."

"Can I read something to you?" I said, referring to the notes I had in my lap. "It's something Eric Lamaze said in *Horse and Hound* about starting horses slowly:

> *I'm a fan of letting them grow and become strong. At three years old, put a rider on him, give him a couple of little fences under tack, then put him back in the field. Bring him back as a four-year-old, teach him the ropes a bit, go to a show or two, and put him back in the field. As a five-year-old, do a few more shows, then back in the field. At six you can do almost a whole year, and then at seven years old, you know what you have.*

"Would you agree with Eric, Eric?"

"Yes," he said with a short nod. "They are not adults until they are seven. I don't believe that they are mature enough to use their abilities until they are nine. If you are careful at seven and don't rush, you have a horse that goes through till sixteen."

I thought about all the sports that didn't let horses 'mature enough to use their abilities.' Most of them. Not even close. "Does it serve a competitive rider in any way to learn to start horses?" I wondered.

"It is very difficult for competitive riders to do," Eric acknowledged. "They are concerned with results. *Now!* In an instant.

Sometimes, with young horses, you have to allow them to make mistakes, and the horses learn from the mistakes. When a horse is on a wrong stride, the competitive person wants to do something about it, then the horse doesn't learn—other than to learn to listen to the rider. One of the issues we have in cross-country riding is that riders are taught how to ride properly—jump things perfectly, see strides—so horses never learn to think for themselves. Horses have to learn how to get themselves out of trouble. And if they learn to get *themselves* out of trouble, then they get *us* out of trouble."

I thought about the certain kind of bravery it took for a rider to allow a young horse to get himself out of trouble, and asked Eric, "What characteristics *should* someone who starts horses have?"

His answer was a familiar one.

"Be very observant to what horses do," he replied with emphasis. "You need to *watch* horses. How do they react? We 'look' at horses, but we don't *watch* horses as individuals. Watch their mannerisms, their characteristics, their reactions. The horseman observes even the slightest reactions from their horse when they walk into the stable."

"What could we all do better or differently?"

"Remove money from competing horses at a young age. Remove *all* the money for two-year-old classes!" he replied without hesitation. "The horses would last longer. Your futurity horses and Western riding horses, they have joints that are gone by five and are useless by six. Racing horses at two years old does not help their longevity. Off-track Thoroughbreds are physically and mentally crocked. I don't think we, as a riding fraternity, think enough about the horses as individuals.

"Give them time!"

20

Jake Biernbaum had lent me three lariats. First, they'd sat in the bed of the pickup. Then they'd collected dust in my trailer. A couple weeks later, I'd hung them in the tackroom. Finally, I'd put them beside the round pen. Each time I moved them to places where I thought I would be more inspired to actually use them, but I never did.

Are you taking this seriously? I asked myself.

Yes, I am, I answered myself. *I'm researching. I'm setting up clinics.*

But what about roping?

I'm exhausted. There are only so many hours in a day.

This could be the most important competition of your life.

Everything feels important right now! Everything feels like a priority!

Don't give yourself excuses! Don't live with that regret!

Then Jake texted me. He had some horses I could start.

Quarter Horses, he said. *Two coming three in the spring.*

Can we try it like a simulation? I asked. *I start them over three days, and you coach and judge?*

One gelding, one filly. Yup. They are catchable, and haltered, and can lead, but I haven't done anything more with them.

I could do this Friday to Sunday… I suggested hopefully.

I like this weekend, Jake texted back. *I have a medical procedure tomorrow and am on light duty for seven to ten days.*

The only time I've told people I was getting a 'medical procedure' was when I got a vasectomy, I replied with a smiley emoji in a cowboy hat.

Jake sent an LOL, then: *Getting my varicose veins fixed. One leg now and the other closer to the holidays.*

My saddle or yours? I asked.

What are you using for the show?

I am 90% sure a jump saddle. But I'm still open to having my mind changed. It's just what I'm so used to.

100% easier to get bucked out of. 100% less exposure and confidence training for the horse. 100% less functional for the dragging obstacle and tying a tarp to, was his response.

I shook my head as I texted, *I mean, just tell me how you really feel, right?*

I knocked the dust off the lariats and threw them back in the bed of my truck.

Ever since meeting Jonathan Field in 2008, I'd wanted to feel included in his scene—the world of "horsemanship."

The first time I saw a rope halter at Bruce Logan's in Texas, during my three years traveling the world as a working student, I walked over to the fence. I took the halter down, careful not to disrupt the way it hung. I held the puzzle in my hands, inspecting it, studying it.

I undid part of it, then did it back up. Then undid it a little farther. Then did it back up again. Fifteen times, twenty times, I practiced, building muscle memory. I would have been embarrassed to ask. *This is something I should know.* I felt I could figure it out with a little effort.

Often it seems like the recipe is pretty simple: *curiosity* and *effort.*

In this colt-starting adventure, I still felt like an observer, sitting just outside the "club," looking in. Did I only get offered the spot at Road to the Horse because I was Canadian? Because they needed someone "different?" Feeling like an outsider only bothered me a little; it was a role I'd played before. And it didn't really matter why I was invited. Natalie probably would tell me it doesn't matter to the apple tree why winter is over...blossom! Make the most of it!

From our place to Jake's it was a straight shot down County Road 316 past Waterworks Farm, Happy Bottoms, Stormy Gray Farm, April Fools Farm, the White Ranch, a Donald Trump 2024 sign, and the Dupree Cemetery, an African-American cemetery—a few acres of low-lying tombstones and cement pads, shaded by a dozen or so live oaks. Many of the trees were wider and taller than the Dollar General down the road. They must have been three or four hundred years old.

County Road 316 isn't quite straight; it dog-legs when it meets NE Jacksonville Road. It's a rural road: sometimes a pickup with a dog leaning out the window will speed past me going ninety-five, other times I'll pass a tractor going fifteen. Two winters previously when Nick was visiting from Wisconsin and helping Jake with welding, I'd put my running shoes on and jogged over to visit. I'd gotten a few honks as I ran down the road in my red short-shorts.

Now Jake leaned against the fence as I worked with his colt.

"You need to find the balance between taking the time to build their confidence and their curiosity, and on the other hand, 'getting it done,'" he announced. "In other words, building their obedience. You really need to think about what you are trying to accomplish there. Given the choice between pushing the horse too hard and winning, and going at an appropriate speed and not winning, pick the not-winning."

I nodded. *Of course*. But what was left unsaid was that somebody experienced enough, and talented enough, could do both.

I believed that going into Road to the Horse with the mindset of *only* trying to go slow would be giving me an excuse before I'd even started. I wasn't going to go in there and just do nothing for three days and say, "I don't want to rush him." I knew what the spirit of the competition was—to go as fast as you could without going *too* fast—and I was determined to play for real.

The first hour and a half of the simulation went quickly. Jake was a fantastic coach, pointing out both details and big-picture concepts. I needed to be more aware of my tempo. *Go slower at the start; go faster at the end.* I needed to give the colt more time to process when he was learning. But then, later on, I needed to push it to get him ready to ride.

For example, I asked the little gelding, now saddled, wearing a rope halter and with a fourteen-foot rope connecting us, to follow the rope around behind him—to "unwind" himself. First, I just had the rope around his hindquarters; once he could do that, I made the exercise more difficult, bringing the rope behind the saddle cantle. Then we made it more difficult again by bringing the rope behind the horn. Each time I asked him to unwind himself I changed the angle so it got a little harder for him. Once he figured it out, I didn't stay with the same exercise, I increased the degree of difficulty.

A second example was asking the colt to go forward into the trot for the first time. He stopped after a half lap. I was ready to keep him going, but Jake said to rub him, give him a break. Later when we tried again, though, Jake said "Push it a little more now." So I did, I kept him going, and at that point we already had the foundation to build on, and it felt right.

What a horse can learn in an hour is absolutely incredible.

Riding in a Western saddle was out of my comfort zone. I was leaning toward the idea of starting with a bareback pad, then switching to a Western saddle, then finally riding in an English jump saddle at Road to the Horse.

Jake rode one of his horses at the same time as I worked the colt. He rode in a saddle that he had won at Road to the Summit in 2014, another horse-starting competition. His sleeves were rolled up, and I noticed a tattoo on the underside of his forearm. It said, *For my ally is the force...and a powerful ally it is.*

I struggled with walk, trot, and canter transitions in the Western saddle. They were abrupt.

"Think of going down and up a ladder of musical notes," Jake suggested. "*Ceeee—Beeee—Aaaaa—Beeee—Ceeee*," he sang. "Each one has a buzz and a pitch."

A few of Jake's students watched the lesson, and already I felt more comfortable with an audience than I had at the simulation in Wisconsin. Although I was accustomed to crowds when I competed in the jumping or dressage phases of eventing competitions, in those instances, I was out there in front of an audience for only a few minutes, and just one of dozens of competitors, demonstrating a skill that I have already spent ages practicing at home. Starting horses in front of spectators felt different; there were more variables, almost anything could happen, and I would have to adjust on the fly. There were also fewer competitors, so the spotlight would be brighter, hotter...less diluted.

I was dragging some extra rope, and Jake side-passed over and taught me the clove hitch for wrapping the extra rope around the saddle horn.

At the end of the session, I made the mistake of starting to undo the saddle's front cinch before undoing the back cinch.

Idiot! I thought. *Rookie mistake!*

Then I called it a "girth" instead of a "cinch."

Another rookie mistake.

I returned the still-unfamiliar saddle to Jake's tack room. On the back wall I noticed two white boards, on which were written:

5 Body Parts: Nose / Neck / Shoulder / Ribs / Hip

8 Directions: Standstill / Forward / Backward / Right / Left / Up / Down / Standstill

4 Stages of Development: Teach / Control / Reinforce / Refine

5 Stages Toward Mastery: Awareness / Understanding / Doing / Reproducing / Teaching

I noted that "Standstill" was repeated as a direction—considered "two" of the "eight directions." I wondered if that was to emphasize the importance of not overlooking where we should start and finish each bit of play, each jump, each ride. Two basic things we teach horses are "to go" and "to whoa," and how many horses don't even know *those* two things well? Riding them is like getting into a car where the gas and brake only work *some* of the time.

Next to the white boards was a bookshelf. I couldn't resist. I got down on my knees to check out the titles. I spied *Warrior Soul*; *Tracking and the Art of Seeing*; *Animal Tracks*; *Mother Earth, Father Sky*; *Nature in Horsemanship*; *True Horsemanship Through Feel*; and the aptly titled *One Man's Opinion About Spade Bits*.

The lists and books in Jake's tack room reminded me he was not "just a rider," he was a fan of horses and sports, and their history. He was thinking outside the box. He was seeking to break stuff down in a manageable way. He enjoyed teaching and wanted to make it accessible.

The list and books felt familiar to me. Like home. I too enjoyed thinking outside the box, breaking stuff down, making it accessible. But mostly, right now, I was just *busy*. I had big goals coming up, and it was a lot. A lot of time, a lot of energy, a lot of money. It was a reach for me, and a reach for my family and our business. There were constant butterflies in my stomach. Or maybe just flies.

I wondered if I was developing ulcers.

Occasionally there were moments when it didn't feel like a reach. Moments where I felt like I had spent decades learning, and these were things I *could* do, *should* do. Moments where it felt like this was what I was put on the earth to do.

But I was acutely aware that even with all the knowledge I was gathering, nothing was a sure thing.

You can spend years learning the theory of how to swim, putting your head underwater, blowing bubbles, and moving your arms a certain way, but you still don't know if you can really swim until you're in deep water.

I was definitely headed toward deep water.

21

The flight was full. I alternated between reading Ray Bradbury's *Zen in the Art of Writing* and Peter Singer's *Animal Liberation Now*.

Bradbury was full of zest! And gusto! And exclamation marks! He wrote that it is neither college nor skill that is the basic requirement of writing, it is ENTHUSIASM!

You grow ravenous, he wrote. *You run fevers. You know exhilarations. You can't sleep at night, because your beast-creature ideas want out and turn you in your bed. It is a grand way to live.*

He also wrote: *The answer to all writing, to any career for that matter, is love.*

Singer was equally passionate, but he was appealing to people's minds, as much as their hearts. Singer argued that we should end the suffering of animals. He approached this mission not from a place of empathy, though of course he is empathetic, but from a place of rationality.

Yes, when I pick up a book, my first action is to read the first line. But in choosing which book to pick up, I am influenced by both the title and the cover.

The Curious Incident of the Dog in the Nighttime. Great title.

Grapes of Wrath. Even better.

I prefer a cover that is simple, understated. It can be art, or a photograph, but not too busy. I want to know the genre just by looking at it. Science fiction. A beach read. A thriller. A horse book.

After reading the first page, I scan the blurbs and look for a recommendation by someone I recognize. In the case of *Animal Liberation Now* it was an endorsement by Jane Goodall, the primatologist. One of my favorite Goodall quotes is: *It actually doesn't take much to be considered a difficult woman. That's why there are so many of us.*

I have a high appreciation for difficult women. Strong women.

In Frankfurt, the plane, swollen with Americans, finally reached the gate. We descended like ants into the airport, then through customs, and then finally out into cabs, and trains, and cafes. I switched my Duolingo language from Spanish to German, and took a few lessons while I waited for the train. *Bitte einen Kaffee und ein Croissant.*

I loved traveling but hated being a tourist.

Wind farms. That was the first thing I noticed. Germany had a goal of setting aside two percent of their land for "wind-parks."

I walked through the train to the café car and ordered a cappuccino and a croissant. I looked around and wished I had trendier shoes. I found a seat that allowed me to watch the landscape rolling by. Hills, towns, narrow streets. There were Fords and Volkswagens, but there were also Opels, Skodas, Peugeots, and Citroens. It was rare to see a pickup; I never saw a dually.

In two days, Sinead would fly over with a client, and we would all go look at horses for sale. In the meantime, I had two days to learn about the German style of starting horses. Juliette, who lived part of the year in Germany, was my tour guide.

She met me at the train station, and we walked to her car, a tiny two-door compact.

Our first stop, she said, was the *Westfälisches Pferdestammbuch,* which translated as "Westphalian Horse Pedigree Book." German breeds were often named after where they were from: the *Hanoverian* from Hanover, the *Brandenburg* from Brandenburg, the *Holsteiner* from Holstein, the *Oldenburger* from Oldenburg, the *Mecklenburger* from Mecklenburg, the *Black Forest Horse* from, yup, the Black Forest.

Trakehner is short for *Ostpreußisches Warmblut Trakehner Abstammung,* which translates roughly as "East Prussian Warmblood of Trakehner origin." Trakehners are from the town of Trakehnen, which is now called *Yasnaya Polyana* and is part of Russia. Toward the end of WWII, as Soviet troops advanced from the east, Germans and their animals fled. Between January and March 1945, the main Trakehner Stud evacuated. Their journey west, known as *Der Treck,* or "The Flight," crossed the frozen Vistula lagoon. The group was bombed by the Soviet airforce and only seven hundred horses, mostly mares, made it to safety.

Juliette pulled up at the Westphalian studbook. There we met Marina Jurgens, the stable manager, and Marco Zimmermann, *Ausbiler* (rider). With them were two *Lehrling* (students): A young lady, Jenny Letters, and a young man, Paul Papenroth.

For three hours we watched them work with three horses that were each at various points along the journey of being started. The trainer and students demonstrated what they were doing, and I filled an entire notebook with notes.

"How many horses have you started?" I asked Herr Zimmermann. He said he had started, or coached others through the starting process of, more than a thousand horses with their method.

But what about more difficult horses? I wondered. Ones that didn't fit into this method?

"What do you do with those horses?" I asked.

"We send them to a specialist."

"Wait a second," I said. "*You* have started, or been a part of starting, over a *thousand* horses, and *you* are not the specialist?"

A thousand horses…was an impressive number.

Herr Zimmermann explained "The Specialist" had more experience with younger horses and also more time.

"How much more time?"

"Some horses need twice as much time," he said, shrugging his shoulders.

Back in Juliette's little car, I asked her, "What was your biggest takeaway?"

"That they had a system. And that they were confident in it."

"It seems like there are a lot of systems here."

"Germans are very systematic. They value tradition. They do things as they have always been done. There are rules for everything. Rules for breeding horses. Rules for learning to ride. If you want to drive you need a license, if you want to tow a trailer, that's a separate license. If a kid in the city wants to ride a bicycle, there is a course and a license."

Juliette pulled into the left lane to pass. The little car responded slowly. "My foot is all the way down," she observed with a laugh. We pulled back into the right lane, and an Audi whisked past us. "I wish I had an Audi," Juliette said wistfully.

Then she slowed her car, as in front of us were two commercial trucks, side by side, heading sluggishly up a hill. The passing truck was only marginally faster than the truck being passed.

"That's called *Elefantenrennen*," Juliette said. "'Elephant racing.' There is a fine if you're caught doing that."

At the crest of the hill, the first elephant made it by the second and then merged right. Before we had a chance to pass, a BMW passed all three of us like we were standing still.

"Geez," Juliette said as she accelerated as best she could into the gap.

"With so many systems and rules and fines, it's so bizarre that the Autobahn is the only place in Europe with no speed limit," I remarked.

The German system of starting horses was clearly effective and efficient. And yet…I wondered if with such a rigid structure, innovation and out-of-the-box thinking might be lost. My guess is it was no accident that "natural horsemanship" was developed in America, a place with immense spaces, horses, and cattle.

The fastest way to move cattle is slowly is one of my favorite sayings. Another is *Slow is smooth, and smooth is fast.*

To move cattle slowly, one must become proficient at reading them. Cows that are worried speed up, and running cattle are difficult to steer. When a cowboy doesn't understand bovine body language, they might be staring at a stampede in a matter of seconds. (A stampede is dangerous, but stress, they say, also affects the beef quality. Reduced tenderness, decreased marbling, less nutritional value.)

Most European methods of starting horses had been born out of the need to start thousands of horses on a journey that would eventually lead to war. Their methods were almost, but not quite, foolproof.

Honza Bláha wore blue jeans, a blue hoodie, and a black cowboy hat.

Honza was a "specialist."

"Finding the solution to a horse running away from you is not in the technique, it's in here," he said, putting his hand on his chest, "and it's in daily habits. It's like going to the dentist. They can fix your cavity, but only you can fix eating sugar and cleaning your teeth. It's so easy to eat sweets, and to be lazy brushing your teeth, and then in two months the problem is deep. It doesn't mean you are bad, it means you are human."

Juliette and I had just sat down to watch Honza teach a liberty clinic in Zülpich, a small town in Western Germany. Honza was from a village in Czechia. He taught mainly in English, but sprinkled in some German.

"Germans are quality! That's why I drive a German car." He pointed out the door of the indoor arena. "That's why I have a German tractor. But it's not good for friendship. I'd rather choose *friendship* now, and precision later. The horse has feelings; he is not a machine. Do it several times and he will hate his job. For him to know to 'come to you' is more important than the exercise. I forgive all in the name of the relationship. Abort the exercise before he leaves. Abort and try again the next day."

I had heard stories about Honza for years. He had spent time in America, and people who had met him had, without fail, stories to tell. He was one of those horsemen you don't forget.

"I have 'green' mistakes and 'red' mistakes," Honza said. "A green mistake allows improvement. Constantly choose the mistakes that are easier to fix later."

In other words, there is no perfection, and so we must decide, each and every second, what to prioritize, and where to compromise.

Honza set up an exercise with poles where the horse had to go around the poles and then back to his person. It was a difficult exercise because the human had to send the horse away without the horse wanting to leave. The horse had to leave *already with the idea of coming back*. Honza helped and managed to read the situation correctly, time after time.

I was almost overcome with a feeling of greed. I wanted to know everything this man knew about horses. I wanted to see what he saw. Feel what he felt. I devoured his words, his body language, his energy. I couldn't look away.

After the clinic, I asked Honza if Juliette and I could take him for a beer.

We drove down the road to the local pub where I ordered in German. *"Drei Bieren, bitte."* I acknowledged to myself that I would have made an atrocious spy—I held a notebook as I spoke; my accent was terrible. We had arrived before dinner, and the place was quiet. We stood out.

The three of us took a table near the window. Honza removed his black hat and put it on the chair next to him. He was clean-shaven, with short brown hair.

After I explained my mission to learn about starting horses and to prepare for Road to the Horse, Honza's first question was, "Why is it in a round pen?"

"Why is *what* in a round pen?"

"Road to the Horse."

It was a good question. There was an argument that round pens have done as much harm as good over the years.

The argument against using round pens was that a trainer could put a lot of pressure on the horse, and the horse couldn't get away because the fence keeps the horse close and there are no corners for "relief." But I felt it was no different than when we have the horse on a rope, except for how we *see* it. I'd heard people say that the round pen appears to represent something "kinder," and so to use it to create stress was disingenuous. To me, the round pen, like a lot of tools horse people used, could be a blessing or curse, for good or evil. In the words of Uncle Ben to the young Peter Parker, "With great power comes great responsibility."

I wanted to think I could start a horse anywhere, in any situation, with, or without, any equipment. One scenario might take longer than another, but that would be the only difference.

That said, you had to be *somewhere.* In the case of Road to the Horse, the round pen, at the very least, delineated space for the competitors and gave the audience a specific focal point in the arena to watch.

The bartender brought the beers. We raised our glasses and looked each other in the eyes before taking a sip.

"How many horses would you say you have started?" I asked Honza.

"I don't know. A thousand? I used to say, 'Bring me a horse you can't ride, and I'll ride it.' I got better at it, and I got more and more difficult horses. But every time I would fix one, they would bring two more."

"That sounds exhausting," I said, meaning it with all my heart. Even just two difficult horses at a time could sap my emotional reservoir.

"At clinics I would have twelve difficult horses, and then the next weekend, twelve more. Then twelve more, twelve more, twelve more. I knew a guy who dealt with problem horses, and he hung himself from a tree last year." He paused. Juliette and I were quiet. Then Honza went on: "In 2005, I gave my last 'goodbye clinic,' and decided to go back to working with computers. That lasted two weeks."

"What changed?"

"I remember someone said, 'Don't be stupid. Don't waste your life with untalented horses.'"

"So you just stopped taking difficult horses?"

"I changed what I do. The biggest enemy of horses is 'horse lovers.' People are looking for non-conflict communication. That's bullshit. People need to go through conflict. Even with a *friend* you need to go through conflict. You can't tell another person, 'Do whatever you want. And don't pay taxes.' It's not conflict-*less*, but how we *deal* with conflict when we face it."

What Honza was explaining was something that I had struggled with. I wanted to build rapport and trust in horses, but at some point, I also wanted to (slowly, gradually, progressively) build emotional fitness. The strength to withstand adversity. I wanted the horse's comfort zone to get a little bigger each day, not a little smaller.

Horses are not "horse lovers," *they are horses.*

I got the sense that Honza was more "horse" than "horse lover."

"If people don't learn this lesson, 'hobby horses' will replace real horses. I've already had two 'hobby horses' come for lessons."

I looked at Juliette. "Is he kidding?"

"I can't tell."

Honza kept a straight face. His lips were still. His jaw line was the stuff of Hollywood. Only his eyes carried expression: they were full of mischief.

"Do you think it's possible to start a horse without him ever bucking?"

"Ninety-nine percent of horses I can get to walk and trot with no drama. The canter can be complicated."

"What's the secret?" Juliette asked.

"The trick is this: *don't canter.*"

I nodded, pondering.

"Trot," he said. "Then trot again. Keep trotting. Have the feeling that you could trot for three days. The other trick is to go from the standstill to the trot. Standstill to trot. Like that!" He snapped his fingers. "Getting the canter through the buck is something I could do when I was younger; it's not a good way to help students."

Honza's face and body grew animated. I could tell that here was someone, like me, who could talk horses for hours.

"If you could send a young horse to anybody in the world to start," I asked, "who would it be?"

"I would start him myself."

"Hypothetically, imagine you are injured and need someone to start the horse?"

"I wouldn't. There is too much to ruin."

I could tell from his face that this was a painful question. He squinted a little and pursed his lips. It was as if I was making him choose between a punch to the face or a kick to the groin.

"If I went to buy a horse, and he was already started, it would not hurt me."

"C'mon," I said, lifting my beer to my lips. "There has to be one person."

"Would I have to watch? That is torture."

"Let's reframe the question. Who would you *not* want starting your horse?"

"The unathletic," he replied without hesitation. "The fearful. Un-educated people. The people who say, 'I don't know anything about reining or dressage or jumping, I just start horses'—that should be il-legal! I want a good rider who knows the basics of dressage, or jump-ing, or reining, or whatever that horse will be doing."

It felt good to be in Germany. I liked the weather, I liked the horses, I liked pubs. After another beer, we made our excuses. I sin-cerely hoped our paths would cross again.

As we parted, Honza said: "Make that five hundred or more."

"What's that?"

"Horses I've started. A thousand is too high."

"Got it," I said. Although I wondered how accurate he could be. Going from a thousand to five hundred was a big drop. Some people inflate their numbers, while others humbly guess low.

"Was he kidding about the hobby horses coming for lessons?" I asked Juliette as she drove us to *das Hotel*. Juliette was looking ahead into the dark, down the Autobahn. She was trying to accelerate, but her little car was as disinclined as ever.

"I really don't know!" She laughed.

22

"The devil is in the details," explained our veterinarian, Dr. Angie Yates. "When I look at the science about ulcers, it's important to look at the details. What was the sample size? What breed of horses was the study done with? Most of the studies are done with racehorses. And say what you want about the racehorse industry, we have it to thank for so much science about horses. They have funded a huge portion of it. That's why I love this study in Canada with show jumpers. It might be closer to the horses we are seeing here in Ocala. And what year was the study done? When I look at a summary of findings from 2023, some of what we knew to be true in 2021 is already out of date. A lot of what I was taught in vet school is *really* out of date."

Science is not the truth, *it's the search for truth*. There are few facts that a scientist will hold to be unimpeachably true. A study that showed us something last year could be contradicted by a different study this year. Does that mean we ignore the science? No. But it is a lot of work to keep up with it. That's why we had Dr. Yates. For her, keeping up with the latest horse science was fulfilling. It was a riddle to keep solving. It was a form of play.

Who could help me interpret the "science of horsemanship"? It was so full of conflicting ideas. Do we want to use positive reinforcement? Negative reinforcement? A combination? Do we want our horses motivated by serotonin or dopamine? Adrenaline or oxytocin? All? None?

I went out to ride. We'd shipped Sam down the road to Barend Heilbron's Island Farms. I had a dressage lesson.

I had never seen Barend lose his temper. I had never even seen his boat rock. When I got frustrated, he laughed it off.

Barend hailed from Holland. Before he trained as a rider, he was in training to be a *Bloemist*, a florist. Bloemists study the Latin names of flowers, the history of flowers, and how to graft and plant and prune.

"What was your favorite thing about florist school?" I'd once asked him.

"Nothing. I wanted to ride."

"What's your favorite flower?"

He'd said he didn't have favorite flowers, he had favorite *horses*, but I'd pressed him.

"Tulips are nice…" he'd admitted. "But so are daffodils…and crocuses."

I wanted to work on Sam's flying changes, but Barend had me just work on the quality of the canter. To just take a step back, work on establishing a stronger and stronger foundation, that was a lesson that I had to learn over and over again.

I sat tall. I tried to sit like a cowboy who called his saddle home. I had it for a moment, but it was fleeting, flitting away as abruptly as a bee leaves a stamen.

Since our kids are about the same ages, and since they attend the same Montessori school, and since we have similar interests, and since they are pretty cool, we had become friends with Will and Katie Coleman—two elegant riders and knowledgeable horse people. They lived, as the flamingo flies, about six miles due south of us. Their farm was named "Okonokos" after an album by Will's favorite band, My Morning Jacket. The title means, according to one fan, "a state of being in which the human soul transcends space and time through a sense auditory nirvana; said state is reached when the pure power of rock and roll is so intense and spiritual that it can no longer be perceived by the eardrums and must be heard using only the heart."

It was a great name for a farm.

After watching the end of the Maryland Five Star, I picked up Will and his daughter, Charlie, and we headed to the old Marion Theatre in historic downtown Ocala. *Monsters, Inc.* was playing. We bought popcorn and lemonade, and shuffled our way in the dark to our seats. Once our eyes adjusted, we realized there were only two other people in the theatre.

The movie began, and for a couple hours I shared popcorn with my son and didn't think about bills or clients or horses.

On the way home I told Will that Tash, my sister-in-law, was coming to compete in an Ironman in Panama City. I was planning to drive the five hours to watch and support her. It was meant to start at seven in the morning. The fastest competitors would complete the triathlon in under ten hours. The slowest would keep slogging away until midnight, when the course was cleared.

"It's fun to watch," I said. "There's a great atmosphere. Food trucks…"

"Food trucks! That's cruel." He laughed. "You're running along, and you see someone gulping down a delicious lobster roll and sipping a lager. The runners must be thinking, 'What am I *doing*?'"

In the back seat, our kids were talking about frogs. And tadpoles.

"Sometimes at events," Will said, "with the pressure…all the pressure…that's what I think when I see someone at the beer garden…*I could be there.*"

"I know what you mean," I agreed. "But when I'm at the beer garden, watching the competition, I want to be competing."

"It's the ultimate 'grass is greener' situation."

That evening Sinead arrived back from Maryland where she had been commentating for the event's broadcast on the United States Equestrian Federation (USEF) Network live stream.

"It used to be that I was so impressed by these five-star riders," I said. "Who won and all that. But looking at the Maryland field, the person I have the most respect for wasn't riding."

"Who was that?"

"The course designer. Ian Stark."

Sinead nodded.

At a five-star event, the highest level of competition under the international governing body the Fédération Equestre Internationale (FEI), there were lots of jobs—from stable manager to marketing director, from dressage judge to groom. But it was the course designer who had the toughest job.

The cross-country course designer's job was to create a track that tested the partnership of horse and rider. Designers could use water, wood, earth, rocks, and light. They could use the hills, valleys, trees, and ditches. Like sculptors, they could take all these elements and mold them into an interactive piece of art.

The competitors then, one at a time, tested themselves against this art. If it was too easy, they'd all pass, and there was no way to determine a winner, and no excitement for the fans. If it was too difficult, someone, or some horse, might pay the ultimate price.

The great cross-country course designer had to be able to listen to feedback and also trust his own inner voice. He could be compared to Ernest Shackleton, the captain of the *Endurance*, the ship famously trapped and crushed by ice in the Antarctic in 1915.

It was Shackleton who said: "Life to me is the greatest of all games. The danger lies in treating it as a trivial game, a game to be taken lightly, and a game in which the rules don't matter much. The rules matter a great deal. The game has to be played fairly or it is no game at all. And even to win the game is not the chief end. The chief end is to win it honorably and splendidly."

Shackleton also said: "I have often marveled at the thin line which separates success from failure."

This was all true for the cross-country course designer who must create a course that challenged the riders and the horse-and-rider partnership, but that was fair to the horse. In other words, the horse had to be able to "read" the tests on the track.

We must only ask the horse questions we know he can understand.

There is a team of course builders who support the vision of the course designer, and each carpenter is an artist in his own right. There are other "masters" at horse shows as well. People who take their jobs seriously, who study, who take their trades and elevate them into art. The grooms with the deep bonds with the horses in their care. The dressage judges who see two horses do seemingly similar tests, but notice the quiet, soft eye in one. The coaches who realize that it is more important to be a good person than to win a ribbon, and yet help students accomplish both.

These are the maestros.

In the 1970s before I, or my brothers, were born, my parents made their living as horse show photographers. They noticed details. Ears, lips, angles, depth of field, sun beams, falling leaves… And later, when they had me and took me to horse shows, they pointed out those details to me.

Now when I watch a horse show, I hardly notice the winner. It's the details that fascinate. Who eased off the pressure at the right time? Who was the smoothest getting on? Who picked just the perfect moment to give the horse a break?

On my way home from another event at Chatt Hills, I called Natalie again. I needed a sounding board for the journey I was on.

She told me the totality of a truth is so large that I am destined to fail.

How I work with horses, what I write in a book, how I live my life, will not land with everyone.

I am destined to fail. But I must try.

Don't wait. You must not wait, she told me. You must try now.

There is no one better to do it than you.

23

I got up early to watch Road to the Horse 2022. The sound wouldn't work, and after struggling with the remote, I just let it play on mute. At first I was annoyed; then I realized, with the volume off, I saw more. I wasn't distracted by the competitors' words, or the crowd, or the interpretations of the hosts. I was reading the body language of the horses, and the body language of the trainers.

As the competitors caught their horses, I watched the "bubbles" of the horses—the area of "personal space" around them that delineated their comfort level. If a trainer "burst through" a horse's bubble—got too close, too quickly, for example—the horse would toss his head or trot off. Some horses didn't trot off; they just stood there and looked uncomfortable. But all it took was misreading a colt's bubble once, and the colt started to think about leaving.

Humans have personal space "bubbles" as well. Just like with horses, the size of them, and how sensitive we are to them, varies. If you are standing in a large empty room and a strange man walks up to you, shakes your hand, and then steps even closer to you when he begins speaking, he has almost definitely invaded your bubble. You may then take a step back to reestablish space, or you may choose to remain where you are and just be a little uncomfortable. Scientists call the bubble the *flight zone (FZ)*. The edge of the flight zone is the *flight initiation distance (FID)*. Swiss zoologist Heini Hediger, a pioneer in nonverbal communication studies, had distinguished between standard interaction distances between animals: *flight distance* (when an animal will flee from a predator), *critical distance* (when an animal will feel the need to attack—obviously, compared to the vast majority of species, most horses will continue to flee at any distance), *personal distance* (how far apart members of the same herd will stand when grazing), and *social distance* (how far apart two bands that don't know each other will stand). Love and hunger, argued Hediger, take second place; knowing when to flee is the most important behavior of an animal.

I watched how the competitors touched their horses. Was it a rub, or a pat, or a scratch? What kind of rub? How hard? How soft? On what part of the body? For how long?

How does a horse like to be rubbed? That's like asking what toys kids like. Some horses like a firmer rub on the withers, some prefer a softer one on the neck, some never seem to learn to enjoy being rubbed at all. Some like it one way one day, and another way the next day.

I reminded myself that rubbing is usually better than patting. I once heard Pat Parelli say: "Horses and women prefer a rub; men and dogs like a pat."

One of the contestants, Mike Major, had his horse saddled on Day One, and I watched as he swung a leg over the saddle for the first time with only nine minutes left on the clock.

Wow, I thought. *That guy has nerves of steel! Nine minutes left!*

At that point in a training session, I would want to be winding down. Letting the dust settle. Looking to finish on a good note. Getting on with nine minutes left is like betting a hundred grand you won't get bitten picking up a rattlesnake—high risk…high reward.

The horse, who was the color of eggnog, started to kick and buck almost immediately and Mike almost came off. The clock rolled on like a freight train and with 6:47 left, the colt spun left, hard! Mike came off over the colt's creamy yellow shoulder. He landed on his feet, holding onto the reins. His body language was surprisingly easy and smooth as he swung a leg up back into the stirrup.

At 6:30, Mike's seat touched the saddle again. He was back up in less than twenty seconds, and with no rush. He was hastening slowly. He was completely in the moment. He was listening to his gut and acting on instinct. For him, *time was slowing down.*

With 4:30 left, Mike's horse trotted smoothly forward. I couldn't believe it.

At 2:40, Mike stepped off. He started working on picking up his horse's feet. He was focused; he was determined.

With thirty seconds left, Mike stepped out of the round pen.

I leaned back in my chair. Wiped sweat off my forehead. I shook my head and thought again, *This guy has nerves of steel.*

I turned the television off. The kids were still asleep. Sinead was in upstate New York, teaching a clinic. My mind was churning, but I had to start packing lunches.

This was the first Road to the Horse I'd watched since I had been invited. My eyes were drawn to so many details I hadn't noticed before: Did they put the saddle on from the left or the right? (Left was "normal," but right saved time and an extra trip around the horse when it came to the cinches.) Did they brush their horses? How much "soak time" did they give their horses to process each lesson?

The next evening, I got the kids to bed early so I could finish watching. Sinead wasn't going to be back from New York until after midnight, and I wanted to wait up for her anyway.

At one point, one competitor had trouble catching her horse. That was one of my biggest fears, and I paid attention to how she handled it. Another competitor had trouble with asking the horse to go over an obstacle. The gelding kept looking right or left. The trainer was quick to add a barrel to one side of the obstacle. By giving the horse one less option, the right answer was more obvious. It would have been easy for the trainer to get stuck trying to explain the obstacle to the horse. I hoped I could be that quick-witted! It wasn't cheating to make confusing things easier for the horse to understand.

Of course, the barrel also blocked the horse's "escape route," thereby creating a situation where the pressure *could have* been ramped up. It was how the situation was used that mattered.

The third day, the final day of Road to the Horse, is traditionally run in reverse order of go. Pat Parelli, one of the competitors in 2022, was first to go. His colt was already in the round pen, covered in shavings from his recent nap. The colt raised his head, ears flicking around. He gazed into the stands.

Pat had two long training "flags" that he brought into the round pen with him. They were twelve-foot telescoping poles—examples from his own line of flags that he'd branded "Parelli Herding Sticks." The flags were similar to fishing poles (as opposed to "rods," which typically have reels). I knew telescoping poles were used for crappie fishing.

The flags seemed like handy things to have. They also seemed light and playful. Pat turned the colt with the flags. Touched the colt with the flags. He sped him up. He turned him again and then funneled the colt in toward himself. In a forty-foot round pen, with a twelve-foot flag in either hand, he could cover a lot of ground quickly. He could move the flags higher or lower, above the horse, and even to the outside of the horse. It was as if he had gone from working in two dimensions to working in three. He had become ubiquitous.

After he caught the horse, Pat brushed him, getting the shavings off, giving him a smooth, peaceful feeling.

"There's a time to go slow with a horse," he said to the crowd, "and there's times to keep things moving." He picked up the saddle pad. "I can put this on him like I put my hat on. I want to be slow, but I don't want to be sneaky. A lot of people are slow, but they're *sneaky*."

Pat sported a gray hat, black shirt, blue jeans, and brown chaps. He wore glasses. His trademark mustache was, as usual, present. After the saddle pad, he slipped the saddle up onto the horse's back. I wondered how many times he had done that in his life.

"I tighten the cinch at least three times before I ride—not in one fell swoop," he said. Next, he mounted. "I do a lot of nothing when I get up here."

There was a twenty-minute limit for time in the round pen on Sunday, and Pat left it till the last second to exit into the main arena. The horse wore a halter—no bit. "I want to stay out of a horse's mouth as long as possible," Pat explained. "A hundred hours! That's part of my program. I'll ride him in this for a hundred hours." Then he drawled, "There ain't nothing better than riding a horse. There ain't nothing better than a horse that's wantin' and willin' to be with you."

I agreed with the second sentence more than the first.

Pat began the obstacle course. The first obstacle was six poles to bend through. What a great expression his horse had at that moment! Not quite joy in the colt's eyes... but...*interest*! At the large tarp, though, the horse started going backward. Pat circled it.

"I have a little saying here," Pat told the audience. "*Nose, neck, maybe feet*. People say, 'Approach and retreat.' I say, 'Retreat and approach.' I'd like to think if this horse's mother was watching us right now, she'd be proud of both of us. I try to be the 'Ambassador of Yes,' instead of the 'Minister of No.'"

Pat asked how much time he had left. As he picked up a rein, he then remarked, "I've never seen a horse wear a watch."

I heard the apartment door open. Ferdinand barked once. Sinead was home. I paused the television and quietly (so as not to wake the kids) hustled over.

"I missed you," I said, giving her a kiss. She wore gray shorts and a long-sleeved green shirt.

"Missed you too," she said. Then, "I'm so tired."

"Want to decompress by watching a few minutes of Road to the Horse before crashing?" I asked. "Pat's on."

She nodded and we settled on the couch together, Ferdinand at our feet, wagging his tail and pushing his nose into my knee. I rubbed him behind the ears.

"He's doing a good job," Sinead remarked after a few minutes. "The horse doubts the things, but he never seems to doubt *him*."

It was a sentence I would remember for months. That Sinead had been so impressed, even with the pair that wasn't winning, made an impression. It gave me encouragement that it didn't matter what place I came in, it would still be worth it to do it…to read the horse, to pay attention to details, to do a good job. Winning the judges over was nothing compared to winning the horse over.

"That horse has not lost his curiosity," Sinead said.

On the television, Pat noted, "Horses don't like applause nearly as much as people do." The cameras flashed to the panel of judges and one of them, normally stonefaced, smiled. Pat asked for a "Big Green Ball" to use for his finale with his colt. It was another tool popularized by Parelli—like a large yoga ball. Horses can push it or kick it. People can bounce it or toss it. Some horses are scared at first; many horses interact with the ball almost immediately. I've seen foals push them and paw them and chase them like a cat playing with catnip.

Pat's horse pushed the Big Green Ball around. The colt was still curious—he still had a sparkle in his eyes.

"Cute," said Sinead. "I'm going to bed."

"I think I should buy this horse and take him home," Pat said, looking out at the crowd. "What do you guys think?"

The crowd roared. Sinead left.

I wondered if the colts would be for sale when I competed in a few months. Would I be able to buy the colt I worked with?

I turned the television off, glanced in at the sleeping kids, refilled Ferdinand's water, then stole after my wife, to bed.

24

"Are you feeling pretty confident?" Glenn asked. "You must be, if you entered."

"More coffee?" I asked.

He nodded. I shuffled to the sink and refilled the kettle. I hadn't started drinking coffee until I was in my mid-twenties, but I was making up for it now. Three to four cups a day, usually with cream, no sugar. I tried to abstain after two in the afternoon, or the caffeine teamed up with my nerves to keep me up at night.

Seated at our big table were three guests: Donna, the clinic host, whom we called our "neighbor" even though she lived seven miles northeast of us, Glenn Stewart, a two-time competitor at Road to the Horse, and his assistant Carli. The four of us were discussing the schedule for the week ahead.

I had three Quarter Horses to start in this clinic with Glenn. They belonged to Dr. Mary Beth Gordon, and were bred and raised by the Purina Animal Nutrition Center in Gray Summit, Missouri. There was Dart, a red roan mare; Bert, a red roan gelding; and Natasha, a chestnut mare with a white blaze.

I set the kettle on the stove and shoveled coffee into the French press. "In some parts of it I'm feeling confident. In other parts I'm feeling in way over my head."

"Well, I'll watch you work with these colts, and we can see what you do. Maybe I have some tips."

"No," I said immediately. I had planned this speech. "I want you to teach me as if I'm *your* working student about to ride *your* horses while you're out of town. I want to know how *you* do it. And I don't want you to go easy on me." Glenn stared at me as I continued: "At the end, we can talk about how what you do, and what I do, can mesh, and at the competition I will do what I'm most comfortable doing, but I want these next ten days to be about doing something new, doing it *your* way…learning *from you*."

He nodded. He understood what I was after.

Glenn had arrived on the twenty-eighth of October, the same day as the cross-country phase of the eventing competition at the Pan Am Games in Chile. Team USA, the favorite, was in first. Brazil was second, Canada was third. (The show jumping phase would show what a fickle sport eventing is when the Americans had one rail too many, and Canada ended up taking the gold.)

Both Sinead and I wanted to be competing there—at the Pan Ams. With the horses we currently had in our string, we had accepted months ago that it would not be in the cards for us in 2023. But *not* being there made us realize we were both still hungry. And when I was hungry a *lot* more got done.

It was Halloween. Brooks wanted to be a dinosaur. Goldfish was too young to know what she wanted to wear. Brooks woke up sick that morning, and after some negotiation, stayed home from school. Goldfish *did* go to school, dressed as a squirmy, cuddly pumpkin.

"People been riding ten years and they can't do that course,"

Glenn was telling six ladies, clustered around a picnic table, as I arrived. He was at the head of the table, in the shade of five live oaks. Two of the women had horses in the clinic. The other four were there to just watch and learn. "It's not hard physically, it's hard emotionally and mentally," Glenn said.

"What a foggy morning," I said, as I sat down. I was late.

"Did you bring your plan?" Glenn asked.

"No," I admitted.

"Did you bring the rules?"

"No," I said.

I wanted to disappear. I prided myself on being prepared. But my mind was being torn in so many different directions—kids, family, barn, staff, horses—I was overcommitted and running on fumes.

What am I doing? I asked myself for the hundredth time. "Sorry, Glenn," I said out loud, trying to keep my voice even.

"This is what I have." Glenn showed me his notes for Road to the Horse 2022. It was three or four pages long, and it broke down a general plan for each day, and each part of each day. He went through it with us; I took notes. The dew from the trees, and the thick fog, dripped onto my notebook.

When we reached the end of his plan, I asked, "How many horses have you started?"

"Three thousand."

"That's a lot more than me," I responded. The ladies around the table laughed. One of them looked at me with soft pity in her eyes, like I was about to show up empty-handed to a knife fight.

"The main thing to realize is that experience is not the same as knowledge," Glenn said. "At the start, I had a lot of experience, but my knowledge was pretty skinny."

"Have there ever been any horses that you didn't want to work with?" a lady with tangled, tawny hair asked.

"When I first began starting horses, I would take on everything," he replied. "For fifteen years, my main deal was to take unbroken horses at the start of the week, and have 'em ready by the end of the week. But now I know there are some matches that are going to be inappropriate. And I'll tell the owners. Often they'll say, 'But I love him,' and I'll say, 'Start digging deep in your bank account 'cause he will be ready for you in about three years.'"

I could relate to those horse owners. Sometimes, we *want* it to work, even when it appears hopeless. We have so much invested in our horses—time, energy, money, love—we *want* it to work so badly.

"What's the biggest difference between what you knew *after* you had started fifty-or-so horses, and then what you knew *after* the next two-thousand-nine-hundred-and-fifty?" I asked.

"Feel and timing," said Glenn. "That, and how to read the horse. It means I can be smoother. I can slip stuff in quietly. You can read a horse *without* feel and timing; it's better to have it all."

Glenn had on a long-sleeved gray shirt that said ROAD TO THE HORSE on the front. He took a sip of his coffee, which I knew, after our meeting the day before, he drank black.

"Five, six, seven thousand people are watching at Road to the Horse, and they all have an opinion," he said. "The poor guys in the ring, you are trying to get a job done without offending the people in the crowd, most of whom have never started a horse."

"Why do you care?" a lady with a brown cowboy hat asked.

"*They* are your business. The crowd. But what they don't understand is that what's best for the horse is not always what's best for accommodating people in the stands." He paused for a moment. "I've been to the Spanish Riding School in Vienna, and the people I was with started picking the riders apart. 'That's not good enough,' or 'That guy's not smiling.' I had to walk away. There we were at the *Spanish Riding School,* and they were judging."

I knew I cared what the crowd thought, but not because they might be customers. I cared, *just because.*

I wished I didn't care, but I did.

I got up to stretch, then mumbled something about more coffee. I wandered away for a moment and called Tash, my visiting sister-in-law, to drive the seven miles from our place with the competition rules, and with my newly purchased bareback pad, which I had also forgotten.

"Are they always colts?" someone asked as I arrived back at the table.

"Usually. Fillies can change dramatically depending on if they are in heat. If you get one that's not in heat, she is like a regular horse. But a filly in heat can have some really strange behaviors."

"What did you look for when picking your horse?"

"Will he be smooth to ride? Will his back hold a saddle? I don't want something too tall—I'll need to be able to jump up on 'em. Can he pick up the right and left lead easily or is he running around, cross-firing? I'll check his conformation. He should have straight legs. Is it a horse I would want to buy at the end? Something I would want to ride?"

Tash drove in. I excused myself for the second time and went over to grab the saddle pad and the paperwork.

I handed the pages to Glenn. He perused the rules; I peered over his shoulder.

The first page began with the Road to the Horse mission: *To inspire people to reach a higher level of horsemanship and develop unity with a horse based on trust and not fear.* And a vision: *We believe through education and entertainment we can change people's ideas and create a better world for the horse.*

It listed the five judges who would be rating my performance: *Jeff Williams, Eric Hoffman, Jesse Westfall, David O'Connor, Cody Lambert.*

"Remember, with the judges, don't be too quick to ask questions," Glenn said solemnly. "They are of the mindset that God gave you two ears and one mouth for a reason. And don't make excuses! Think about it—across from you is this guy who has started five thousand colts, and he's from Texas, and he's spitting Copenhagen right there on the floor. They don't want to hear you talk. You get in there and impress them in the arena."

One of the ladies at the table tentatively raised her hand, waiting till Glenn nodded at her to ask, "Is this Road to the Horse competition an appropriate thing to ask of a horse and trainer?"

Glenn, rarely a sentimentalist, said, "Remember, everything changes with two things: the talent of the person, and the time that you have."

It was a wonderfully cool day. Blue sky, white clouds, massive green-leafed oak trees shading the round pen.

But I was not totally *there*. Mentally, I mean. I kept catching myself thinking about the leaky hose and broken fences back at the farm.

At one point I was allowing Dart to get used to a blue tarp, and I progressed too quickly from having the tarp crushed into a small ball and letting her smell it, to having it drape wide open over her withers. As I brought the open tarp toward her, she tensed her neck and flinched away from me. Fear was plain in her eyes.

I knew I had screwed up. The ladies watching knew it too. *What an idiot I was!*

"Too quick," Glenn said.

Later that day Glenn brought it up again. "You dropped the tarp too fast. You went from a green light, to an amber light, to a red light.

You missed the sign! Now, the next time you introduce her to something new, it will take a little longer."

That evening, I drove home, pulled myself up the stairs, and collapsed into a chair. This clinic was a big test, the first major milestone on my way to the competition in March, and I was failing.

"Take those boots off," Sinead said sternly, "I just swept."

I took them off. I sighed loudly.

Sinead was typing away at her computer. I looked at her. I wanted to say something, but the more stressed I got, the harder it was for me to communicate. I was overwhelmed, frozen.

Finally, I schlepped over to the table. I sat down across from her. I waited for her to look at me, and then I told her how I felt.

"Tik, you have a four-star horse," she said. "You're writing a book. You're entered in Road to the Horse. This is all stuff *you* asked for…. Pressure like this, it's a privilege…it's going to mean extra organizing, and extra hours, and early mornings, and extra stress."

I nodded.

"Look," she continued. "This is going to be the hardest year of your life. But if you work harder and smarter than you have ever worked before, you will be able to do it."

The second day with Glenn began at the picnic table again. A timid lady in a white hat asked, "If I go up in phases, will I lose draw?"

The "phases" she meant were increases in pressure. "Phase One" might mean I could touch my horse as lightly as a fly landing on him. "Phase Two" might mean as hard as raindrop might land in a puddle. The phases, depending on the wisdom and strength of the handler, could go higher and higher.

"Have you ever seen somebody with as much draw as I have?" Glenn asked and looked around the table.

"No," chirruped the group.

"Well, then, let me ask you this: Would you rather be nagged for the next three hundred and sixty-five days before you understand what I want, or know today, even if I have to kick your ass?"

"I would want to know," someone said.

"There isn't a bone in my body that doesn't think that is what I would want. I would want to know. Be as clear as you can. Show the horse what you want, then *go away*. The longer the horse is wrong, the more he feels like he is right. Don't be a nag!" Glenn raised his hands, palms facing toward each other. "This is what some people think is a 'soft deal.'" He moved his left hand a bit and looked at it. "And here is where they are firm." He waved his right hand and looked at it. "But more range is needed." He moved his right hand, widening the distance from his left, the way a fisherman shows how big the fish he caught *really* was.

Glenn was showing us we needed to have the ability to be both *softer* and *firmer*.

"Expect more from the horse. But you can't expect more from him unless you expect more from yourself. If the foundation is not there, you are leaving so much potential on the table. I think ninety percent of people are accessing less than five percent of their horses' potential."

There was nodding around the table. I stood up and put my sweater on. The day was colder than yesterday. Perhaps our first fall day.

"My problem is me…" began a soft-spoken woman in a purple Ariat sweatshirt. The song by Taylor Swift, one of Sinead's favorite singers (and often playing at home), popped into my head. "And the trouble with me is, I tend to feel sorry for her," she finished quietly.

"Do you want somebody to feel sorry for *you*?" Glenn asked.

"No. Of course not," she sputtered immediately.

"Often the perspectives we pick," Glenn said, "are the ones that make us feel the most comfortable. Comfort is a place you can visit, but then get the hell out of there."

I raised my hand. Glenn nodded at me.

"Sinead gave me a book a few months ago. A book on writing by Lawrence Block. It turned out to be more of a self-help book than a technical book. I kind of rolled my eyes a little bit when I saw the cover," I admitted. "But I started it. In the book it asks the reader to write down this phrase: *I am now willing to act in the presence of fear. I hereby resolve that I will never again allow fear to keep me from doing something I genuinely desire to do.*"

Everyone was looking at me. Glenn's expression encouraged me to go on.

"Road to the Horse scares me," I said. "A lot. Everything about it. But I wholeheartedly want to do it. And there is a little spark in me that believes I *can* do it, and do it *my way*."

The lovely lady in the purple sweatshirt, bless her, said: "At my level, I feel that too. *How is that going to look?* I think, when I try something new."

I blinked. I wanted to hug her. Instead I shared another quote I knew: "*We all have two lives to live, and the second one begins when we realize we only have one.*"

This prompted another woman to pipe up, "You know, I used to perform. I was a singer. And it gets easier every time you do it. Just remember, that round pen is your stage."

I smiled. I imagined a younger version of the woman crooning and dancing in a smoky bar, patrons holding cocktails, unable to take their eyes off her. She was right—it *was* a stage. For a few days it would be *my* stage. I was determined to have something to do, something to say, on that stage.

With the morning's discussion over, I brought Dart, Bert, and Natasha to the round pen, one at a time, to play with.

Starting horses on a timeline was out of my comfort zone. Working with Western tack was out of my comfort zone. Having Glenn coach me was out of my comfort zone. I was doing all three, and in front of people watching. Some of the mistakes I made were embarrassing. But I kept going and the former singer was right. It got easier with each horse.

That afternoon I had to leave before Glenn's clinic day was over. He was coaching one of the ladies on a small dun-colored horse, and I approached them to apologize for my early exit. Glenn sat on a big black horse that looked like a trotter.

"What were your takeaways today?" he asked.

"A big one is that I need to be quicker about stuff that is not specifically about the horse," I said. "The logistical stuff that wastes time. It takes *you* about a minute to get the saddle cinched up; it takes me three to four minutes. If it takes me a minute to get the halter on and tied, it takes *you* thirty seconds. These are things that have nothing to do with the horse that I need to be smoother at. I need to be handier and more efficient."

I felt guilty about leaving early, but I had to help at Copperline, and then help with the kids. As I drove home, I realized I was sure glad the competition wasn't the following week. My confidence was not high.

Sinead asked me what my takeaways were as well. I gave her a different answer.

"I'm not good enough yet," I replied bluntly. "What I will need to get done in three days in March takes me five or six days, at least, now. And these three Quarter Horses I'm working with are pretty straightforward horses."

There was another takeaway, though. I didn't share it with Glenn or Sinead, but it was very much on my mind.

I was afraid of the bucking. *Really* afraid.

I never used to be afraid of a horse bucking. Or rearing. Or bolting. It was the combination of getting older, knowing more, of being hurt a few times, and in particular, it was my groin injury. When tweaked, it would still pluck the nerves in my lower body in a way that I would feel all the way up into the back of my neck. It was like an electrical shock that began between my legs and headed straight for my brain. And the anticipation of the pain was as bad as the pain itself. It was a kind of torture.

This takeaway, this fear was so embarrassing…. Riding horses that bronc'ed and twisted had been my thing for years. Dealing with "difficult" horses was my career. *And* I had just entered the most prestigious colt-starting championships in the world.

I needed to *not* be scared.

All through the day at Glenn's clinic, I dreaded that one of the horses I rode might buck. *I shouldn't be doing this*, I thought that night. *It would be so easy to back out; so easy to say it was about the ethics of the competition, or about spending more time with my kids, or about writing my book.*

All my reasons had a ring of truth to them, but really it would have been about my fear.

A lie to myself, one with a virtuous aura of truth shrouding it, would be the easiest lie to tell. It would also be the most deceitful.

As Glenn told stories, and the ladies chatted, and the squirrels chased each other around the oaks, my mind began to wander. In training a horse there were so many "quitting spots"—moments that would be a good note to stop on. What was the right one? Maybe there were no "right" ones—just the ones I found.

With an "emotional" horse, I'd be looking for that first good quitting spot from the moment I started. It might take five minutes or fifty minutes, and when I found it, I'd stop and end for the day. With a mature horse, one that I had a good relationship with, there might be twenty good quitting spots, and I'd feel more free to choose any of them.

Before lunch I worked with Natasha and Bert. As we walked back to the round pen after break, I wanted to let Glenn know I appreciated him.

"Thanks, Glenn," I told him. "I'm pretty lucky to have you here helping me for ten days."

"I don't know if people realize," he said, "but it's pretty rare to have someone like you. To listen so much. To not argue. To put themselves out there so much."

His words were the highlight of my day, and I walked back to the barn feeling a little better. A few kind words could be the light in a dark room. I skipped out to the field—it was time to play with Dart.

I couldn't catch her.

Really, I couldn't catch Dart. Not *at all*.

I had caught her the first day because she wasn't quite expecting me to catch her, and I had gotten the halter on her before she really knew what was going on. And then the second day we had put grain in a bucket that brought all three horses to the gate, and I had caught her while she was eating. But now she wouldn't let me walk up to her. It wasn't that she trotted off or showed a lot of fear. She was simply keenly aware of where I was, and where she was, and where the other two horses were, and she easily kept herself just about a foot or two away from me. She would just kind of slip her head to the other side, or turn her bum to me, or position herself so that another horse was between us. I tried for ten minutes, and then turned to go back to the barn. Ten minutes might not seem long, but it was long enough for me to know that I could have kept trying what I was trying for two hours, and I wouldn't be any closer unless something about the situation, or about me, changed.

I walked halfway back to the barn, about the distance of a football field.

"You have time to give me a hand?" I shouted to Glenn.

Glenn nodded and headed my way. Behind him I saw my mother stand up to follow. She was visiting from Vancouver to watch the clinic, visit her grandkids, and watch Tash compete in her first Ironman.

Some people like to be told what to do as they figure it out. Others like to read, or guess, or learn through trial and error. I learn best by watching, and although a small part of me was shy to ask, that part was immensely overshadowed by the part that was looking forward to watching how Glenn handled the Dart scenario.

I was not a beginner at catching horses and had even written how-to articles on the subject. In one I noted that horses should never learn they can't be caught. At the least, it's time consuming; at the worst, it's an emergency. And what does it say about the relationship?

Even with a horse that is easy to catch, it's worth asking, *How can I make this better?* Everything we do with horses can be improved upon. Our lives with horses are made up of tens of thousands of small moments. Catching a horse can be broken down into hundreds of habits that we have. All these tiny actions are like dabs of paint on a canvas. They add up, and after a time, I'll stand back and I'll take stock. And that's when I realize what kind of painting I've created. Is it a relationship as sincere as a Van Gogh? As intense as a Picasso? Or is it a mess, no kind of painting at all?

Over the years I'd asked other trainers for their hard-to-catch horse advice. Florida horseman Pete Rodda gave me his top tips on creating good catching habits:

- "It is not a race."
- "If they have a halter on, do not grab it. Catch 'em as if you have to put it on."
- "Don't trap them, or catch them 'just for today.'"
- "Sometimes leave when the horse is in a better spot, *even though* you have not caught him."
- "Have them learn to catch you instead of you catching them."
- "Don't catch 'em at the gate."

"Do not be in a too-big area!" recommended my friend Jonathan Field. "I want to practice success. So if I have a horse that already has a history of playing the 'You can't catch me game,' then I will keep him in a smaller pen close to the barn and go out to catch, rub, and turn that horse loose as many times in day as I can. This way I practice a new pattern and also show the horse every time I come to his stall, pen, or pasture he won't always be taken away for a ride."

Repetition is a strong reinforcer. In other words, habits are reinforcing. Actions will get easier and more natural as time goes on. These are some of my favorite horse-catching habits:

- Allowing them to touch the back of my hand once, twice, or three times before I ease into their space and give them a rub.

- Not thinking of horses as being "caught" or "not caught," but having a gray area in between. For example, could I put the rope around a horse's neck and give him a rub, then a minute or two later put the halter on? When I let him go, could I unsnap the bottom of the halter, then lead him a few more feet, then rub him, then let him go? The last thing I wanted was to have a horse feel completely disconnected when I didn't have him, and trapped when I did, then spin and gallop away as soon as I removed the halter.

- Greeting my horses with treats. The treat could be a carrot or a cookie. It could be grain, or hay, or some grass I'd picked. A treat might also mean a rub, or scratch, or undemanding time. But never, ever starting a pony's day by heaving the halter over his head, yanking the rope, and dragging him into the barn.

If how smoothly a horse can be caught is on a spectrum, most horses fall somewhere in the middle. Occasionally there are really difficult ones. (Once it took me an hour to catch a horse in a stall. And Pete said it once took him forty hours to catch a two-year-old filly in an eight-acre field.) Even more rare, however, is to see the ones really exceptional at being caught. What might that look like? How good could a catch get?

Come to think of it, we shouldn't call it "caught" at all. What do you call it when two friends meet up?

There is no one way to catch a horse. It depends on why he can't be caught—is he scared, or is it a learned habit? It depends on the size of the space he is in—large or small? It depends on how dangerous he is—timid or an alligator? It depends on how many people are around, and what skills and experience they have.

We want horses to *want* to be caught, and that is created by good habits and by understanding what motivates horses.

My mother and I stood about twenty feet back and silently observed Glenn catch Dart. As he sauntered his way around those three horses, there was a lot going on. The level of detail he noticed was exciting.

"Think about how you walk up to a horse," Glenn talked as he went. "Is it with a hand out? Palm up or down? Or with your arm by your side?"

Glenn never gave Dart the feeling that he was *trying* to catch her. He didn't give her the feeling that he was coming *at* her. He was smooth and unhurried. Once he caught her, he gave her a quiet rub, and she didn't *feel* caught.

"That was the best part of the whole clinic," my mom said later as we were driving home.

"It was *insanely* good," I agreed. I turned onto County Road 316, then swerved to avoid a dead armadillo.

"His skill and timing were one thing, but what he did so well with that filly was to meet her where she was."

We had a sit-down family dinner. Bernadette came, so the kids had both their grandmothers at the table—a treat. My dad was back in Vancouver. Sinead's dad, Eamon, we all missed every day.

I opened a bottle of Tobin James, Eamon's favorite wine. It was a 2019 Syrah. *Berries and smoke with a wild spicy finish*, said the label.

"You know what I find so amazing?" Bernadette said.

"Brooks?" I guessed, rubbing his hair.

"Well, Brooks, yes. But no. It's that you do this for a living, and you're pretty good, but there is so much more to learn."

"*Glenn* is pretty good."

I poured the wine. The adults sat back in our chairs while Brooks and Goldfish ran to and fro around our feet and under the table. Ferdinand swung his tail against my leg.

Then Ferdinand abruptly flopped onto the floor, and Brooks started a game he called "Ferdi-crockin." The game involved "tacklin'" and "wrestlin'" Ferdi, then using a shirt or towel to "tape" his muzzle shut, as if he and Goldfish were crocodile wranglers in the Outback.

I put my wine down, spilled it, and leaped across the floor to save our dog.

"Poor Ferdi."

The fourth day of the clinic, I never found a rhythm.

With Bert I had to back up and work on saddling again. As soon as I got the saddle close to him, he would push into me with his shoulder, or he would lift his head over the fence. I just took my time; I just took the saddle on and off him a few times. Finally, I found a place where he was relaxed, the first good quitting spot, and I turned him out with the mares again.

But then I had trouble catching the roan mare, Dart, again. She would wait till I was an arm's length away, then pin her ears and either walk behind one of the other two horses, or turn away from me. If I gently put a hand on her withers, she would stand for a moment, but when I went forward to her head or produced a rope, she would quietly walk off. After only a few minutes, I knew I wasn't going to catch her.

It was the same as the day before. I wasn't bringing the right energy to the table.

Energy. Body language. Intention. I use the terms pretty interchangeably.

I didn't have the goods. I was not in the right head space. I thanked Glenn, made sure the horses were fed and looked after, and left the clinic.

I hoped a day off supporting Tash at her Ironman competition would refresh me, put things in perspective. I hoped watching Brooks and his two cousins play on the beach and race around the RV park would help. I hoped eating ice cream and cheering on my sister-in-law as she pursued her dream would give me a reboot in the pursuit of my own.

We watched two thousand two hundred and twenty people race, jog, and hobble across the finish line after they challenged their bodies to swim, bike, and run for miles. The professionals were antelopes with long bodies and tight clothes who finished in under eight hours. These athletes showered and strolled around town, long before many individuals were even close to finishing, looking fresh and ready to race again.

Tash finished with an extremely respectable time: 13:47:41

While waiting for her, I looked in the window of the Tequila Taco Bar and saw my reflection: Receding hairline. Nose protruding from the center of my face. Bright eyes. Soft belly. Wrinkles around the eyes and mouth. An ordinary middle-aged dad.

I was as young and fit as those gazelles once, I thought, *but I never will be again.*

We left Panama City at four-thirty Sunday morning in order to get back in time for Glenn's clinic. Brooks slept. I dozed. My mother drove.

Figuring out what time we had to leave had been a little confusing. It was Daylight Savings…and while most of Florida is on Eastern Time, a few counties in the Panhandle are on Central Time.

I arrived late, again.

I had trouble catching Dart, again.

"She is giving you the middle finger," Mary Beth, the owner of the three Quarter Horses I was *supposed to be* starting, said with a laugh. Mary Beth hadn't been present every day of the clinic as she had to work, but when she did come, it added another element of pressure.

I *was* learning from Glenn, and my skills *were* improving, but I still felt way out of my comfort zone, and my confidence was dropping.

On Monday, I wandered away from the group chatting beneath the oak trees, refilled my coffee, then meandered toward the barn. I looked left and right. *No one there.* I slipped a handful of grain into my back pocket. Then I walked out to the field.

Dart, the roan mare I was having so much trouble catching, looked at me. I waited. I held out my hand with some grain in my palm. After a few minutes the filly eased forward, then nibbled around my fingers with her lips, then took the grain. I made no move toward her. I took a breath…then walked away.

I repeated the visit with grain six, seven times—then, on the eighth time, I rubbed her on the neck while she ate from my hand. And I repeated *that* three, four more times. Then I left her, refilled my coffee, and went back to the chatty picnic table.

I knew Glenn was not the biggest fan of using food in training. I also knew I was replacing skill and patience with food rewards. But I needed a win in my life, and I wanted an easier relationship with Dart.

When coffee talk finished, I filled my pocket with grain again and headed to the paddock. I started the same process over, and after six or seven minutes, and nine or ten nibbles of grain from my hand, I was able to let the rope slide over Dart's neck. *Grain, nibble. Grain, nibble.* Then I slipped the halter on, but I didn't lead the filly off immediately. I fed her again, I backed up to the end of the rope, and approached her again, pausing as I hit her bubble. She sniffed my hand, I rubbed her around the muzzle, and on her neck, then I turned and led her to the round pen.

Later that day, one of the other horses bucked, and I stayed on.

"After 2012, I went on the road," Glenn told us. "Visited a few people I'd met at Road to the Horse. Some of the judges, they'd seen what *I* did, and so I wanted to see what *they* were all about. I wanted to see these guys….What's their place like? What's their operation? How are they making money? Are their gates nice—do they swing free? There was one guy I met, he was doing thirty horses a day. You'd be miserable. I don't care how much you love horses; you'd hate your life."

Glenn had competed at Road to the Horse twice. The first time was in 2012 when he was on what had been called a "Nation's Cup" team with Jonathan Field. The second time had been 2022.

Dart was easier to catch that day, and I used less grain. I made a point to not be in a hurry with her, and to rub her and feed her after catching her, as well as before.

That evening, Glenn and I appeared on the Horse Radio Show with hosts Louisa Barton and Pete Rodda. Pete asked Glenn what his advice was for me, as I prepared to compete at Road to the Horse in 2024.

"Sprinkle it in," Glenn said. "Keep sprinkling it in."

I won't forget that, I thought.

The next time I walked to the front of the paddock, Dart walked over. I probably didn't need to, but I gave her a small handful of grain. I still hadn't let anyone see I was feeding her.

I had a good session with her, then I caught Bert, and took him to the round pen. I rubbed him on the neck. Then I asked him to yield his hindquarters.

"Talk to 'zones,'" Glenn said. "He's not a big glob of meat out there. Talk to a *part* of him. Then see if it moved."

"I've got a question that's been bugging me for years," I said. "I saw a horse in New Jersey with his halter tied tight to the girth, so he was bent in the neck, almost ninety degrees. The trainer explained how the horse was too dangerous for him to work with, and by tying him in this way, the horse was only struggling against himself, not against him as the trainer."

"That's archaic," Glenn responded without hesitation. "Anytime you are thinking you're training your horse and you're not involved, that's the wrong mindset. How is that working on partnership? How is that working on *you*?"

At the end of the day, the end of the clinic, Glenn asked our group—me and all the ladies—"Why don't more people come to these clinics?"

The soft-spoken lady raised her hand. "I know for myself," she said, "I struggle to do these things because I don't want to look like an idiot."

"A lot of English riders don't come because you're a cowboy," offered a woman holding a coffee mug that said IT TOOK ME 3 YEARS TO LEARN TO TALK AND 60 YEARS TO LEARN TO LISTEN.

"The question you need to ask, that *everyone* needs to ask is, 'How can I change my perspective,'" said Glenn. "It's a form of 'proving' when others are influencing how you feel about it. I'm not trying to prove nothing to nobody. Nothing to the crowd, or the judges, or nobody. I'm here to *im*prove."

Ten days starting horses under Glenn's watchful eye had flown by. My skill level was up...my confidence level was down. I knew I could not sustain this kind of learning right up until Road to the Horse. I would need a few weeks to find myself, and my own way, before I entered the round pen in March.

I knew I needed to continue to learn, but I also needed to find my own way of relating to horses. I didn't want to be Linda, or Pat, or Glenn, or Chris, or Jake, or Eric, or Shawna, or Ren, or Jonathan.

I wanted to be me.

25

I sat at my desk. I stared at the wall. No coffee. Just a glass of water. Half empty. My mother always used to tell me, "Some people sit and think; some people just sit."

Questions I face daily are: How much adversity should I let my kids face? How much should I coddle them?

One surprise I've had as a parent is how easy it is to say, "Yes." *Yes, yes, yes!* "Yes" to the candy, "yes" to the screen, "yes" to staying up late.

It's much more difficult to say "No."

I face similar questions with horses.

The better I get to be at reading horses, and the more present and creative I am, the more I can make learning feel more like play than like work. But, inevitably, there is adversity. Is adversity bad? What's the difference between adversity and suffering?

Suffering, perhaps, starts off the same, but is prolonged and inescapable.

Adversity, maybe, is struggling to face something outside of a comfort zone. Learning to face adversity can, in the right context, offer growth. It can make us more emotionally fit, more emotionally balanced, ready to face the world. It will make our comfort zone bigger.

When I was a child, my parents did a tactful job allowing me to be introduced to adversity gradually. If anything, they erred on the side of "babying me" too much, and as I grew older, I was shocked by how much adversity there is *out there*, in our big world, to encounter.

Adversity is like rain for plants. To grow tall and strong, we need a steady supply of it. We can have too much, a flood, or too little, a drought. Most of us don't need to go looking for adversity. Just like water for plants, it will mostly find us wherever we are. What matters is how we face the rain.

I was forty-one years old, two kids, a wife. My father was eighty, and he was still looking out for me.

He had sent Vicki Wilson a message because she was from an English-riding background and had competed in Road to the Horse. He was worried that I was worried—about not catching the horse, and about not being able to throw a lariat, and about not being a cowboy in a cowboy competition.

"Being a professional cowboy…I don't think that is important," Vicki responded to my father from New Zealand. "Most of the horses can be caught with a rope over the neck. Picking the right horse or asking the wrangler the right questions can help set that up…. Lassoing, to me, scares the horse—the horse gives in, but there will always be an element of fear. Get him to explain that his brand of horsemanship doesn't feel roping is necessary."

My dad forwarded me the message. *One more reason to not waste time with a lasso,* I thought, which was great, as I was really struggling with it, and I had lots of other things to practice.

What I was forgetting was that when something is uncomfortable, that's probably *exactly* what I should be working on.

In the 2019 Road to the Horse, Vicki had tried to catch her first horse for ages. The gelding stayed constantly a couple feet out of reach. The horse was not petrified, just nervous enough, and savvy enough, to be able to stay a whisper away from being caught. Watching it again on television, it reminded me of trying to get a halter on Dart. I felt for her.

Horseman Craig Cameron had made a guest appearance for some color commentary, and he'd drawled: "Patience is waiting without worry. Going slow is the fastest way to get there. Give 'em the time it takes for them to understand. When done right it is an art form."

Sinead walked into our small office.

I'd been thinking about Vicki's note to my dad, but I'd also been thinking about the "horse hunt" Sinead and I were on. We had two "syndicates" operating, each of which owned two competition horses for our eventing careers. There were six shares for sale in each syndicate. If we managed to sell all the shares, the horses would pay for themselves. The problem was, only half the shares had sold, which meant each year operated at a significant loss.

But we continued regardless, as you do when you are passionate about something.

We had recently sold one of the horses, and that money, due to the syndicate agreement, was meant to go toward purchasing another horse.

Besides our kids, all our money went into horses, and we tried to be fair, when money came in, about whose turn it was for a horse. At the moment, we were looking for a horse for me. But we had run into a string of bad luck: four horses in a row that didn't pass the veterinarian's pre-purchase exam, and then one, a liver chestnut (my favorite, that I loved), that was sold to someone else at the last minute.

"I've been putting this off," Sinead said, standing just inside the doorway, "but why am I doing that? I need to be able to talk to my husband."

"Good," I said, swiveling my chair to face her directly. "There's something I want to talk to you about too."

"This is nothing personal. Just the universe speaking, I think."

"Do you want to go first?" I asked. Sinead hesitated, caught off-guard. "Okay," I continued. "How about I go first? You look tense. Why don't you sit down?"

Sinead hovered above the other desk chair that sat just a couple feet from me.

"I was thinking," I said, "that with me getting ready for Road to the Horse, and Sam going Advanced, and this book that I'm working on, that we should spend this money on a horse for you."

Sinead sank into the chair. "That's what I was thinking."

"I decided this morning."

"I decided this morning too."

"It was *ikigai* that helped with the decision."

"No way."

"Way."

"*Ikigai* helped me too."

"You know what that means?" I raised my eyebrows.

"What?" she asked carefully.

I rested my hand on hers. I smiled. "That we're soulmates!"

She rolled her eyes, but I caught a twinkle in them.

The sky was dark and rain sprinkled our camper. We huddled in-side—my mother and I, and Olivia—watching the television. Olivia, big-hearted and quiet, was helping with the horses, and was seeing Road to the Horse for the first time.

It was interesting watching people's first impressions. Olivia was silent and thoughtful. My mother, also, was completely absorbed.

"You don't get this done unless you have the goods. Unless you have the skill level to get this done," the host announced.

The three competitors, all cowboys, could have been in a band together, or been characters in a Larry McMurtry novel. McMurtry wrote *Lonesome Dove* and helped adapt the screenplay for *Brokeback Mountain*. In the biography *Larry McMurtry: A Life,* Larry is described as a writer to the core: *If you leave a cow alone, he'll eat grass. If you leave Larry alone, he'll write books. When he's in public, he may say hello and goodbye, but otherwise he is just resting, getting ready to go write.*

Some cowboys need to cowboy the way Larry needed to write. They would rather wither, shrivel, die, and rot than live in a high-rise in the city.

One of the men swung a rope and his colt skittered away.

Roping was a skill, like throwing a football, that had a lot of nuance. Just tossing it a few feet was a primitive skill that could be learned by a two-year-old. But throwing it with spin, throwing it straight and true, throwing it accurately, throwing it far, throwing it to a moving target, throwing it under pressure, and most of all, throwing it with a sense of where a horse is going, what he is thinking, and how he is going to react *when* it is thrown and after he is caught—*that* takes an artist.

After ten minutes, one of the competitors was still trying to catch his horse, and I was sweating. Here it was again, that first fear. *I could see that happening to me.*

Rain began pelting the camper windows. I turned the volume up.

"How can one minute we move the horse off with the flag, and another minute expect them to get used to it?" the host asked the audience.

How would I answer that? I wondered.

- First, consider a horse under saddle who feels our seat and leg. Initially, we want him to *not* move when he feels our leg—just stand there, not nervous. Tame.

- Second, when we use our leg and seat with a different pressure and intention, we want that to mean, *Go forward.* There are a lot of horses that never even truly understand these first two steps. They walk when we ask them to halt, and they stand when we ask them to trot.

- Third, we might want the horse to learn that when we use our leg and seat *this way*, it means go *that way*: *Leg-yield. Shoulder-in. Haunches-in. Haunches-out.*

- Fourth, maybe we could use our leg and seat to say, *Bring your balance up and look ahead.* Like when we are coming to a jump.

- Fifth, my leg and seat could say, *Without speeding up, can you stretch your neck out and down and look ahead, like we are about to walk across a stream?*

- Sixth, they could say, *Collect. Can you be quick, and light on your feet, like a ballet dancer?*

When I start a horse, besides gait and speed, I also consider "forward thinking," and energy level.

- I Gait.
- II Speed.
- III Thinking forward.
- IV Energy level.

Gait and speed are the most obvious; the last two are the most important. Just because I can get *gait* and *speed* does not mean I can get *forward thinking* and *energy*. But if I can influence the last two, I can achieve the first two.

On the television screen, a saddle was being cinched up. "He's at what I call 'The Point of No Return,'" the host declared. "There is nothing worse than a saddle halfway on."

Darn straight, I thought. One of my biggest Road to the Horse fears was getting the saddle on but only partially cinched up, and then the horse flinching, causing the saddle to fall off—or worse, get caught under the horse's belly.

At fifty-three minutes left on the Road to the Horse time clock, competitor Wade Black sank into the saddle for the first time, and I stopped breathing.

He sat there smooth as a king born to the throne who knows no other place. He looked to his left, totally present, taking in his kingdom. He looked about my age, maybe a few years older—in the middle part of his life, where he had skill and knowledge, and also still some of the athleticism of a young man. Wisdom often comes later, at the expense of, or perhaps due to, the loss of some of that athleticism.

I clicked the remote. *Pause.*

"Do you think someone can learn that? To sit like that?" I asked.

Olivia was silent, thoughtful.

"No," my mother said; then she said, "Yes."

"I remember standing with Karen O'Connor at Terra Nova two years ago, watching riders gallop by. I asked her, 'Do you think you can tell just by watching someone gallop for a second or two how good they are? I mean, without seeing them jump, without knowing anything about them?' 'Absolutely,' Karen said. 'Without a doubt.' That's what it was like watching Wade sit on that horse. If I could soak up those few seconds, where he just settles into the saddle and sits, it would be enough to know."

"Can you make some tea?" my mother asked.

"Yes, of course," I said, and got up to put the kettle on. "Olivia?"

"No, thank you."

"And it's not just about what Wade *does*," I said, waiting for the pot to whistle. "He is *doing less*, and exerting less energy, than the other two competitors."

In the book *Tiny Beautiful Things* by Cheryl Strayed, she writes:

> *One of the basic principles of every single art form has to do not with what's there—the music, the words, the movement, the dialogue, the paint—but with what isn't. In the visual arts it's called "negative space"—the blank parts around and between objects, which is, of course, every bit as crucial as the objects themselves. The negative space allows us to see the nonnegative space in all its glory and gloom, its color and mystery and light. What isn't there gives what's there meaning.*

"He looks so relaxed," my mother said. "There's not a tense cell in his body."

"Look at how he *sits!*"

"Even when he leans forward, he is still deep in the saddle."

The rain picked up again. I put the television on mute because we couldn't hear it anymore anyways. We watched a few more minutes in silence while the kettle boiled.

"Cigar?"

"I used to," Matt Feeney said, giving me a hug.

I offered him a cigar, and he took it. I lit it with a steady hand.

"Thanks," he said.

"I got into them three or four years ago when I was hanging out with Sinead's brother and her stepdad. I wanted to have something in common with them, so I just kept trying them. I have a theory that if I keep trying something, I'll grow to like it."

"Did that work?"

"Yup! Worked with bourbon as well. And gin."

"I wonder what that says about you."

Matt held his cigar at arm's length. We watched it smolder. Dark threatening clouds marched overhead, a column of tanks heading to war. Half a mile away, light spilled out from the cathedralesque barns at Terra Nova, but at this time of night, and overcast, I couldn't see Matt's face, only his silhouette.

"Who do you have here?"

"Sam," I replied. "He's in the Four-Star Long. His first one. *Our* first one. How's your business at home?"

Matt was an actor and director by trade. He'd even been to mime school in Paris. Now he helped his partner with her horse business. Over the past few years, watching Matt learn to interact with horses had been like watching a Lab learn to retrieve. He was a natural. Maybe it was his actor's awareness and control of his own energy, body language, and intention. Maybe it was his ability to read the horse, like a mime reads a crowd. Maybe it was his intelligence.

Matt was the kind of guy who had all kinds of theories. He had a theory that there were three types of people: those who led with their head, those who led with their chest, and those who led with their hips. He had a theory that horse owners don't *really* want to learn.

"Most horse owners don't really want to take the time," he explained as we walked. "Their horse is a pet, like a dog. Look at your dog." He glanced at a dark shadow that I knew was Ferdinand, trotting along beside us. "You just want him to come when you call him. And be happy. He's a little out of control but that doesn't bother you. Most people just want their pets to be happy and to not be a nuisance."

We were walking on a dark path that meandered around the showgrounds. Due to the dark and the wind, we were the only ones out. My cigar went out; I turned my back to the wind, then relit it.

"You are the 'fire,'" Matt said, beginning another theory. "Lighting a fire here, then another fire there. Sinead is more like the 'arrow.' There's a target she's aiming at, been aiming at it since she was a kid, and she's not going to deviate."

"I'm the fire?"

"You're an explorer," he said.

"Hmm. Your cigar out?"

Matt turned his back to the wind while I tried to light his cigar again, but the wind that was tearing in from the Gulf of Mexico thwarted me, and the lighter was low on fuel. Then my cigar died as well. But we were happy to just walk and talk.

Matt was in town only for the evening; he had been in Orlando with his extended family on vacation. We talked late into the night. My mother and Olivia were long asleep when he left. He had a flight back to England the next day.

An explorer. I smiled. I liked that.

I lay in the camper, smelling of cheap cigar smoke, and thinking. Eventually I picked up a book—*Counting Sheep: Reflections and Observations of a Swedish Shepherd* by Axel Linden.

> *I finished the fence by the shed and yelled a few times like Astrid Lindgren's fearsome Ronja. It was so great to be finished. I hope none of the real farmers heard me. I hope no one heard me. Or actually, I hope the sheep did hear me. They probably need something to think about. They're doing fine and all, but it must be a bit boring to just trudge around. Just imagine only having your basic needs to concern you. Am I hungry, thirsty? Am I cold? You'd be going crazy. Or completely at peace.*

My mind was busy, occupied with competing Sam the next day, but also with Road to the Horse, and the kids. I wanted to go to the mountains with them to teach them to ski...I wanted to build a tree fort with them in the back yard...but all I was doing was making myself crazy.

I craved peace.

Three days later, Sam and I completed our first Four-Star Long. The cross-country was longer than I had ever ridden before. It was an eleven-minute novel—a whole story that played out between us. Hope, expectation. Good jumps, bad jumps, then good jumps again. Fresh, then tired. Adrenaline, then fatigue, then adrenaline again.

Our emotions were heightened, and we lived a lot in that quarter-hour.

Time flew by.

I thought after about the real gift that horses gave me. It was not galloping or jumping or a way to make a living. People spent thousands, traveled to India, took classes, spent decades trying to learn to be present...and the gift horses gave me was they invited me to be present.

Sometimes, they insisted on it.

26

At the end of November, I started a young Quarter Horse with Tom Pierson at a beautiful farm in Alechua County. Tom was, at a guess, almost a couple decades older than me. He had kind, competent eyes. He was quiet and knew his way around a horse. He'd started about four hundred horses himself and had overseen another four hundred being started when he worked at a college in Wisconsin.

The most important thing I learned was so small I will never forget it. It happened right after I got in the round pen, and I was letting the colt get used to me. I was looking for a moment when he looked at me, in which case, I would back off to encourage him.

"You missed it," Tom said.

"Pardon?"

"His ear just flicked toward you."

I had been looking for a tiny change in the eye, but Tom had noticed an even tinier change in the ear. I prided myself on noticing little details—but I hadn't noticed what he'd noticed.

I sure paid attention to the ears after that.

Good Apple Equine: Florida's Largest Equine Consignment Store.

I walked in.

"Good morning," said the lady behind the desk, without looking up. She was short-haired, tattooed, and reading the *Eclectic Horseman.*

"Morning. I heard you have books."

She pointed to the back wall. Hidden behind some saddles were four shelves of books. I counted the number of books in a section about a foot wide and did some quick math. Maybe three hundred in total—all horse books.

I picked up Alexandra Kurland's *Clicker Training for Your Horse* and skimmed through it. I put it on the ground next to me. Then I picked up *The Horse Whisperer* by Nicholas Evans. I had read it years ago; time for another go. I put it on the ground next to me. *Wait a second…Horses in Focus. No way!* The book my parents had published in the eighties. I paged through it. *There it was.* A photo of me, with my brother Telfer, and my father, and Honey, our dog. It was a photo my mother had taken on the River Trail in Southlands in 1987, when I was the same age as Brooks.

Thirty minutes later, I was sitting on the ground and had a stack of books next to me. I was getting ready to go when I spotted a book for which I had been searching for years—a small hardcover copy of *The Jeffery Method of Horse Handling,* first published in 1973. The Jeffery Method has many components, but it was most well-known for a technique that involved jumping on the horse bareback, lying on him, crawling on him, and taming him with lots of body-to-body contact. I added the book to my pile.

After paying for the books, I drove an hour out of my way to the office of Dr. Carissa L. Wickens at the University of Florida. The "L" stood for Lee. "It was mother's middle name as well," she'd told me. I texted her as I left: *I'm just passing through Gainsville. Can I stop by?*

Anytime, came the reply.

I parked at the animal sciences building. Her office was on the second floor—202B. Dr. Wickens was about my age, with sandy brown hair, and young friendly eyes. She wore a striped, hygge sweater.

Dr. Wickens sat down, and I eased into a chair on the other side of her desk. The desk was cluttered with dozens of magazines, books, and papers. I looked at her bookshelf. *H is for Horse: An Equestrian Alphabet*—an illustrated book. *Statistical Methods and Data Analysis* was another. There was an immense white book titled *Statistical Methods for the Social Sciences* by Agresti and Finlay. Then I recognized one: *Why Zebras Don't Get Ulcers* by Robert Sapolsky.

"I've got that one." I pointed.

"I've only read half of it," Dr. Wickens admitted, "but I saw him live once."

"There are a couple things in that book that changed how I think about training."

I knew the thirteenth chapter almost by heart. It was titled: *Why Is Psychological Stress Stressful?* Operating under the assumption that training could be stressful, I wanted to see how it could be *less* stressful, or if possible, not stressful at all.

Someone who is really stressed will not learn well, but there is always a *little* bit of stress if we are truly out of our comfort zone, because while the *act* of learning is physical or intellectual, the *experience* of learning is emotional. I know when I'm learning Spanish on Duolingo even though it is fun, there is hint of tension in me. The same goes for playing Scrabble, taking a test, or participating in a clinic.

"What have you been working on?" I asked.

"One of the things I look at a lot is *stereotypic behaviors*, like cribbing or weaving."

Stereotypic behaviors, like a teenager chewing his fingernails, were often called *vices*, but Dr. Wickens encouraged me to think of them as *coping mechanisms* instead.

"When they perform a stereotypic behavior, they are really bad off," said Dr. Wickens. "But those animals that are cribbing may actually be coping better in that environment than the horse that has *not* adopted that strategy or is being prevented from enacting the behavior. It is an OCD behavior. If we try to stop it, is that fair? And how do we measure that?"

"That's what I want to know: How do we determine what is fair?" Veiled behind *my* question were *these* questions:

- Was starting a horse on a timeline fair?

- Was starting a horse in a competition fair?

- Was starting a horse using negative or positive reinforcement fair?

- Was punishment fair?

- Was starting a horse *at all* fair?

- *What is fair for a horse? And who determines that?*

"One of the things I study is behavior and welfare science. What we see being done in practice informs our research questions. It is always evolving. We are always looking for answers, and we are always looking to be more informed."

That didn't answer my question. "Everyone is claiming to have science on their side," I said. "How does someone navigate that?"

"We have a one-credit class here. All we do for the class is sit there and tear apart a peer-reviewed journal article. We ask questions about the study like: 'Was this well run?' 'Did they account for confounding variables?' 'Was there a big enough sample size?' We look at their statistical analysis, how it was designed, and how they interpreted the results."

"I would love that class."

"That's the scientific method. It's not perfect, but when something goes through the peer-reviewed process and has multiple reviewers, it makes it more robust. So when it gets to the point of an accepted publication, it has some rigor."

She was reaffirming what our vet, Dr. Yates, always said: science is not fact; science is the best answer *at a point in time.* That answer could change, and often did change, as new studies were done, old studies were replicated, and current studies were peer-reviewed.

Science is not perfect, but it is the closest to the truth we have *at that moment.*

"But what about for the average person? How do they know what to listen to when there is so much pseudoscience, junk science, and out-right lying-science?" I asked. "Facebook is so annoying—not only can *anything* be posted, and often is, but it is done in a way that polarizes the horse world. *This way is good; that way is bad. This person is good; that person is bad.* It feels like the last thing we need. How do we sift through it all?"

Dr. Wickens shuffled some of the papers on her desk.

"The average person doesn't have access to peer-reviewed journal articles," I went on. "And I don't know how many of those I could read through anyway."

I was fishing for an answer to what was a "right way" and a "wrong way" to train, but she never bit.

"So what's your advice then?" I asked one more time.

"Be aware of biases," Dr. Wickens said. "Even I have them. Everyone has them."

I thought about a man I knew who was brought up in a household that was strict, but fair. His father was good-natured, but set black-and-white boundaries and would immediately enforce them. That man later grew up to join the Marines. He excelled in places of rules and discipline. *Discipline is good for people,* he thought, and he raised his own kids, and trained his horses, and dogs, the same way.

Then I thought about the woman I'd met who had been sexually abused by a family member when she was twelve. Her mother was an alcoholic and not really present, and her father was not in the picture at all. She grew up believing that we should never force anything on anyone. Everything should be a choice.

Then I thought about my own biases: I liked to be pushed, but not too hard. I like to be around people, but not too much. I agreed that rules were important, but I thought there should be exceptions to many of them. In arguments I searched for a compromise. I was a walking, talking, middle-aged, middle-of-the-road, middle-income, white Canadian. I leaned a little left here, a little right there. My biases were pretty tame.

"Also, be more aware of how your horse is actually responding to what you are doing," Dr. Wickens said. "At least people are searching and trying to do better."

"It seems to me that what you keep coming back to is observation," I said. "Watching your horse, being more aware, and then asking questions."

"Exactly, those are key components to being a good scientist. Encouraging people to observe their horse's behavior is especially important. If I don't know what his normal behavior looks like, how do I know if he is suffering? And fads…liberty…certain bits go in and out of style. 'Bitless' is a craze right now. Some students get convinced that it is the only way to go. The 'right' way."

"How do you help them navigate that?"

"I encourage them to ask questions. I'm just excited when we get people thinking and asking questions. These kids get excited by one idea, or one methodology. And that's a start. We do need, or we *will* need, social license to operate. And we will shut down our own industry if we don't make some changes. Dog racing in Florida is a case in point."

Florida had once been the Mecca of American Greyhound racing, with over twenty racetracks spread around the state. The last race, after the sport was outlawed by a state-wide vote, was run in 2021.

"I want you to plunge this morning," Sinead said as I stood in the doorway leading to the kitchen, staring at her.

I tilted my head. "Hmm," I said.

"You're completely useless in the mornings. Look at your face."

"That's not a *hundred* percent true."

"Don't forget. We have your call later today."

I grunted. I hobbled to "The Plunge" and studied the stern water that sat, still and clear, at exactly forty-five degrees Fahrenheit. The Plunge was basically an outdoor bathtub with a water cooler attached to it; the opposite of a hot tub. It was still dark outside. I stripped, groaned as I got in, dunked my head, and then resurfaced, eyes bright and skin tight.

"You're right," I said, back in the kitchen. "Better than a coffee!"

We went into kid preparation mode. Normally Sinead was in charge of mornings: clothes out, lunches packed, breakfasts made, clothes on. And I would organize the evenings: pajamas on, clean teeth, potty, read books, light off, sing two or three choruses of "You Are My Sunshine," the same song I remember my mother singing to me.

We alternated dropping the kids off at school, and Bernadette might help as well. It was my day to make the drop, then I rode a couple horses, then I brewed a carafe of coffee in the French press and got the computer ready. At eleven sharp I joined a Zoom call, and within seconds I saw four rectangles on the screen—my face and three others.

"So, this is it," I announced. "Jake, Nick, Juliette, good morning." Sinead, carrying a mug of coffee, walked in at that moment. "And Sinead is here too—say, 'Hi,' Sinead."

"Hello," Sinead said.

"Hello," the others sang.

Jake had been my final addition to my Road to the Horse Support Team. Not only did he live close to Copperline, but he was willing to help and coach me in the essential skills I knew I lacked. Jake had quickly turned into a source of experience and knowledge I was depending on.

"This is the three-month countdown. I need to continue to be out of my comfort zone as much as possible," I threw out to the group. "I want to learn as much as I can. I want to work with different people, study new techniques, and experience other perspectives. Nothing is off limits. Then the plan for the final three weeks leading up to Road to the Horse, starting March first, is I will work on my strengths. I'll have incorporated new ideas, but I will be doing things *my* way. I don't want to have any outside voices in my head; no coaching. I want to feel like I can get in the zone."

"The 'flow state,'" said Sinead.

"Exactly."

"The 'unthinking place,'" said Nick.

"Yup."

"That place where time slows down," added Juliette.

I nodded.

"Totally *present*," agreed Jake.

I sipped my coffee. I pondered my team. Jake was patient, but he was also a man of action. Juliette, the youngest of the group, looked dressed for class. Nick stroked his beard pensively, his rich eyes taking everything in. Sinead sat beside me, making notes.

"I want to take this chance, with all of us together, to voice my fears," I said. "These aren't *horrible* fears. They aren't giving me nightmares or anything—at least not yet—but they do keep me up at night."

The others were silent, the rectangles on my screen staring at me.

"My first fear is not being able to catch my horse," I began. "I can imagine myself in the ring, in front of the audience, and he is just out of reach, constantly turning his head away from me, or methodically positioning his hindquarters toward me. The clock mercilessly counts down. I feel the urgency of the time and move more quickly; he learns my tells and starts to leave me more quickly.

"My second fear is the first saddling. I am afraid he will flinch away and the saddle will hit the ground, or I will get it partially on, *then* he gets scared, and it ends up around his belly. Either way, he loses a lot of trust in me, and I'm not able to build it back up in the time remaining.

"My third fear is the first ride."

I didn't have to say any more about the third fear; the others nodded. They understood. I could be hurt or killed. It was not likely, but it was possible. I had known people that had been killed by horses.

Thinking about the first ride at Road to the Horse felt like standing on top of a cliff in North Vancouver, looking over the edge at the glacial-cold water in Lynn Canyon far below. My body telling my mind, *No way! You're crazy!* and my mind saying, *I'm not crazy, I've done it before.* I could inspect the water, measure the depth, watch others do it, make it as safe as possible, and still, my body will seize up on the approach and say, *Forget it.* If I waited too long, or thought too much, it only got more and more difficult. I needed to *just take the leap.*

The others were still silent. Dreading what would very likely be a vulnerability hangover later, I plowed on: "My last fear is when I start riding, I try to steer too much, stop too much, bend too much, or go over obstacles too early, and my colt shuts down. The fear is that I start to lose 'try.' The fear is that I lose sight of the first two things I need—relaxed and *forward*. If I get in a hurry about details, I risk losing him mentally."

That fourth fear was the least dramatic, but the most insidious, and probably the hardest on the horse. If it happened, it would be like my car seizing up and needing a new engine, or my kid no longer communicating, going inside himself, shutting off the outside world.

There was silence from the rectangles on my computer screen. It felt like they were waiting for me to continue, but I had hoped the team would talk through my fears. A slight disappointment twinged inside me as I slowly spoke: "Well...I guess the next thing to talk about..."

"Hold on," Jake interrupted. "Those are *big* moments. Those are the moments I would be scared of too. They will go as good as they can go, but that's that."

In other words, Jake was telling me it was okay to be scared, that anybody would be scared, that we could never be totally sure how those moments were going to go.

"We can practice to be ready for those," he said. I saw nods in the other rectangles.

I wished we were meeting in person, over a beer. I would have given that big tough cowboy a hug right then. I took a breath and continued: "The next thing is, 'What does success look like?' It would be nice to win some money, but I know very well it's possible to win and feel bad about it, and to lose and feel good about it, so I've made up a set of principles that I feel like if I can follow, if *we* can follow, will determine our success."

I cleared my throat and began reading the list I'd drafted to my team. Saying them out loud gave me a little sick feeling in my gut. I contemplated the group before me: Juliette was taking notes. Jake, who had peach sideburns that jutted down toward his jaw like cleaving knives, was adjusting his reading glasses. Nick was studying me, his eyes twinkly behind his enormous beard. I felt like Nick still didn't quite believe we were going to be successful. "Skeptical" wasn't quite the right word; neither was "pessimistic." *Maybe "realistic" is the word,* I thought ruefully.

They all looked thoughtful, so I let them all soak. Then I moved on to the last item on my agenda.

"The last thing I want to mention is the booth," I said.

Road to the Horse contestants could have a booth during the event to provide a "homebase" for meeting the public, as well as a retail shop. It was my chance to educate the fans about what I did and also make some money. Preparing for Road to the Horse was turning out to be an expensive endeavor, and this would be a chance to recoup.

The only problem was…other than my first book *In the Middle Are the Horsemen*, I had nothing to sell.

Some competitors showed up at Road to the Horse with sales staff, merchandising teams, certified instructors, club memberships, and online streaming platforms. They had rope halters, bits, hobbles, and T-shirts. They had twice-life-size banners featuring photos of them sliding to a stop with dirt flying toward the viewer.

I had none of that.

I knew I wanted to sell books, and not just my own, because the educational piece is such an important part of developing as a horseman. But books could be a tough sell to crowds accustomed to soundbites and social media. At one of my recent lessons with Karen O'Connor, we'd got to talking about a clinic she'd just done in Alabama. She'd told me she had begun the clinic by asking the assembled students what horse books they had read recently.

"What did they say?" I'd asked.

"Nothing." Karen shook her head. "Just blank stares."

"My vision," I told my team now, "is to make our booth a comfy library-meets-coffee-shop kind of vibe. We can have a bookshelf with some of my favorite books."

One of the titles I wanted to sell was *Horse Brain, Human Brain* by Janet Jones. I knew Janet had spoken out publicly against colt-starting competitions, so I wasn't sure if she would want me selling her books at Road to the Horse. Juliette had written to Janet, explaining my plan and requesting her approval.

"Thanks for asking," Janet had responded. "I would be honored…. Yes, it is a controversial event—I have gone on the record several times against colt-starting competitions because I believe they encourage people to push young horses too far, too fast. However, that is all the more reason for people at Road to the Horse to develop greater knowledge of equine brains, and I believe my book can help provide that. I also believe that Tik is a true horseman who would stop for the horse's sake and withdraw from the competition if he felt he was pushing too far too fast—and what a powerful lesson that would be!"

Janet's email was a reminder that *I could stop*. Entering a competition didn't fate me to finish it…or to follow a certain path. Because we will be rewarded for doing something does not mean we are necessarily going to do it. Humans have many competing and complex motivations. We all have a choice. Those choices with horses happen every season, every day, every minute, every second.

Making a mistake with a horse once is not a mistake—it's finding your way. That's how we learn. Making the same mistake with a horse the eighth, thirteenth, hundredth time? *Those* are mistakes.

And losing is not always *losing*. If we keep our wits about us, we can lose and still learn something, *still win*. Lately, I had been wondering if, in fact, "losing" was the *only* way to learn something.

Books about winners are ubiquitous. However, one of my favorite sports books is about losing: *My Losing Season* by Pat Conroy. He writes:

There is no teacher more discriminating or transforming than loss.... Loss invites reflection and reformulating and a change of strategies. Loss hurts and bleeds and aches. Loss is always ready to call out your name in the night. Loss follows you home and taunts you at the breakfast table, follows you to work in the morning. You have to make accommodations and broker deals to soften the rabbit punches that loss brings to your daily life. You have to take the word "loser" and add it to your resume and walk around with it on your name tag as it hand-feeds you your own shit in dosages too large for even great beasts to swallow. The word "loser" follows you, bird-dogs you, sniffs you out of whatever fields you hide in because you have to face things clearly and you cannot turn away from what is true.

That's what I wanted, I wanted to know what was *true*. I wanted to know *me*. How would I react if I stepped into that round pen and I couldn't catch the horse in front of eight thousand people? Would I run? Would my mouth go dry?

Winning does not encourage us to know ourselves; it might not even allow it. But when we lose, when we break up, when we leave home, when we get fired, *those* are events that allow us to grow. Why? Because when we tie our self-identities to something else, we end up shackled to that thing, be it a job or hobby or sport or horses. And when I lose at that sport, if I lose with horses, *who am I*?

I had to know.

The ten-minute Zoom countdown clock suddenly flashed across the screen. Our forty minutes of "free" were about to run out.

"Anything from you guys?" I asked. "Anything to add before Zoom kicks us out?"

"I like the list of principles," Nick said slowly. "It's beautiful, actually. With those things in mind, this isn't so big anymore."

I thought I knew what he meant. The list gave us permission to just do the best job we could do.

I went to the dark wooden cabinet in the kitchen, what we called "The Bar." I poured Sinead a Tito's and soda. I poured myself a bourbon—the last few drops from a bottle distilled in New York, in the Hudson Valley. Sinead stood in the kitchen, making dinner. The kids were playing with Legos, mercifully quiet for a few minutes.

"How many horses *have* you started?" Sinead asked.

"Maybe thirty," I said.

My wife raised her eyebrows.

"Maybe twenty-five."

Sinead's eyes twinkled. I loved it when they twinkled.

"Twenty?" I offered.

"Really?"

"Well, the first horse I started was with Bruce Logan in 2009. And then I didn't start any for a while, and then maybe one or two a year on average."

"So how many is that?"

"I don't know." I laughed. "But I *do* know I have learned more about horses in the past few months than I have in the past few years. That's one thing I will get out of this project, win or lose. I'm learning a ton, and without this deadline, I wouldn't have ever put this much into studying colt starting."

"Then it's worth it," Sinead said.

I was in the midst of a turning point. How I thought about my family, my home, my kids, my career, *myself* was all changing. Road to the Horse, I suspected, was going to do one of two things: bring out my best or reveal my worst.

The kids ran into the kitchen, squealing like puppies. Brooks wrapped his arms around my thigh; Goldfish koala-beared onto my shin.

27

In December I started a filly with Jake. After three days there was a big change in the filly—but not big *enough*. Not for Road to the Horse. Not even close.

I still hadn't saddled her, much less ridden her.

She still wasn't tame. She still didn't trust me.

The filly had gotten better with me getting on and off bareback. She had become more responsive, and less reactive, when she felt the rope touching her. There were even moments where she was really relaxed with the flag, not just staying still and tolerating it.

The filly was the color of tangerine, with four white socks and a big ol' blaze. Her birthday was Memorial Day, and her name was Liberty, but since she was the only filly on Jake's property at the time, we had taken to simply calling her "the filly."

Jake sat in a wooden rocking chair next to the pen. "Give her a back rub so nice she wants more," he said. "If *you* want more, you have two options: have a lot of slick skills, or pick an easier one."

Initially, Jake and I were just going to do three days with her, but we kept going. On the fourth day I tried the saddle. I had it part way on, the heavy horn up near her withers, and then she flinched. Her eyes were fire and ice.

After the flinch, just a twitch of the skin and her head brought higher, she froze, and I hesitated. She felt my uncertainty and bucked. The saddle hit the ground.

I immediately asked Jake to take her. Partly because it was his horse and his saddle, partly because I was tired from a flight home from a clinic in Nebraska the day before, but mostly because I just wanted to see what he would do, how he would handle it.

Jake took the rope attached to the filly's halter. He placed the saddle on and off, on and off. He was rhythmic and persistent. Jake gave off this feeling of underlying confidence; he was a strong leader with a plan, and this *was* going to happen—he knew it, I knew it, and the filly was learning it fast. It was a hot day, and Jake's shirt began to darken with dirt and sweat. The filly was sweating too, on her chest and near her hind legs.

Then the saddle hit the ground again.

Jake said, "Everybody makes mistakes. Don't let it get to you. Just stay persistent."

Jake picked up the saddle and kept going. In less than fifteen minutes he had the saddle on. Once the filly had the saddle on, she started to bronc. Jake asked her to turn in, essentially shutting down the bucking.

I said, "You've told me that in situations like this, you would get out of the round pen and let her buck, and now you're staying in there."

Jake didn't take his eyes off the filly. "With her, right now, that's not an option."

After fifteen minutes, when she was a little more used to the saddle, Jake unsaddled her.

It was a reminder that every horse, every situation, was different.

I went back the next morning, early, so I could fit in a session with the filly before I rode the rest of my horses at Copperline. It was cold out, refreshing.

I looked at the filly, and she looked right back at me. She moved away from me. Again, I asked Jake if he would work with her.

Jake took his time. He talked me through what he was doing. He was patient. He thought ahead. He had good ideas. But this filly was the most sensitive horse I had ever seen. And not just sensitive—there are sensitive horses that are looking to connect, but she wanted nothing to do with us. Progress was slow. *Really darn slow.*

I leaned on the rail of the round pen, watching. Jake was breaking out every trick in the book, and still she struggled. Suddenly, she bucked and twisted, as if to say, *Don't fucking touch me.* A cold sweat broke out on me. *I can't do this.* Jake was struggling with this horse, and I hadn't started half as many horses as Jake. I had an overwhelming urge to sit down, but I made myself keep standing. I kept watching. It was still chilly, and I picked up my coffee; I couldn't drink, but I needed its warmth between my hands.

If I drew a horse like this filly at Road to the Horse, I would get nowhere.

The next day I went to Jake's again.

I was walking over to greet the filly when Steph, Jake's wife, arrived with grain for all the horses. Breakfast time. I figured I'd wait outside her pen till she was done eating.

Jake wandered up, holding a rope in one hand. "Why don't you go on in there with her," he suggested. "Hold that feed out for her. She can eat while you're holding the bucket."

He was right. I was missing an opportunity to offer her a good deal.

I squeezed in between the fence rails and held out the bucket. She backed away from me, her eyes wide and wary. She didn't trust me; she was ready to flee.

I inched over to her, until I ended up just in front of her, and slightly to the side, as close to her neck as her muzzle. She stood still. Still holding the bucket of feed, I took another step. I was now an arm's length away. I held the bucket in my left hand, and I brought my right arm up slowly. *Easy does it.* I touched her, as smoothly and gently as I could, on her neck, near the withers. She jumped. She jumped and landed on my toes. It was as quick as a snake bite.

Damn, that hurt!

I grimaced and bit my tongue. Not a sound escaped my lips. There was a tiny blip in my rhythm as I stepped back and then stepped in again. I offered the bucket again, and this time she ate out of it. I took a deep breath.

Then another. Then another.

And that was all I did with her that day.

I went back again the next day. Clouds covered the sky; the temperature was tepid. I was in a t-shirt.

Every horse has the potential to be wild, and every horse has the potential to be tame. This mare, after six days, was still more bobcat than house cat. I still could not saddle her.

Jake and I discussed her. We agreed that horses learn on their own timeline, and I needed to give the filly, and myself, the time and grace to go slow if we needed to go slow.

"Let's try something different today," Jake said.

"Let's."

Jake disappeared into his little wooden shed and returned with two twelve-foot, lightweight retractable fishing rods. He attached pieces of plastic, about eight inches long, cut from plastic bags, to the ends.

And *voila,* he had the same flags I had watched Pat Parelli use with his colt at Road to the Horse.

I watched Jake artfully steer the filly around the pen, sometimes with both flags behind the filly, sometimes one in front (*way* in front so as not stop her thinking forward), and one behind. He asked her to go, to stop, to turn to the inside, to turn to the outside. The filly, with her four socks, glided along. After a few minutes Jake retracted the flags, exited the round pen, and offered them to me.

The flags had enabled Jake to work on the same things we had been working on a few days before but from a greater distance. This allowed the filly to be farther from him, and to feel freer. The long flags also meant that Jake could be in many places at once without actually moving his feet.

I took one pole in each hand. Then I sliced one through the air and the momentum caused each section to smoothly extend away from me. *Click click, click*—it locked into place. Then I cut the second one through an imaginary foe before me, and it also extended. For their length, they were almost magically lightweight. I grinned. I was a young Jedi with twin light sabers.

I entered the round pen and initially I tried what Jake had been doing, but then I started to experiment. Could I have both flags on one side of the filly? Could I twist my body, so sometimes I was walking forward, and sometimes walking backward, but without changing the direction I was traveling? Could I ask her to trot to me while I jogged backward? I knew that in deep footing the trick was to move my feet in short, quick strides, not long strides, so I didn't trip.

As we waltzed around the pen, the young horse relaxed more and more. Her head lowered, her eyes softened, her tail hung quietly, and the rhythm of her hooves became even. I could have matched them to a metronome. Or a song.

"You Can't Hurry Love," maybe.

"I love this so much," I said as I took the flags behind and above me, away from the filly, and we took a break.

"You're doing awesome."

It *felt* like I was doing awesome. It felt like I could see everything that was happening in space and time. I envisaged what was going to happen next in my mind's eye, like Jack Reacher rehearsing a fight, or like Beth Harmon in *The Queen's Gambit* playing chess on the ceiling—and then I did it. It felt…amazing! The learning was happening so fast it was addictive.

I can't rope. But I can do this! I thought.

I tried to explain it to Sinead later, but I couldn't.

"It was like a band had been playing, and they invited me onstage, and I borrowed someone's guitar, and joined in, and sang, and rocked along to the beat," I said.

"Uh huh," she said, distracted.

"A rockstar!"

"You can't sing," she murmured.

"That's only if you judge singing on quality over enthusiasm."

She gave me a funny look. I didn't mind.

"I can't afford it."

"Mum, you *can* afford it."

"That's what you don't understand. Your brothers don't understand it either. If you watch the cents, the dollars take care of themselves. I'll never understand how your father and I made it work all those years. We had so many adventures. Went to so many horse shows. And on no money."

Frugal begins to describe my mother. Cheap, inconsistent, hypocritical, intelligent, caring, tough, and matriarchal are only the beginning. I love her very much and can't imagine a world without her.

"I'll share a room with you and your brother," she said.

"I can't hear you very well, the reception is bad."

"*What*? We all lived in the same house growing up."

"We did, you're right. We did. And we all shared one bathroom too. This trip is supposed to be fun, though. Why don't you get a room for yourself, and Jordan and I will get a room. I'll pay the difference for you."

"Dad." Brooks pulled at my sleeve.

"A penny saved is a penny earned," said my mother.

"I gotta go. I'll call you later."

"Who was that?" Brooks asked.

"That was Granny. I'm going to see her tomorrow."

"You're leaving…"

"Just for a few days."

"Dad." His lip softened. "Don't go. Who will I catch the blue-bellied lizard with?"

"Brooks, while I'm gone, I do have one piece of advice for you: never listen to your mother."

"By *never* do you mean *always*?"

"Yes, Brooks." I smiled. "Exactly right. In this case, by *never* I do mean *always*."

My own mother, I suspected, was right. One definition of happiness might be spending one percent less than you are making each month, something we hadn't figured out yet. Here I was going on a trip for five days. Spending money; making none.

The trip was to Seattle for "Chicken Camp," and that evening Sinead asked me once again: "I don't understand—what's the end game with this?"

I stared at her. While I understood I was asking a lot of her to watch the kids and run the farm, the trip had been on the books for weeks.

"Where is this going?" Sinead asked.

"This is a work trip," I said. "Research. Training."

She looked at me, suspicious.

"It's not a vacation," I said.

28

I caught the briny smell of the Pacific Ocean. It smelled like Vancouver, where I'd grown up. Home. I heaved on my puffy jacket, then slipped my toque on my head.

I held my arms out to the sides, palms up. I closed my eyes, and tipped my head upward, letting the rain soak my face and hair. A group of airline attendants with umbrellas surged around me, staring.

I schlepped my bag across the road to a restaurant called The 13 Coins. High-backed chairs and Christmas decorations greeted me. Martini glasses shone behind the bar. I took my wet jacket off and approached the table where my mother and my brother Jordan, who had driven down from British Columbia, were lunching with a childhood friend of my mother's—Joan.

"People are the way they are, I meet them there," Joan said to my mother as I sat down. Her statement made me think of how I meet horses. When I step into a round pen with a horse, when I'm at my best, I'm not thinking about his past traumas, or considering our future goals. I'm simply reading how the horse is *right in that moment*.

Horsewoman Mary Kitzmiller, another member of our party, landed an hour later, and we all squeezed into Jordan's little Subaru Crosstrek. We drove into twilight, then into pitch black. The road twisted as it followed Hood Canal, part of the flooded valley known as Puget Sound. Puget Sound is a series of fjords that were chiseled out by glaciers. Its average depth is four hundred and fifty feet, its maximum depth nine hundred and thirty feet—a lot deeper than the waterways around Florida.

To our right was the darkness of a large body of water. Clusters of lights twinkled in the distance. Cottages on the other side, I guessed.

The conversation turned to ways to motivate animals, and Mary offered an observation that surprised me.

"Balance," she said. "It makes them feel more comfortable, and the more you put them in a good balance, the more they like it, and the more they look to you."

Balance as a motivator. I imagined how it felt to be on ice in slick shoes, constantly wanting to grab something, worried about falling, or how it felt to be skiing out of control. Awkward. Unsettling.

"There it is," my mother suddenly said. We turned left over a small wooden bridge and arrived at the Seabeck Conference Center on Seabeck Highway, nestled on the shore of Seabeck Bay.

"What's that?"

"Headlamp," Jordan said as he pulled his toque on, with a light attached to it. "Let's go!" We were already late for dinner, but I raced to get my shorts.

The backroads smelled of fir and cedar and salt. It was inky black, almost wet, and we ran shoulder to shoulder so we could both see the ground from his light. Our footfalls quickly got in sync. We explored a few dead ends on the backroads, then ran into the cedar forest until the path dwindled out. We turned around again and in another few minutes arrived back at the water's edge near the convention center.

Jordan turned his headlamp off. There were no stars. We felt our way down over the rocks until we felt water. *The Pacific.* The skin of the ocean was dark and flat in front of us, even darker than the sky. I heard Jordan adjust his footing on the rocks. In the distance three or four lights twinkled. In the silence we heard the voice of someone arriving home. It always amazed me how clearly sound traveled over quiet water. I felt a seducing pull toward the depths.

I waded in. I glanced to my left; Jordan was right beside me. I took another step into the water. It was chilly-to-the-bone in a way that I always associate with the Pacific Northwest.

I dove under, opening my eyes underwater. *Blackness.* My stomach was firm, my fingers and toes extended, reaching.

Jordan and I were unable to stay in even two minutes. We slipped our shoes back on and jogged back to civilization.

There is something that approaches perfection about the first few days of spending time with someone who is both kith and kin who I have not seen in an extended time. It is like re-reading a much-loved book, a book that reminds me of a favorite place, or time in my life. Like *The Power of One* or *The Time Traveler's Wife.* It's a combination of being absorbed in the moment, while experiencing at the same time a sense of nostalgia or *déjà vu.*

I was reading in bed when Matt arrived. I was on Florida time and struggling to be, as Sinead always told me, "normal." Matt had just flown a direct London to Seattle flight, and his unpacking was labored, as if gravity had unfairly singled him out for a double ration. Meanwhile I peppered him with questions. I hadn't seen him since our cigar at Terra Nova. We chatted until we fell asleep, mid-sentence.

"Chicken Camp" was feeling a lot more like a vacation than I was going to admit to my wife.

The sun, pink as a peach, broke through the mist as Jordan and I finished up four easy miles by headlamp. The shore was wet and rocky. We stood and took in the clean, rippling water, like we had hundreds of times before.

In the distance, Olympic Mountains rose straight up out of the water like swimmers short on air. The side that faced the Pacific was still wild, and one of the wettest places in the world. Soupy mist hid the white mountain tops.

Drops of rainwater slipped and ran off those mountains into the ocean. Those drops turned, when the currents were just right, and were hustled north around Cape Flattery, through the Juan de Fuca Strait, and up into the Strait of Georgia, into the waters that I know best, where the Fraser River runs into the Pacific.

"We have time," I said to Jordan.

"If we're quick."

Three long steps and a dive. The water was a temperature where exhaustion would overtake the average swimmer in an hour; death most likely within three. *Welcome back,* the salty bay said with its embrace.

We held our shoes and sprinted barefoot back to our rooms. I toweled the water off my face and chest, but didn't shower, which left a film of salt on my skin. Like the scent of bread in a bread machine, it reminded me of my boyhood.

"Camp" began at nine in the morning. Lectures were upstairs in the building called "Colman." The actual training was on the ground floor, which I figured must have once been a garage, as it had three sliding garage doors and a concrete floor.

Jordan and I took our seats. We were the last ones to do so.

Dianne Canafax, with shoulder-length chestnut hair and clear oval glasses, was our instructor. "KARE" was printed on her t-shirt, which was short for Kitsap Animal Rescue and Education, the nonprofit that was hosting us. Pat and Vicki, also KARE members, were there to assist with the fowl logistics: feeding, watering, and cleaning up chicken poop. Linda, from Alaska, was there to help as well.

We started with a quick refresher on positive reinforcement, which most of us had a working knowledge of already. I thought about what I knew about clicker training, and what I had learned from Shawna Karrasch.

For the "in-crowd," positive reinforcement was called "R+," which annoyed me sometimes, especially when I caught myself tossing it around in front of someone that was new to the scene.

The idea with R+ is that when there is behavior that we like to see, like a dog sitting, or my son reading, and we give the dog, or Brooks, something nice, like a treat, we will see more of the dog sitting, and more of Brooks reading. They are rewarded for a desirable behavior with something they like, therefore are more likely to repeat that behavior. Simple.

"Clicker training" is *one* training method that uses the principle of R+. It is simply a type, or brand, like Kleenex is to facial tissue. I was familiar with the clicker, which was about the size of a large beetle, and its sound (similar to opening a can of soda), because Shawna had used one and I had practiced prior to her visit to Copperline.

A 2018 NPR "Morning Edition" episode explained how clicker training was adapted to train surgeons in certain skills—for example, how to tie a better knot: "I'll click when your fingers are in the right position," the instructor told them. The surgical student *wanted* to be there, and therefore was intrinsically motivated, seeking the little rush of satisfaction humans get from working at something, facing some adversity, and figuring it out.

With R+, according to some, there is no forcing, no coercion, no *aversion*, nothing that an animal might dislike. But that is not always true. If the only way an animal gets food is by performing, that could easily be called coercion. Which was why, for animals of a higher intelligence, humans (surgeons), chimps, dogs, there was that other motivation to consider. The *want* to learn. The *desire* to understand. The *puzzle*. The *play*! Was it also true for horses? Yup. Or, at least, it could be. In some cases, the understanding of the exercise is an even greater reward than food for a horse. Horses are highly motivated by curiosity, and they dislike inconsistency and confusion. I might even say they hate being confused.

Dianne stood up at the front of the classroom. *Click*, came the sound from her clicker.

We all looked at her.

"You also have to use negative reinforcement sometimes," she said. "I've never been able to say I've trained an animal with one hundred percent R+. Maybe because I'm just not good enough."

Dianne had been a dog trainer for twenty-five years. She had sixteen years of shelter experience. She was Karen Pryor Academy (KPS) certified, but she wasn't about to get on a high horse, so to speak, about how she trained animals.

No fundamentalists here.

"When it comes to Chicken Camp, I started puppy doggin' Terry Ryan twenty years ago," she went on. "Terry is…. Who knows who Terry is?"

I raised my hand. I looked around. I was the only one.

"Didn't you read the handout?" I whispered to Matt. He shook his head.

"Terry is a professional trainer and author and speaker," Dianne said, absently passing the clicker from one hand to the other. "She has run Chicken Camps for years. I've done forty Chicken Camps with her. She still does virtual ones, but she donated her gear to KARE, and she has given me permission to run them going forward.

This is my first one without her." Dianne paused and smiled. "Terry gave me some advice last night: be kind, but be honest."

She put her fingers to her laptop on the long table in front of her, and a slide appeared on the large drop-down screen at the front of the room: *ETHOLOGY*.

We all looked at it.

"In order to train chickens, you need to understand chickens," Dianne said. "That's ethology." She pressed a button on her laptop again. *WHY CHICKENS?* appeared on the screen. "With chickens, if they aren't doing something, *we* are the reason. *We* haven't made it achievable." Dianne pressed the button and *ETHOLOGY* appeared again; she apologized, and pressed repeatedly until she found the correct slide.

"I am a little nervous," she admitted, and I liked her for that. "With chickens," she continued, "we need to leave our ego at the door. What we learn with chickens we can apply to any animal. And remember, it's not about the end result. In the big picture, it doesn't matter what the chickens can do. It's about *your* learning."

Dianne led us through some facts about chickens:

- They can see colors.
- They have poor night vision.
- They can't see directly in front of them. But they *can* if they look sideways or bob their heads, which is why they are constantly ducking and bobbing, like a needle on a sewing machine.
- They like shiny things.

"If you have on shiny dangling earrings," Dianne said, "I would suggest you put those away. I turn my rings backward. Also, your eyes can be shiny, so maybe keep the chickens away from your face."

I imagined a hen pecking out someone's eyeball. A downer for Chicken Camp for sure.

We learned that all fowl were not created equal. Ours were to be white-and-brown Leghorns, originally from Italy. ("Good layers," Jordan, a farmer, told me later.)

"They are flighty and curious," said Dianne. "Leghorns are motivated, like Border Collies. They are much better than say, Buff Orpingtons. Buff Orpingtons are loving, but sedate. They don't offer much in terms of behavior. I'm looking for an active bird. Not a mellow one!"

I looked around the room. Five women, three men. One instructor at the front. Four white plastic tables. Two people per table, all facing forward, arranged like many other lecture halls around the world. Three assistants arranged in a group to the side, chatting quietly. I looked at the window, and the thermometer just outside it. I could see it was thirty-eight degrees Fahrenheit. Five days of damp cold. Five days away from the kids, and Sinead, and the farm. Was this chicken adventure really going to help me with colt starting? Or was it one big waste of time, as my wife had seemed to suspect it might be? Dianne flipped through slide after slide after slide.

As we reached the end of the lecture hour, we prepared to go downstairs to begin chicken training.

"Sessions are thirty seconds," Dianne explained. "You will have a partner who will be your coach and 'chicken wrangler.' As a coach, you tell your partner what you liked about the training effort. As a wrangler..." She looked at us. "...as a chicken wrangler, you will need to be pretty agile. You will need to pay attention! Get the chicken from the cage, and bring her to the table. Most of the chickens are comfortable on the table and are not afraid of the clicker. *But* we never know the behavior we are going to start with."

Matt raised his hand. "Why thirty seconds?" he asked.

"Thirty seconds is a long time in chicken time. Then they need a break. They will need to drink a lot as well. Also, the more they are trained, the more they 'fill up.' Each learner has different abilities, and different attention spans."

"So, some chickens can do more than thirty seconds?"

"Thirty seconds is not a hard rule," Dianne said patiently. "Yes, some chickens can handle more. It just makes sense for the way the class is set up."

Her last slide stayed up on the screen as we stood to head downstairs. It held a quote: *Advanced training is just the basics done well.* It was attributed to Ken Ramirez.

I knew who he was, too.

Hundreds of elephants migrate each year from Zambia up to Tanzania. And each year they pass through the corner of the Democratic Republic of the Congo, where the poaching laws aren't as strict as they are elsewhere. Fifty to seventy elephants are slaughtered there each year, just in one short stretch of country.

Ken Ramirez, a noted biologist, animal behaviorist, and trainer, was brought in to see if he could teach the elephants a new migration route that avoided that one area. He first visited the route in June 2017 to create a plan, and his team fell under heavy machine gun fire, their vehicles upended by a rocket launcher. His crew, airlifted to safety, survived the attack, and Ramirez vowed to continue with the plan to help the elephants.

In 2018, he and his team dug three hundred and twenty-five waterholes along a new route, each one within sight of the last, some of them in dense clusters. Each year that followed, they reduced the number. By 2023, there were just over a hundred waterholes, some four or five miles apart. It was an expensive project, and one that required the support of more than a few organizations and governments, so they were given ten years to complete their task. Ramirez had to hurry, but he knew if he reduced the number of waterholes too quickly, they risked the elephants returning to their old migration route.

Ramirez and his team were using what's called "Remote Training." As Ramirez explained on YouTube: "Reinforcers are delivered in creative ways that appear to come from the natural environment. This type of training is increasingly being employed in wildlife-conservation projects to prevent habituation or any contact whatsoever with humans. This technique also has increasing applications in pet management to deal with separation anxiety and other behavioral challenges while the pet is alone at home."

When Ramirez began the project, he wondered, "How can a guy train three hundred and seventy-five elephants?" But then he realized: "I don't need to train *all* of them, just the 'matriarch.'"

The matriarch. The one who remembered the migration routes, where the waterholes were, where the best grazing was.

The young have energy and ideas, but wisdom is hard won.

There were two short flights of stairs, with a landing midway that led to a hall with bathrooms. We all trooped down to the ground floor, excited for our first session.

"How do we determine who wins and who loses?" someone joked.

"I'm going to have trouble with this group, aren't I?" Dianne said with a laugh.

We drew cards for partners. I drew Mary Kitzmiller.

"Let's talk about chicken handling," Dianne announced. "Carry them by the wing joints. Cradle them like a football. Slide them on the table—don't drop them. Be smooth! Be decisive! If they are flapping their wings, they are anxious. We don't want that. If a hen freezes, gapes, scratches her beak, scratches the table, or wanders off, she might be stressed."

We were learning how to "read" a chicken. I loved this part. I knew right away that no matter how stupendous a trainer was in a lab, how fantastic her thesis, how many books she had read, how many lessons she had taken, how many PhDs she'd collected—it was all for nothing if she couldn't read her chicken. In theory, theory was great…

Then Dianne warned us: "If a chicken flies off a table, yell, 'Chicken down!' Then everyone should pick up their chicken. Do *not* chase the downed bird! Let the assistants take over."

Mary set up her video camera, so she could review our training sessions later. We huddled and decided she would train first, making me chicken wrangler first. Mary prepared the table for her hen. She cleared off everything—books, pens, crumbs…all might be distracting to a chicken.

I'd handled my fair share of chickens and felt confident as I reached into the enclosure and put my hands around a hen. Her cluck was eloquent and her feathers soft. I lifted her. She was light, weighing less than my MacBook. I carried her close, her shoulder against my rib cage, then eased her onto the table.

"The first exercise to practice is clicking and treating," Dianne said.

Click. Mary immediately offered the bowl of cracked corn. *Click*—corn. *Click*—corn. *Click*—more corn. For thirty seconds.

The sound of the click was mechanical and consistent. It was also satisfying, like a bite of a Kit-Kat or a camera shutter opening and closing. The click carried none of the emotional connotations of "Good!" Or "Great!" Or "Almost!" The click was sincere. In educated hands, it was honest as a typewriter, and as accurate as a scalpel. The Leghorns were quick, but the click was too.

It was an open room with a bunch of tables and clicking everywhere, but the tables were far enough apart (five or six feet) that our clicks were noticeably louder to our chickens than our neighbors', and therefore distinct. I also suspected, given their responses, that our chickens were intelligent enough to discern that what was happening close to them was more relevant than the sounds and movements that were farther away.

For thirty seconds, Mary rewarded anything she saw. Any microbehavior, like a head tilt or an eye shift. After thirty seconds, I picked up the chicken and we took a break, discussed how it went, and tried again.

"Good," Dianne encouraged.

"*Good* doesn't cut it with me," I whispered to Mary.

Mary smiled, then nodded seriously. "We want to be *great* chicken trainers!"

"Remember, the click is a *promise* that you will feed," one of the assistants told us. "The click is a dopamine release. Think of slot machines, think of the high people get."

Is a slot-machine-high really what we want? I wondered. *Do we want our hens to feel like zombie-eyed retirees in Vegas?*

Mary trained her chicken. Four times thirty seconds, with discussion and coaching in between. Then I trained mine. And then we trooped back upstairs to give the chickens a break.

The cards fell like rain drops. Three of spades. Five of clubs. Jack of clubs. Ace of spades.

I watched Mary drop each one. I clicked only when black cards hit the table. I forgot about the other tables. I saw only the cards. My fingers cradled the clicker, and the hand muscles were taut. I was in the zone.

Click. Click. Click. I grinned as my timing improved.

"Now, switch to red," Dianne called. My focus changed from clubs and spades to hearts and diamonds.

Queen of hearts—*click!* Five of spades. *Silence.* Seven of diamonds—*click.* I was doing well, and it was satisfying.

"Clicking on red or black, that's called the 'criteria.' I'll keep changing it rapidly throughout the session," Dianne explained. "Black," she called. Then, "Red," she called again.

My focus was complete; the cards came so fast, I had no time to think about anything else.

Dianne then explained the concept of *rate of reinforcement,* which we then started to call "R-O-R."

"How *often* is the animal reinforced?" Dianne asked. "If the ROR is too high, time to move on to the next thing. If it is too low, you need to break the behavior down more."

In other words, when we are constantly being told, "Good job!" things are too easy. When we aren't getting any "Good jobs," we might get frustrated, we might get angry, we might give up. Different species, and different individuals, will do better with different rates of reinforcement.

"For your hen, you want seven to twelve reinforcements in a thirty-second session," Dianne explained. I wondered what rate horses learned best with. I wondered what rate kids did best with. I wondered what rate *I* did best with. "Some reminders before we head back downstairs: Mistakes have no consequences. The reinforcer must be something the animal will work for. (It's best if they are small and quickly consumed.) And last, reinforcers are situational."

Bad behaviors had no consequences—that was one of the beautiful principles of this kind of work. Ignore what we don't want, reward what we do.

If you can't say something nice, don't say anything at all.

"Coffee?"

"Please." Linda from Alaska nodded.

"There is an acronym for how to improve groundwork," I explained to Linda as I poured two coffees from the spouted pot next to the sink. We were on a break. Every hour or so we had a coffee break, whether we wanted it or not. It was to keep us fresh—and it was working. I was itching to get back to the chickens.

"SADDLES," I said. "*Speed*—not just fast, but the speed you *want to go*. *Accuracy*—if you want to be on *this* track, *that* track isn't good enough. *Distance*—how far away can you be, and still have the animal respond? *Duration*—can you trot six circles or only two? *Lightness*—do you have to bribe, coerce, pull, or kick, or do they respond to a light feel, like a dancer? Milk?"

"Please."

"*Expression*—and do they respond with a pleasant expression? Eager eyes. Focused ears. *Sequences*—can we connect a few behaviors? Circle, figure eight, draw to me, jump the barrel."

I handed her the coffee. We raised the mugs towards each other. I took a sip, let her process.

"What about 'Generalization'?" Linda asked. "Can you do the same thing in new places or with new things?"

"That's a good one!"

"And 'Distractions?' Can you do it with all kinds of other stuff going on?"

Geez, I thought. *She's good.* I was going to have to think of a new acronym.

"Here are a few ways to get the behavior we want." Dianne put up a new slide:

- *Capturing.*
- *Luring.*
- *Targeting.*
- *Shaping.*

"Luring can help them find what you want them to find," Dianne explained, "but it can also take away their ability to think. Terry Ryan's rule is three lures, no more, for a particular session."

Horses trainers sometimes talk about using food as either a reward or a bribe. Usually, they mean a *reward* is something unexpected at the end, while a *bribe* is something promised beforehand. The problem for the newbie, the layperson, or the semanticist is that there are so many words: *bribe, bait, lure, reinforce, encourage, treat, reward*. Some of the words are part of the scientific vocabulary, and some are just words we apply willy-nilly. Even trained, credentialed animal behaviorists, with letters after their names, don't use these words consistently.

"For example," Dianne continued. "Put corn on the red poker chip. It can help them find it, but it may also mean they aren't looking for the red chip, they are just looking for the grain. You need to fade it out pretty fast."

"Why three lures?" Matt asked. "Why not two or four?"

"This is a tough group. You're really pushing me. All I'll say is this: You get three trainers in a room. The only thing two of them are going to agree on is what the third is doing wrong."

We all laughed.

EFFECTIVE SHAPING was now up on the screen.

"Decide what you are looking for," Dianne said. "That's called 'choosing the criteria.' If your chicken gets it, you can 'raise the criteria.' If they are struggling, you need to 'split the criteria.' If they continue to have trouble, you break it down into smaller steps. And then smaller steps."

We hustled downstairs again, eager to train. Dianne put a red poker chip in the middle of a table, then asked for a hen to be freed in front of the chip. As soon as her feet hit the table, the chicken immediately tilted her head a quarter inch toward the chip. *Click!* Then Dianne held out the cup with the corn in it. The hen pecked. Dianne removed the corn and held it behind her back. The hen looked around… left, right, quickly, abruptly, then glanced at the disc again. *Click!* Corn.

"Dianne has a phenomenal read on that chicken," Mary whispered.

The hen lowered her head. *Click!* Corn.

The hen almost touched it. *Click!* Corn.

Then the hen pecked it. *Click!* Corn.

She pecked it again. *Click!* Corn.

"Day One, and I already feel like I've gotten my money's worth," my mother piped up.

"I just bought a coffee from the little shop across the road," Matt said. He cradled the cup close to his chest, like a baby. The morning was both brighter and colder than the day before. We stood on the front steps and looked at the frost on the evergreens. I took a deep breath of that cold, wet, fresh air I had grown up on.

"What does Hanna think about all this?"

Matt laughed. "What does Sinead think?"

"How's the coffee?"

I knew Matt and Hanna well enough to know that Hanna was

probably feeling the same way as Sinead. Trying to be supportive, but also not able to help feeling slightly resentful that their partners were off playing with birds, while they were at home managing staff, riding horses, paying bills, making money, and just doing hundreds of other things that running a small business entailed.

Matt offered me a sip.

I put my own coffee down and tried his. "That goes down good."

"The coffee lady asked what I was doing in Seabeck."

"Did you tell her we are training chickens?"

"I did. Then she asked if I could come train her chicken not to be a bitch."

I snorted into my mug.

"And I bought a cookie," Matt said. "I feel guilty when I go into places like that. Guilty when I only buy a drip coffee. I feel like I need to buy something else."

"You're the opposite of my mother," I said, because she had just wandered up. "My mum would have no problem ordering the drip coffee, arguing with them about the size, mentioning the exorbitant cost, getting them to transfer it to her to-go mug, and then asking for any leftover food scraps for the chickens."

"Good morning, Jen," Matt said.

"You two look like you're up to no good."

"I feel like I'm at camp." I grinned.

"Me too," said Matt.

Jordan asked, "How do you use this with humans?"

"I use it a lot," Dianne said. "When I am training an animal, I constantly ask myself: *How can I break this down?* So when I train a human, if they are not getting the task, I ask myself: *How can I break this down?* Think about how we developed the timing for this exercise. If anyone has trouble, we can go back to a 'pen-chicken.'"

The "pen-chicken" was one person holding a pen as if it was a chicken's beak, and "pecking" it at the ground or the poker chip. This allowed us to practice "clicking" without involving a live hen.

"It's the same with horses," I said. "Some of the best riding and training 'Aha! moments' I've had have been without horses."

Making mistakes as we learned was inevitable, and if we could make those mistakes *without* the horses (or chickens) in the picture, so much the better.

"The whole concept reminds me of a book I read once," my mother said. "It was called *The One-Minute Manager.* Catch 'em doing something right—*that's* what we are trying to do here."

"I don't think that concept originated with that book," I pointed out.

"Well, maybe not," she admitted. "But I didn't say it did."

I nodded. "You are right," I admitted.

She grinned. "Say that again," she insisted.

"That again," I replied.

Most of the exercises we would be teaching the chickens were similar to those in dog agility. That day, we were asking our chickens to move through a plastic tunnel about a foot high and half a foot wide, with a curved top.

"What is the cue we use to ask them to go through the tunnel?" Matt asked.

"Simply the presence of the tunnel is the cue," explained Dianne. "If your hen is on the table, and the tunnel is there, they should go through the tunnel."

"Could you add in a cue later?" Matt asked.

"When you're teaching the weave to dogs," my mother piped up, "you teach the whole thing *before* you give it a vocal cue."

"Exactly." Dianne nodded. "We add in the cue for the final behavior."

The idea of introducing the cue *only once the final behavior was learned* was not something I was familiar with. My mind immediately started imagining examples—not just one or two, but five or six. I pictured when that idea would be helpful, and when it might not, and not just with horses. I imagined how it might apply to dogs, or chickens, or kids.

"Now, in order to teach the tunnel, are you going to use *luring*, or are you going to use *capturing*?" Dianne asked us.

Obviously *luring* chickens into the tunnel would be the easiest way to get started (like asking my son to follow a bowl of ice cream into the bath), but then…then the problem is they are not *thinking* about the tunnel. It would be like driving somewhere while only following the instructions from the GPS. Maybe it would be better to allow my hen a little longer to explore, and then when…*if*…she went through the tunnel, to reward her. That might take a little longer, but long term, it would pay off. It was what was called *capturing*. I'd set up a situation where my hen was *likely* to do something, and then I'd reward her when she did it.

Of course, more than likely, my chicken would *not* go through the tunnel the first time. That was where *shaping* came in. In shaping we were looking for tiny improvements, like building a house one brick at a time, and like when Dianne had demonstrated teaching the hen to peck the poker chip.

In shaping, the smaller the bricks, the easier it is to build the "house," and the faster the progress. Big bricks are harder to move. Big bricks try to get the chicken all the way into the tunnel the first time. They can be exhausting and frustrating. Smaller bricks and "This is easy!" thinks the chicken. When the hen struggles, if the ROR is not high enough, we can split the behavior into smaller pieces, smaller bricks.

"Be a splitter, not a lumper," said Dianne. Then, "Click for action. Feed for position," she reminded us, taking off her glasses and wiping her eyes.

Clicking for action meant marking the behavior I wanted with a click, *right* when it happened. *Feeding for position* meant following up with the corn *where I wanted my hen to be the next time*. For example, if I wanted her closer to the tunnel, I'd give a click when she glanced at the tunnel, but then offer the grain at the entrance to the tunnel. If I offered the grain behind her, or in another direction, she would start to anticipate turning *away* from the tunnel rather than *toward* it.

I thought about how that might apply to horses. "Feeding for position" might mean I take a break after Sam jumps well (the break or rest being the motivator in this case). But the second part of the question was then: *Where* should we take the break? By the in-gate or away from it? Near other horses, or away from them? If we always rested *near* other horses, we increased the draw to them. If we took the break by ourselves, we might end up with a horse that was more comfortable by himself. When I really thought about it, the concept, like most concepts, had lots of intricacies and exceptions, which is why it is impossible to learn animal training from reading memes, and soundbites on social media. Another example: When I am done a round pen training session for the day, do I take the saddle off *facing* the barn, or in the middle of the pen, facing *away* from the barn?

Both choices involve positive reinforcement, but the details of the application could have—would have—consequences, good or bad.

All our chickens learned to go through the tunnel.

It was still dark, but I was wide awake, unreasonably anxious. I knocked on Jordan's door.

"Jordan, let's go for a quick run. I need to blow off some steam."

Jordan rolled out of bed, said nothing, grabbed his shorts, laced up his runners. We crossed the bridge, which was covered with a thin film of ice, then opened up our stride and headed west. After half a mile, we hooked a right up a winding road. There was the occasional house, but it was mostly woods on either side of us. Ahead we saw a deer, alert and still; she bolted into the trees as we got closer.

"I've been playing bow-and-arrow tag with the kids at the farm," Jordan said. "Half the kids are hunters, and half the kids are deer."

We were running uphill at that point, and he was in better shape than I was, so I just panted and looked at him questioningly.

"The arrows are soft-tipped," he explained. "And after playing bow-and-arrow tag I ask the kids, 'Would you rather be hunted by a gun or by an arrow?'"

Jordan organized farm camps for kids. He had a rare talent for setting up games and scenarios to get kids thinking.

"Do the farm kids actually participate in slaughtering anything?" I asked.

"No. But I've killed over a thousand chickens by now," he said in a quiet voice. "It gets easier. I'm not sure if that's good or not."

Jordan and I crested the hill and started down. It was a relief. I had been struggling to keep up.

"And I've been wondering, is it better to let Mera see death or not?"

Mera was his daughter. "How old is she?"

"Three."

We turned a corner, and I sped up a little so I could run shoulder to shoulder with my brother. "Maybe wait a bit."

"But at some point, there is still that question. When does she learn that meat comes from animals? I don't want her to think meat comes from a package in an air-conditioned store for a few dollars."

"What do you teach the kids on the farm?"

"The goal on the farm is *not* to give an answer. And certainly not *my* answer. The goal is to have the kids *think* about food, to be thoughtful, to question."

And that was it.

That was my epiphany. The answer to one of my biggest fears.

I didn't need to have the answers to all my ethical questions about horses. I didn't need to teach people a method. I didn't need to be able to say, "Train with positive reinforcement" or "Train with negative reinforcement" or "Do things *this* way" or "Do things *that* way." I had been looking for answers as if I would eventually find a single truth, when all along, just to be asking the questions, and to be surrounded by people asking questions, and to encourage others to ask questions, *that* could be my path forward.

Maybe there was no *one* answer. No definitive truth. How we trained horses, and *if* we should train horses, could only partially be answered by science. The rest of it needed to be answered by our own morality, our own ethics, our own philosophies.

Maybe what I could do with horses was what Jordan was doing with his farm: help people figure out *what questions to ask*. Asking questions and searching for answers, that was our way to explore.

Maybe Matt was right. Maybe I was an explorer, because every day I wanted to explore what was possible with horses. I wanted to question what was right. I wanted to ask questions no one had asked before. And I wanted to know how far we could go.

We were running in a steady rhythm when I offered, "When it comes to influencing people and the choices they make, I doubt we will change the top ten percent. They have been doing what they do a long time, and they are set in their ways. And we can't change the bottom ten percent that doesn't know what they are doing, because they aren't searching for answers. But I believe that most people, the eighty percent in the middle, want to do the right thing, and they just might listen to the right person. That's who we are trying to reach when we teach."

"Eighty percent, eh?" Jordan ran ahead of me. "Did you know sixty-three percent of statistics are misleading?"

I caught up. "And fifty-eight percent are taken out of context."

Jordan sped up again. "Forty-eight percent are generated by bots."

I tried to catch up, but couldn't. I managed to stay just on his heels. "And seventy-eight percent," I puffed, "are made up on the spot."

Mary and I warmed up by simulating with a "pen-chicken," and I was pathetically late on my timing three or four times.

It took me a moment to realize what was going on. Two of the camp attendees had left that morning, early, before camp was over. My mind was distracted by it, anxious that maybe they had not had a good time, anxious that Dianne would be insulted.

Idiot, I told myself. *Focus!*

I slowly settled into the day and gradually found my rhythm.

"You know what I love about this camp," said Mary out of the blue. "It's really about the journey, not the end. It doesn't matter at all if these chickens are traincd. It's about what we learn. It's really, purely, about getting better."

"Maybe we should have chicken competitions," I joked.

"Road to the Chicken!" Matt said dramatically.

"One hundred grand to the best chicken trainer," I said. "We could have a dog trainer, a horse trainer, a dolphin trainer, and a football coach, all competing against each other."

"Sponsored by Red Bull," added Jordan.

"I can see it now," my mother said.

Dianne put nine dots up on the screen in the front of the room. They created a square with a single dot in the middle.

"I've started training my *lateral thinking*," she said. "I really struggle with it. I think my struggle originates in my childhood. I was taught not to question; to follow direction. Let's try this exercise: See if you can join all the dots with only four straight lines, and with all the lines connected."

I gazed at the screen. My mind was blank. Once again I told myself to focus.

"You will need to think outside the box," Dianne said.

Jordan, at the table in front of us, was the first to talk. "I've got five ways," he quietly announced.

Dianne put her hands out, palms down, and leaned toward him. "I bow down," she said. "Now see if you can do it with three lines."

Creative problem-solving forces people to break away from their usual patterns of thought. Dianne's exercise was illustrating how difficult it could be, and with animal training, approaching problems in unique ways could be a superpower.

For most of us in the room, Chicken Camp itself was an exercise in lateral thinking. Most of us did not use clicker training at home. Many of us did not even use positive reinforcement training at home—we relied on negative reinforcement. Being in Seabeck was our attempt to find new ways to connect the dots.

We also all wanted to better understand how positive reinforcement affected us and our animals. Clicker training and giving treats was associated with dopamine release. Was that a good thing? Or was it rewarding with the wrong kind of pleasure, like encouraging someone to be addicted to drugs?

We set up a video call with Dr. Theo Jankowski, a school-hood chum of Jordan's who worked for the British Columbia Centre on Substance Abuse. We mirrored the call on the large screen in the upstairs classroom so Dr. Theo's face appeared in front of us, twenty times life-size.

"I'm an internal medicine doctor in Victoria," Dr. Theo said. "I've been here five years. I primarily deal with adult humans. It's interesting studying the physiology and also working in practice. We think about that day-to-day, because the actual practice of providing care is far removed from the biology. In fact, a lot of our substance abuse policies are more influenced by politics than by science."

Matt held a toy chicken in front of the computer camera. "While you are saving lives," he said, "we are playing with chickens."

None of us knew exactly how to ask the question we wanted, which was, essentially: Is there a downside to clicker training chickens, or horses, or any other animals?

"You're talking about using *pleasure* and *happiness* and how those two things are experienced," Dr. Theo said. "Yes, if we purely release dopamine, and we continue to stimulate dopamine pathways, we dull them, and it does *not* lead to long-term happiness. The thing to avoid is the pathological pursuit of pleasure *despite* harmful effects. If you partake in an activity that is pleasurable but has negative consequences, and you continue to participate, that qualifies as an addiction. But you also need to look at the bigger picture. By some definitions, for example, I would meet the criteria for having a 'running addiction.'"

"So…is dopamine bad?" I asked.

"Yes…and no. It is so nuanced. That we should 'not seek pleasure' is the wrong message to take away from this conversation. We should all be seeking pleasure. But in your body, everything is striving to be in balance. I think when it comes to the dopamine pathway, especially through substances, we are overusing one pathway. What can happen is we can't feel normal without the chronic stimulation of that pathway. It's an unsustainable way of living."

"What about adrenaline?" Matt asked, moving to a different hormone. "A common thing I hear is we need to longe horses, run them, to get adrenaline out of their system. Do we have to do that?"

"I don't know anything about horses," Dr. Theo said, "but it boils down to a stress response. When fearful, the heart rate goes up. Adrenaline enters the body. The question is not so much how you make it go away, but how you *turn off the production*."

I nodded. That made sense. I imagined a horse that was worried in a new place, and someone longeing him to help him calm down. Yes, he would get tired eventually, but it did not solve the problem of what created the fear for him in the first place.

"Adrenaline is not a long-lived hormone," he said. "It lasts a few minutes at best."

"Is there an amount of stress that could be beneficial?" I asked.

"For sure. On one hand, anxiety and stress will get in the way of learning. It will become too distracting. But apathy, disinterest, and no stress at all will not help someone learn either. Whether stress can be helpful also depends what you are going to be learning. Memorizing or writing a story might require one mindset, while learning to waterski might require a different one. Rather than thinking about stress it might help to think about *engagement.* And *trust.*"

Someone asked Dianne, "What are your fears as a trainer?"

"That I will set up a situation for fear or frustration. That I have no wisdom."

I could relate to that.

Day Four. Our last day of Chicken Camp. We learned why cues are important, what makes a good cue, when to add a cue, and how to layer in a new cue.

We learned about "poisoned cues," when a cue has been associated with something aversive and begins to cause anxiety or fear.

A cue is just like how it sounds. It *cues* something.

A cue could be simple and mechanical, like a red light means stop, and a green light means go. Cues could also be more fluid, like a conversation with a friend. We ask, we listen to her response. Did we ask the right amount? Did we ask too much? Does she understand us?

With horses, that conversation, that back and forth, is key. Listening is as important as talking. Like throwing a pass and catching it.

Matt, of course, had a question. "What about the 'energetic space'?"

I'd once cringed when people talked about energy, but now I embraced it. It all came down to how I thought about it.

Dianne was easy to read. *What are you talking about?* her eyes said.

"There was a study where, after being in the desert for a few days, people's awareness of their surroundings increased from five feet to fifty feet," Matt said.

"What are you asking?"

"I'm saying, being in the 'energetic space' feels like another way of working with an animal."

"Look at Clever Hans," someone offered.

Clever Hans had been a horse in the early 1900s that could seemingly add, subtract, multiply, divide, work with fractions. He could read, tell Saturday from Sunday, June from July, and had an ear for music (he knew a "C" from "D").

Although Hans' trainer had not realized it, his horse had learned to read him. Learned to read what would excite him, and what would disappoint him—like a poker player that zeroes in on another player's tells.

"Clever Hans' owner was cueing," said Dianne. "Using energy, reading energy, that is cueing."

"Like teaching a horse to back up just by bringing your intention up," said Mary from her seat. "When done well, you feel like you can move your horse just by thinking. But, of course, you aren't only thinking, there are tiny changes in your body language that your horse is picking up."

"When I met Fred Pignon," said Matt, referencing a liberty trainer from Southern France, one of the best in the world, "he changed my ways. A lot of what we do in the horse world comes from the military. Drills, really. Work. Pretty much the opposite of play. But of course, the military is about keeping order. Having control. Being efficient. We should be playing. We should be artists. Like Fred Pignon."

Matt was on a real roll. He appreciated and understood the clicker training we were doing, but his soul cried out for artistry.

"The artist reinvents order. Breaks order. When you are learning, it is mechanical. If you are dancing, you learn, 'This is a dance step.' But in order to find the poetic, you need to leave that. The real artistry is in the energy."

I looked at Matt. "I don't think anyone disagrees with you," I offered. "It's like you just said about learning the dance steps. Look at most painters. Picasso had a foundation and a knowledge of the basics before he became the artist he eventually became."

"You have to know the rules to break the rules," someone else said.

"Exactly," I said. "That's why I'm here. Can I learn the rules?"

"Yes," replied Matt. "And at Road to the Horse, if you know all the rules, you can break them. You can take this trade and make art."

I smiled but shook my head. *No.* That was pressure I didn't need. I really just wanted to see if I could start a horse well. Smoothly. Without annoying him too much, and without embarrassing myself too much. If I could do that, I'd be content.

The final day finished with each of us presenting what our chickens had learned after four days. Mine could go through a tunnel, climb and descend an A-frame, and then knock a pyramid of twenty-one red solo cups off the table.

I flew home overnight, and then landed, stumbling bleary-eyed out of the Orlando airport. I was immediately bombarded with the heavy smell of the tropics. On the drive home, Florida's Turnpike to I-75, I listened to country music. Garth Brooks. Dolly Parton. And I read the billboards. Personal injury lawyers. Vasectomies. Machine guns.

29

In January of 2014, with sand between our toes, Sinead pressed her lips against mine. They tasted of salt and champagne. Fifty people, our family and friends, clapped and cheered.

In April of that year I flew to Paso Robles, California, for the "Horsemen's Re-Union." I stayed with Eamon, my father-in-law.

The premise of the Horsemen's Re-Union was simple: forty un-started horses, and twenty of the best colt starters in the world. The trainers would work for five days in a collaborative fashion to start the forty horses. A paying public would watch, and at the end, the horses would be auctioned off.

Jonathan Field was one of the colt starters. When he was on a break, I ran over to see how it was going.

"I'm here because I want to learn," Jonathan said. "I teach a lot of clinics every year, and it's important to make time for things like…" Jonathan broke off, looking over my shoulder toward a commotion at the end of the arena.

"Let's go," he said. I jogged to catch up.

In the far round pen stood a man and a horse. The man was maybe in his mid-sixties, but it was difficult to tell because white hair sprouted from his cheeks, chin, and neck, like a hermit. Or a sage. He wore loose comfortable-looking clothing. Around his waist was a brown-and-red sash.

And he was barefoot.

The man held his head high. He walked elegantly towards a short-legged, skittish bay. The man's limbs moved gracefully, like those of an antelope.

Jonathan leaned on the fence. "Let's watch," he said, without taking his eyes off the man.

I studied the trainer more closely. He wore small St. Nick spectacles and moved with rhythm and self-assurance. He stepped closer to the horse so his hip touched the horse's shoulder. Then he wrapped a leg around the horse's front legs—inside one, outside the other, like a snake. Then he took it back, and he placed his other foot up on the withers of the horse.

Jonathan and I watched the entire session, in silence.

Afterward I sought the bearded barefoot man out. His name was Oscar Scarpati, and his son Cristo, also a horseman, was with him. They were from Argentina, and they had a book for sale. I bought it and read it on the flight home.

Then I hardly thought about Oscar and Cristo for almost ten years.

When I was invited to Road to the Horse and I was making a list of how I wanted to prepare, and who I wanted to train with, I remembered them.

*But Argentina…*I thought. *How could I pull that off?*

One morning in January I woke up in a bad mood. Although I had been anxious every day from the moment I had been invited to Road to the Horse, I had managed to keep it under control enough that I could still go about my daily business, teach clinics, play with my kids. But that Tuesday, the second Tuesday in January, my mood darkened as soon as my eyes opened.

The trip I had planned for Texas was falling through. There were a number of people in Texas I wanted to meet, and I had built a story in my mind about how important it was to my preparation.

One of those people was Chris Cox, the only four-time winner of Road to the Horse. *He is the key,* I told myself.

The last time I'd tried to get hold of him, someone on his staff had told me to buy his DVDs.

After sulking for a few hours, I pulled myself together. I would try one more time. I had finally gotten his personal number from a friend of a friend, so I gave Chris a call.

He answered on the first try. His voice was soft and firm, with a vibrant energy and confidence behind it. The voice of someone who was great at what he did, knew it, but didn't need to flaunt it.

I explained that I wanted to come train with him for a few days.

"I'm not sure I can help you," Chris replied, matter-of-factly. "I don't know you. I don't know your style or what you need to work on. I don't know if I can help you in a day or two. When I helped Dan James, he came out for two weeks. A lot of stuff goes on mentally. And I'm the middle of showing season right now."

I told him I understood. I asked a few questions, trying to keep him on the phone. *Maybe,* I thought, *maybe if he gets to know me a little bit…*

The conversation came around to where I lived. I told him Ocala, although that wasn't totally true, as we lived in Citra, north of Ocala. But Ocala was the bigger town, and one that most horse people knew.

"I used to live there," he told me. "By Classic Mile. That was twenty-five, maybe twenty-six years ago. I'm teaching a clinic just south of Ocala, Lady Lake. I think they have cuttings there. End of January."

"I've just ordered your DVDs on starting horses," I noted with a glimmer of hope.

"That stuff is old. I purposefully haven't put new stuff out there. I haven't done colt-starting clinics in twelve years. Because the people that show up can't ride a saddle horse, so I end up starting twenty-five horses. Defeats the purpose."

I appreciated the honesty.

"Well, thank you. I appreciate your time. I'm just trying to do the best I can to get ready," I said. "I'm trying to read, and watch. Trying to find horses to start. I'll be doing the Martin Black clinic."

"Well, then, do me a favor," Chris said. "When you see Martin, kick him in the nuts for me."

"Sure," I said, lying. There was absolutely zero chance I would do that.

We hung up. My mood was not much brighter. But I made up my mind to look up that clinic that he would be teaching in Florida at the cutting horse place.

I hadn't started any horses in a few weeks. I had forgotten how to cinch up a Western saddle. I didn't even have a Western saddle of my own yet. I was still borrowing Jake's.

Like Texas, the trip I had planned for Argentina had fallen through. I couldn't find dates that worked for the Scarpatis as well as for us. Even without those two big trips, there was a lot on the calendar: riding, lessons, clinics, shows, writing, kids, barn chores. In any spare second I watched films or read books on colt starting, like I was desperately cramming for a final exam. It had the combined effect of me not being totally present with Sinead at the end of the day.

I wasn't present for the horses all the time either.

A friend of mine, visiting from Costa Rica, said to me: "Americans. Everything is so fast."

He was talking about me. About how I was living my life. I immediately knew what he was talking about.

I didn't mention I was Canadian.

30

"There's Buck!" I pointed excitedly at the silhouette of a tall, thin man in a cowboy hat. We cruised closer. "Nope," I acknowledged. "That's definitely not him." We scanned ahead for a parking spot. "There he is!" I exclaimed. The man looked up as we approached. "No," I said. "I'm wrong again."

"There are a lot of cowboys in cowboy hats here," Olivia noted dryly.

It was Sunday, just before nine in the morning. It was overcast and chilly. Men and women were bundled up, trudging from vehicles to cold metal bleachers. Some lugged blankets to sit on or to wrap around their legs. As I pulled into an opening between pickups, it occurred to me many were probably skipping church to be there.

We hustled over to the entrance. Two signs flanked a table. *Thirty Bucks to Watch*, the first sign announced, *for Ten Minutes or All Day. Kids and Seniors Free.* The second sign said only: *No Photography. No Dogs.* Three high-school kids in Wranglers and ten-gallon hats stood behind the table. One of them collected our money. The second kid tightened orange bands on our wrists. I was not sure what the third kid was there for—teenage moral support, perhaps.

"And you get bucked off, and you say, 'But Buck, I did what you said,'" we heard over the loudspeaker as Olivia and I found space in the crowded grandstand.

I knew Olivia was a "Buck fan," so I had invited her to the Florida Horse Park to watch one of his clinics with me.

"No, you didn't!" Buck grumbled. "Don't create your own reality! You *didn't* do what I said. And you didn't *get* what I was saying."

Buck Brannaman. The Man. The Legend. The demigod. He'd become a household name after the surprise commercial success of the 2011 feature documentary *Buck*. The man had even been a guest on the *David Letterman Show*—an uncommon turn of events for a "horse trainer."

Buck held a rope in his hand. He turned and lifted it, as if leading a dance partner onto the floor. A chubby chestnut at the other end of the rope trotted off.

"It eventually takes less and less. We don't want them flinging their head."

He stood with his shoulders back, his chin level with the ground, like the classical statue of David—but fully clothed, and with a neckerchief around his neck. His presence was something to behold. He somehow filled the arena. Like a matador. Or a gladiator. His eyes glimmered. His chest stuck out.

"I want my horse to learn," he said. "Clearly. If my leading hand is neutral, his feet are still…not busier than a cat burying crap."

We were seated at the back. I leaned forward and looked right, past Olivia, eyeballing the crowd. There were a hundred and fifty, maybe two hundred, people seated in the stands that filled the length of one side of the open-sided indoor arena. Twenty-eight horses stood quietly before us. With one exception. One handsome chestnut carrying a stone-faced cowboy kept backing up. *Confused*, I guessed. Two of the twenty-eight were in dressage saddles, one was in a jumping saddle, and the rest…Western saddles. Three of the horses were being handled from the ground.

I looked past the group, out of the arena. In the background, in a distant ring, were ponies carrying colorfully clothed riders. I could see they were grouped into teams. I knew instantly what they were doing, and it filled my heart with nostalgia. I thought of Gail, Justina, Deborah, and Katie, my Pony Club teammates when I was young. And I thought of Margot, our coach. I remembered our practices in the wind, in the rain, in the dark, and our Games Days in the sun, on the weekends, with our families cheering us on. When we were kids, ponies could be partners with us in a way that horses could not be our partners as adults. It was because of the way we existed, rather than thought. We were animals; they were animals. It was just us and the ponies. All we had to do was play, and we did that, and that united us.

My gaze shifted back into the arena. Buck wore tan chaps, a dark blue jacket, a white cowboy hat, and yellow deerskin gloves. He passed the rope attached to the chubby chestnut back to the horse's owner and took the rope of a skinny bay from a bird-like lady with a narrow nose.

"Change direction," he said to the bird-like lady. "Ninety and ninety, that equals one-eighty where I come from. He does it…but he has a sorry expression. I might do that and say, 'Don't you flip me the bird. Don't you lean on that lead rope.'"

Buck's body language was so consistent, it was almost robotic. I wondered if he knew how consistent he was, and how unusual and difficult that was to achieve. I wondered if he grasped how intimidating he was. I'd come intending to ask him some questions about starting horses, but I'd changed my mind.

"You gotta say, 'Hey, Bud, stay the hell off of me,'" he said to a lady to his right. "You've tolerated way more than I would have."

It reminded me of one of my favorite sayings: *Do less sooner, rather than more later.*

"You need to understand, when you're backing up that's a *draw*.

And you've just taken about thirty steps backward."

The horse was all over the lady, like my son on a toad. Like Goldfish on Sinead when my wife tried to take a few minutes to meditate. Like a cat on a mouse.

The idea of *draw* and *drive* had been first introduced to me by Jonathan Field. It was one of the most effective ways of learning to look at the world when training horses. There are things horses are *pushed away from*, and things they are *drawn toward*. Drive and draw are created not just by what he sees, but what he feels, smells, hears, and tastes. These things can change based on the horse, and the situation, and the day, and the minute, and the second, but the general idea is always there, and when you begin to pay attention, patterns emerge fairly quickly.

Buck said, "It's like you're in the twelve-step plan. The first step is admitting you are being run over by your horse. And *you're* making it happen."

Buck took the rope from the woman and asked the horse to move his hind legs away from him. The leg closer to him, the inside one, stepped forward and over. Buck paused, then asked the horse again. "I just 'rolled the hindquarters over,'" he noted, as if he was saying he just boiled water. "We could have spent the whole three days just doing that, and it would have changed your life."

After a few minutes of silence, Buck spoke again, his voice quiet, but now with an edge to it. "The only thing the lead rope is for is to tip the horse's nose off the center line. To let them know…*WHICH. DIRECTION. THEY. ARE. GOING.*" The words fell like hammer blows. "The rope is *not* to *pull* them there. The only way you can move a herd animal is by *driving*, not dragging."

I knew what he meant, but when I heard the words "always," "never," "all," or "only," my mind immediately went to the exceptions. A few years before I had seen a scared horse pulled into a water jump by a tractor. The owner had used a nylon halter, a thick rope, and a John Deere.

I realized Buck probably meant that the only way you can move a herd animal with *softness* and *feel* was through driving. But even then, I knew there were exceptions. A horse could learn to follow the feel of a rope—if I had good timing, if I looked for small improvements, if I was aware of what motivated him.

Buck continued to stand in the middle of the arena. My thighs were numb from the cold, and I shifted position. *I should have brought a blanket.*

Buck turned back to the horse. The horse looked back at him. "'Who the hell are you?' this horse says," remarked Buck. "I'm the guy that can move your feet, that's who. If you ask and you get a big fat 'nothing sandwich,' and you stop, you told him, 'That's right.'" I watched as he prepared to ask the horse to back up. "I'd offer this," Buck said, as he gently lifted the rope and brought his energy up, like a balloon that had slightly inflated. The horse didn't move. "So I'd offer this." Buck bumped the rope toward the horse. Startled, the horse backed up. "I'd offer this." Buck gently inflated again, and this time the horse backed up. *Yes, sir!* the horse seemed to say. "That's called presence," Buck said, describing himself. Presence was something he had in spades. "I'd offer this." Buck tried again. The horse was slow. "You're late," Buck reproved, and bumped hard again on the lead rope. "I'd offer this," Buck said, gently lifting the rope. "That's a good deal I'm offering…but that good deal expires in about a second." The horse backed up. Buck relaxed. Then he spoke directly to the lady again.

"It's not just in your hand. It's in your body. You ask with your hand, but your body is dull. Lifeless. Your horse has a six-foot bubble around him. I push on that bubble. I don't want to be right up next to him with his snot on me. If I move that bubble it *stays* at six feet."

I thought about Matt's lecture about energy at Chicken Camp. Buck's energy was a cue. A very clear and consistent cue. And Buck's timing with the horses was impeccable.

When I watched clinics, I took in information on three levels.

The first was the *techniques and tools* the trainer used. This was the most surface level, the most obvious. Tools and techniques can vary a lot from person to person and discipline to discipline.

The second was the *theory* the trainer employed. I'd found there was not much variation in theory between good trainers. Horses only learned a certain number of ways.

The last level was the most interesting, the most profound. It was the trainer's *philosophy*. I believed no two trainers had exactly the same philosophy. What was more important, for example—trust or respect? Do I break down everything and explain it for my horse, or do I let him make mistakes and figure it out on his own? How important is discipline, cooperation, submission? What kind of timeline are they on?

We can all learn technique and theory, but how we apply them comes down to philosophy.

"Olivia, what do you think?" I whispered.

"He's pretty good, isn't he?"

"He sure is."

Buck took another horse from a young woman. The horse was the color of dark chocolate; he carried a Western saddle.

Buck put a foot in the stirrup. He swung up and sat in the saddle in a way that is impossible to fake. It reminded me of watching Wade Black settle into the saddle at Road to the Horse. It was so smooth and confident, like the way Simone Biles stands on a balance beam. It was the animal confidence of an apex predator in its element.

"I get 'em well halter broke before I ever start riding 'em. First thing I'll ask is, how well do you bend? Most of you guys have never been around really bronc-y horses. But if they are a little twitchy, I'll ask the hindquarters to move. Otherwise, I might have to make a little bit of a bronc ride. I'll kinda feel my way. I'm not gonna beg, but I'll ease my way into it."

I wondered how old he was—sixty? He had more slouch in his shoulders now than he'd had in the documentary about him.

"I'm looking for a moment when he is light to my hand *and* light to my leg," Buck went on. "If he is only light to one, I'll keep traveling. Then, when he is light to both, I'll give him a little break."

I was cold and stood up to stretch. I bent side to side at the waist. Then I tried to touch my toes. I couldn't.

I wondered what Buck would have done if he hadn't discovered horses. If he had joined the military he'd probably be a general by now. He appreciated rules. Discipline. Clarity. Truth. He wanted purpose. Boundaries gave freedom. Respect was important. So was watching and learning. And honesty. He was ambitious. He strived. A relentless forwardness, like the flying migration of the Arctic tern, the longest of any bird.

"Ray Hunt told me the only time you're ever going to say something to a horse's foot is as it leaves the ground," Buck said as he stepped off the chocolate-colored horse. "He had us do that for *hours*. It was so damn boring. But once I figured it out, I realized you can't do anything with a horse until you know where his feet are. Until you *feel* all four feet. It's hard to imagine you can do it. But it's a game-changer when you can."

He led the horse back to the owner. He stopped and backed the horse up.

"'What the hell's the matter with you?' Ray asked me when I was struggling to feel the horse's feet. 'You ride more in a week than most people do in a year!' he said. He was so disappointed in me. I wanted him to think a lot of me. I just needed to put out the effort. Once I figured it out, it blew my mind, the things I could get a horse to do with his feet. 'Cause I had better timing. I was so mad at myself then. I'd just wasted a year *not* knowing. But luckily, I was pretty young. Maybe sixteen."

Buck had learned horsemanship from Ray Hunt, one of the early teachers of natural horsemanship. Ray'd worked a lot with legendary American horse trainer Tom Dorrance, who'd mentored Ray and encouraged him to share his method with others. I'd heard Ray called "The Horse's Lawyer." Ray would start clinics by saying, "I'm here for the horse, to help him get a better deal."

Ray believed, as I do, that to change the horse, we first need to change ourselves. And changing ourselves is a lot more difficult than changing the horse.

Buck faced the crowd. It was nearing lunchtime.

"All you're trying to do," he said, "is get the horse to hunt that relief. But you have to *get 'em to believe*. They have to believe you can give it to them. It's a promise. Once that promise is made and they believe you, then they will *hunt* it. But at the start you have no street cred. Why would they believe you?"

Buck walked, with a stiff elegant walk, toward us. "You've been a really good group," he said. "It's been a pleasure spending time with y'all."

The crowd clapped, and half the horses in the arena skittered away from the bleachers like ripples from a fallen stone.

"Don't fall off," I heard Buck say, and then static for a moment as he removed his mic.

Olivia and I walked to the car. On the way out, we stopped and watched the kids and ponies. They did the balloon race, then the ball-and-bucket race. They cantered fast. There was a purpose to what they were all doing. It was play, but it was clear. And kids and ponies were doing it together.

I motioned to Olivia that I needed a minute, finding a contact on my phone, and pressing "call."

"Yes?"

"Hey, Jake," I said, leaning against the fence of the Pony Club ring. "I'm kinda freaking out. I'm not nearly ready. Not even the simple things."

Watching Buck in that saddle had just reminded me of what it should look like when I ride. I felt like I was about to enter a chess competition but still couldn't even name all the pieces. The feeling of unpreparedness was overwhelming.

"I don't think you just need to be starting horses," Jake said. "You need to be at my place, riding young Quarter Horses, in a Western saddle, every day. You need to get really comfortable with the equipment."

He was right. I told him I'd be at his place tomorrow.

I'd thought about Road to the Horse for months and months, for as long, and as often, as I had thought about proposing to Sinead. Constantly. Morning till night. With as much excitement. With a lot more fear.

But with all that thinking, and even with all I had been doing and juggling and balancing, there wasn't as much action as I would have liked. I was itching to be starting horses every day, practicing, but I wasn't. Most days I was still doing the same thing I had been doing for the last few years—riding horses, teaching lessons, raising kids.

The day after the Buck clinic, it was windy and chilly, but the sky was blue, and the sun was sharp and clear. In the morning, I taught and rode for a couple hours, then competed a horse at Majestic Oaks. In the afternoon I fit in another session with Jake's filly, Liberty.

I parked at Jake's house and jogged to the round pen. Liberty was already inside. I was climbing in to greet her when Jake showed up. He wore denim, top and bottom.

"Find a rhythm," he said. "Get in your zone."

I picked up the rope, looked at the little filly, and stopped. I reminded myself to go slow. "My plan is to work on on-and-off bareback," I told him, "then the short flag, then the two long flags, then the bareback pad. Then look for a good quitting spot. I've got about an hour and a half."

"Why don't you get the bareback pad on first, then use the flags?" he said.

"Good idea. Two birds, one stone."

"Remember, just like I taught you about riding transitions, think of your session like musical notes. Up and down the scale. Like music," he said.

I nodded as I played approach and retreat with the filly. I made a mistake and went half an inch too far. She trotted off.

"*Deee-dooh-soooo*," Jake sang. "Like notes."

I changed plans. I retrieved the two twelve-foot extendable flags I had bought from the edge of the round pen. I began again, but soon felt I was getting stuck again.

"Am I doing something wrong?" I asked Jake.

"You just need to keep going; you're on the right track."

But it wasn't getting better. The filly would look at me, and she would come to where she was five feet from me. But she stayed just out of reach. Her eyes were intelligent and her ears alert. If I couldn't get close enough to touch her this wasn't going to work. *Nothing* was going to work.

I asked Jake to take over.

I felt like I was always asking Jake to take over.

Jake stepped in and took the two flags from me. He tapped the air behind the filly and above her. He used them in the same place I had, but with a quicker rhythm, like a pulse. I could see how his plan was clearer. There was a feeling of inevitability when he interacted with the horse. What he wanted *was going to happen*—he wasn't sure how long it was going to take, and he was in no hurry, but the way forward was plain.

"What I'm doing is tapping her up farther, so her head is right near my chest. Then I can put the flag on one side of her, then the other. Then both sides at the same time."

In less than fifteen minutes, she was right up close to him.

"Then I can put one of my arms on her neck. Then the other arm. All the way until I can hug her."

"I didn't want to use the flag to tap her up," I said. "I didn't want to get her scared of it…"

And as I spoke, I suddenly realized what I had been doing wrong.

"Jake…I was training the horse I had twenty minutes ago. Not the horse that was in front of me."

"Yup," he said.

Damn it, I thought. *Jake should be competing. Not me.*

"It's those little things," Jake said. "You have a lot of horse experience, but not a lot starting them."

I took a breath. I reminded myself that I had just learned something I needed to learn. That was a good thing.

But we were on day ten or eleven with this filly. I had lost count. And she was still so sensitive. She was wild, really. Her instincts and reflexes were off the charts. We still couldn't get a saddle on her easily. I was frustrated, but only with myself. I never felt frustrated with Jake's filly. All her problems were *horse* problems. Things she was born with. In other words, *they weren't problems.*

I took over again. I spent some time getting close to her, then I put the flags away. I gave her a rub. And then I jumped up, my body sideways across hers like a sack of grain. Limp, letting gravity hold me there. Then I slipped down and jumped up from the opposite side. Then back to the left side. On and off I went, finding a rhythm.

Eventually I found a quitting spot and let her rest. Jake and I talked again about how each horse has his own timeline. At Road to the Horse, there would be no shame in going at the speed the horse I drew needed to go.

"There are a lot of people with more experience than you," Jake told me. "You want to win the horse…and win the crowd."

"Want me to hose her off?"

"Nah. She isn't sweaty. We can leave her alone for now."

I took the filly's halter off, then hung it tidily from one of the rails.

"I'm learning lots, but if I draw a horse like this at Road to the Horse, I'm not going to get him saddled, much less ridden."

"You can learn more from this filly than you can from ten easy ones."

"And I *want* to learn. I *want* to do this. I *want* to know colt starting, and all the nuances…. I want to know it all."

31

"You have the passports?"

"You have the phone charger?"

"Why are you taking off your clothes?" Sinead's tone was sharp as glass. "We need to leave in seven minutes!"

"I've got the passports," I said, taking off my pants. "I'm going to cold plunge for two minutes!" I darted for the back door.

Even though we left late we stopped at Best Buy and bought an iPhone 13, unlocked, for Cristo's wife, and Nintendo controllers for his kids, who had broken theirs.

They are twice as expensive here, he had texted me.

How many kids do you have? I texted back.

22 the oldest. 4 my little girl, and 7 and 11 the boys.

That's amazing. I have two. 5 and 1.

Lovely, kids are the best, Cristo wrote. *Family, it's all.*

It is all, I agreed.

Sinead's phone buzzed at the airport as we schlepped our bags up to the counter. She answered it.

"Any bags to check?" the attendant asked.

Sinead put her hand over the phone and looked at me. "It's my mother. She wants to know if we have a will."

"Geez," I said. "Talk about timing. Didn't we write a will when we applied for the mortgage?"

"Bags to check?"

"No bags," I replied to the attendant. "We can carry these on." Then, to Sinead, "I think we made a will, but it was before we had kids. Is she planning on something happening to us?"

"I think she is concerned about us flying together to South America."

As soon as we had checked in and made it through security, I got on my laptop. I looked up templates for a will. And I entered in what was to happen to our kids if we didn't make it home from Argentina.

At the end of the template there was a box where we could leave a message to our children. What do you say when you are sitting in an airport, imagining a world where your children will never see you again? It was at once both unimaginable and despairingly sad.

"Maybe," I suggested to Sinead, "we leave a note making things into a contest, like in *Drops of God*. We devise a series of tests in which the winner receives the farm. Initially the tests drive them apart, but in the end, it brings them closer together."

"Good idea," said my wife. "It could be labeling the colors of a horse."

"'Is that a brown or bay?'"

"Violet will win," Sinead said.

"We'll put some questions about frogs in there."

On the plane to Miami, I started reading *In Patagonia* by Bruce Chatwin, published in 1977.

Splendid, said the *Sunday Times* on the front cover.

Pure pleasure, said travel writer Paul Theroux on the back.

Sinead had on a new necklace that said "MOM" and a white shirt with blue stripes that reminded me of the Navy. But a trendy Navy. A cute Navy. She read *Ten Percent Happier* by Dan Harris.

Our second flight was four thousand five hundred and thirteen miles to Buenos Aires. Eight hours and seventeen minutes.

We landed and booked a cab to *Aeropuerto El Palomar*, a small airport on the other side of the city. Our driver was old and bald. Like me. He wore sunglasses that were broken on one side. His cab was old too, but it was clean.

Sinead and I were quiet. We looked out the open windows; we felt and scented the wind. It smelled like cars and commerce and the ocean.

Sixty minutes and forty American dollars later, we stepped out of the cab and entered our fourth airport in twenty-four hours. On the plane, I continued reading *In Patagonia*:

> *"The Indians rode better than the gauchos," he said. "Brown limbs! Naked on horseback! Their children learned to ride before they walked. They were one with their horses. Ah! Mi Indio!"*

I leaned back and thought about riding naked.

I looked out the small plane's window. Below I saw hundreds of squares of dark-green, brown-green, pastel-green, and brown, dividing up the land. They were crops; some of the most fertile soil in the world was here.

I admired the hardworking adventurers, and later, the farmers, who had settled and tamed this land. I also felt a sadness for the land and people that used to be. One feeling did not cancel out the other. Wildness; civilization. Mustangs on the range; tame ponies to cuddle. The ability to start a horse in three days; the patience to take a year. The wish to eat meat; the empathy for the bovine that gave the ultimate sacrifice. All these things could exist.

Then I saw a strip of hills in the landscape, like a fold in an otherwise even bedspread.

The plane lowered toward a runway so narrow it was like walking the plank.

"It feels like we are landing on grass," I whispered. "This place is so romantic. It's the kind of place where they test foreigners. They will probably send me barefoot into the hills to catch and tame a horse… I'll catch one for you, too, if you like?"

I looked at my wife. She rolled her eyes.

"This plane is too big to land on grass," she stated.

"Ah, but the pilots here are one with the wind. Like the fisherman who works the currents. Like the cat that toys with the sparrow. Like the politician who rides the ratings. No wind is bad, no horse can't be tamed."

"I stopped listening about five minutes ago," Sinead said.

We met Cristobal and his daughter Abril on the tarmac in front of the little airport. We greeted each other with hugs, which seemed appropriate, despite having only met him once, almost ten years before. Cristo, I guessed, was a couple years older than me. He had shoulder-length, chestnut hair, which he periodically ran a hand through.

To keep it from falling into his eyes, I thought.

Abril, Cristo's daughter with his first wife, was red-cheeked and smiling. She was in her early twenties, and I could sense in her a desperate wish to explore the world. I watched her take it all in—our conversation, our strangeness.

We crammed into an old truck and headed out of town. When we stopped at a toll, a friendly woman selling empanadas approached. Cristo bought four and handed them out.

I half-turned in my seat. "How do you say your name again?"

"Ah-breel," Abril said. "'April' in English."

A few minutes later when we slowed for a red light, a smiling Rastafarian stepped in front of the truck. He was manipulating a diabolo on a string between two sticks. Faster and faster he went, accelerating with urgency to impress us before the light changed. His body danced and convulsed. The diabolo flew into the air, and then fell to the ground. *Wait, wait!* he signaled. He renewed his act, grinning clumsily. He whipped the diabolo over his head, then wrapped it around itself, finishing with a cat's cradle.

Cristo gave him some money, and we drove on. The gray of San Luis City turned to green corn fields. We saw cattle. Sinead pointed out goats. Horses walked in a creek that ran parallel to the road.

"I like helping people that have this *feeling*," Cristo said, putting his hand near his heart. "That man, he had a nice…*feeling*. He was not *demanding* money from me. That is what I want to share as well—a calm, relaxed joy."

We had lunch at his place. I filled my plate with thick cubes of fresh tomatoes, drizzled them with oil, then sprinkled them with salt and pepper. I didn't take any chicken.

"You want eggs?" Cristo asked.

"No, no. I'm fine," I said.

"It's no trouble," he said, and fried up three eggs in a pan over a portable gas grill in the kitchen. The grill sat in a stone fireplace, a propane tank next to it.

We chased our meal with red wine. Lunch ended well after five in the evening. Almost dinnertime for us back home.

Sinead and I had rented a room in the house next door. It was a three-minute walk, and we moved lazily, feeling satiated. The house sprawled across the hillside, surrounded by trees, ponds, and a small creek. It had seven bedrooms, seven bathrooms. Horses grazed in the yard.

After a nap we explored the property and found a cement and metal dam that created a pool fed by waters that trickled in from the nearby *Sierras Centrales de San Luis*.

I stripped and jumped in. A perfect day.

"Fill and pass," Cristo instructed.

I sipped the maté, then topped it up with hot water from the thermos, and then handed it to the gaucho next to me. Each of us partook, then shared. A ritual. Like passing a joint.

In front of us, Flor was playing with a horse. Flor was Cristo's second wife. Her eyes were sunny, and her cheeks smooth. The round pen was on the side of a hill, fabricated out of reclaimed wood. Tall wide-leafed plants emerged around the edges. Flor wore slip-on shoes with blue tops and a rubber soles. They were tapered and had no laces. They looked comfortable.

Since Flor spoke no English, Cristo continued a running dialogue for those watching, which included us and a group of a dozen men and women who had also come to spend a few days with the Scarpati family. They were part of a retreat that was there to learn horsemanship and participate in the "Scarpati way of life."

"I had two accidents," Cristo said, while Flor saddled the chestnut. "Then I wrote an article."

Accidents, he explained, were something you couldn't have prevented. Something that you couldn't have seen coming. But…in retrospect…his accidents were not *actually* accidents, and he *should have* seen them coming.

I immediately thought about my torn groin. *If I had trusted my gut, if I had been less impatient, I wouldn't have gotten hurt.*

Suddenly we heard the shouts and cries of their younger kids, and Cristo sprinted off toward his house, just a hundred yards down the hill.

"Flor," I said. "What is the horse's name?"

She didn't understand. I tried again in broken Spanish. *No use.* We could still hear the crying of the kids, and she was distracted. She made a motion with her hands to wait for Cristo, then she put her weight in the stirrup and climbed aboard her horse. She looked at home. She took a breath, gave her horse a rub, then trotted off.

Oscar hobbled up. Mid-seventies. Massive white beard, just like I remembered from the Horsemen's Re-Union. Maybe less gray and more white. He was handsome in the same way as his son, with an inner glow that I imagined began in his heart, then spread to his complexion and into his eyes. It was the best way to be handsome.

"He is feeling his age," Cristo had told us earlier, in the truck. "We may not see him work with a horse."

As Oscar spoke with the retreat group, he put one leg up on a round pen rail and stretched. I copied him, but on a lower rung, introducing myself to a lady from the group standing near us. She explained that she, and five other women, had traveled together from Santiago. Four of the six spoke English.

When Cristo returned from the house, he saw me stretching. He put his foot up on the lower rung of the round pen, the same as mine.

"Tik, there are three levels of Scarpati Horsemanship," he began. "*This* is Level One." He then put his foot on the middle rail. "This is Level Two." Then with a pantomimed effort, he swung his foot up to the top rail of the pen. "This is Level Three!"

I laughed. I knew he was poking fun at all the "levels" that American horse trainers have created. The Scarpati way did not fit neatly into different levels.

Cristo introduced me and Sinead to everyone in the retreat group, explaining that I was getting ready for Road to the Horse. One of the ladies from Santiago asked what the rules were. A young man from Brazil with blue eyes asked who would win.

"Who will win?" Cristo responded. "The best person! Kind, smart, nice, firm at the right moments. There must be confidence so the person can say, 'Yes!' or 'No!' at the right times."

In front of us, in the round pen, Flor went from the trot to the walk. Dust rose from around the horse's legs. Two roosters entered between the rails, and swaggered through the dirt, chests out, eyes beady. One was jet black, the other was mottled cream and milk-chocolate brown.

"If I never disappoint you," Cristo said, "I can keep asking for more. The difference is not the method, it's the philosophy. After I visited the United States, I realized many people were teaching technique and method: 'A, B, C, D.' '1, 2, 3, 4.' I realized my calling was teaching *philosophy*. The way I teach horses is the same way I raise kids, the same way I cook, the same way I eat."

The entire property was on the side of a gentle slope. Each building was on a new level. First the guest house, then Cristo's house, then the garage, then the round pen. Near the top of the property, and about halfway up the rise, was a second round pen with a thatched roof. The effect was soft, natural, endearing.

"I had a dream of going to Road to the Horse and losing," Cristo said softly. "I would go slow. Nothing against the others, but to get them to *think*. My intention right from the start would be to go, to go slow, and to lose."

"I get it." I nodded.

"You may find out the truth. The horse may not want to do the job."

I thought of my kids. The last thing I wanted to do was pressure them to do something *I* was passionate about, rather than let them find their own passions, and to let those passions run their course in *their* way, on *their* timelines. But I could see, and feel, how tempting it would be to push them.

Flor and her chestnut picked up the canter. They floated through the dust.

"Don't get on till you feel one hundred percent. The horse has to say, *Yes*. It has to feel *right*." Cristo then placed a hand on his belly. "It has to feel *right*, right here. Even then, when starting horses, get on ninety percent ready to get off. If you get on to stay on you might grip; they might feel it."

I was desperate to watch Oscar play with a horse. But before I could introduce myself, he limped down the hill, back to the house. I noticed he put his hand on his right thigh with each step of that leg.

Night was upon us, and people were suddenly hungry. We all made our way down the slope behind Oscar. We passed the garage, in which the truck and a small CUV resided. In the house, we all sat around a large table and began to pour wine.

I wandered into the kitchen where Cristo showed me how to make mayonnaise. "Two eggs, then add sunflower oil." I held the bowl while he poured the oil with one hand and managed the blender with his other. There was a lovely rhythm to it. The emulsion thickened leisurely. Cristo poured salt into his hand, then dumped it in. Then he squeezed two lemon halves and poured the juice in. He blended one last time, then found a good spot to quit.

I tasted it and gave him a hug. He went back to chat with the group at the table, and I took a glass of red wine and explored the house. The walls were stone. The ceiling had old, pock-marked, wooden beams. I found the bookshelf and introduced myself. There were horse books, kids books, a novel, and a few new-age books. Most were in Spanish, a few in English.

At dinner, I was next to Abril's boyfriend. He was not a horse person; he was a long-haired musician. He strummed the guitar. He had a helpful face and wore a black Foo Fighters shirt. Oscar sat elegantly at the head of the table, mostly happy to let others talk. I asked him what he calls it when he trains a horse: *Teaching? Playing? Mentoring?* A Chilean woman with the sharp chin of an actress translated what I had said.

Oscar spoke in Spanish for a few minutes. I could follow none of it. The Chilean lady thought for maybe ten seconds, then translated: "He calls it a…a conversation."

"That's *all* he said?"

She shrugged.

Sinead and I were exhausted and left before the plates were cleared and guitar was brought out and the singing began. We strolled in the dark in the direction of our rented room. After a few minutes we noticed a shadow behind us. Something was following our footsteps. It was a kitten. I picked her up and ran her back to the house. Then I jogged back to Sinead, who was standing still, looking up at the sky. The air was clean and unaffected. Stars upon stars upon stars shone down on us. I hadn't seen that many stars for years. The last time might have been in Texas, over a decade before.

"I love you," I said.

My wife took my hand in hers.

Sinead sat in a chair, facing the bed. She had a book in her hands, but she was staring at me. "You ready?" she prompted.

I grunted, swung into a standing position, and pulled my pants on.

We set off up the scrabbly path to the Scarpatis'. Sinead was keen and led the way. She wore shorts that showed off her firm legs. I scrambled behind her, dreaming of coffee.

At the entrance to Cristo's driveway was a sign that said *Los Alazanes*. "The Chestnuts." ("Our favorite color," Abril explained to me later.) A breakfast of rolls, yoghurt, and peaches was on the table. We were the first ones to arrive.

"It feels like Europe, doesn't it."

"It's the stone walls and low ceiling."

"And the old wooden chairs. Nothing from Target or Ikea or Amazon. Everything is authentic. The table has been fixed instead of replaced."

After breakfast Sinead and I left the retreat group at the table and made our way up the hill to the top round pen. On the way, we met Oscar. He walked with a cane. I fell in beside him.

"*Buenos dias!*"

"Good morning, Tik." He spoke the English words hesitantly.

We followed him to the covered round pen. I pointed at his leg and asked what had happened. He lifted his pant leg. The muscle tone was evident, but the foot was very, very swollen.

He moved his arm in a wave.

"Ocean?" I said.

"Snake," Sinead guessed.

Oscar nodded grimly.

He had been bitten by a *yarará,* a pit viper that usually hunted at night. Although considered highly venomous, only one percent of pit viper bites were fatal. Its Spanish name meant "large snake."

The upper round pen with its thatched roof was a thing to behold. It had an attached pavilion with tables and a rough stone fireplace. A horse stood quietly on the far side.

"What's going to happen today?" I asked Sinead.

"No idea," she said.

Then Oscar surprised us by taking his shoes off and slipping through the rails into the round pen, like a boxer entering the ring. He walked lightly. He held his head high. As he approached the horse, his limp disappeared.

"*This* is what we came for," I whispered excitedly to Sinead. I leaned against the rail. Suddenly, Oscar jumped. The horse flinched, then trotted off, and Oscar landed like a cat. The horse was not much bigger than a pony. He was the color of coal, with a long, tangled mane. He trotted lamer than Oscar, and Oscar sighed and sort of shrugged.

"Damn it," I said out loud. There would be no playing with that horse today.

Oscar limped back over to us, then began to speak. He started slowly. I only understood words rather than phrases, and Sinead's Spanish was not much farther along than mine, but she kept nodding, and together we pieced together what we thought he was telling us.

"There is a hierarchy in the herd," Oscar said. "Three-year-olds are bigger and stronger than two-year-olds. Foals follow their mothers. The problem is *humans*. It is because we *think* like humans."

The lame horse had wandered over, and now he pushed his hindquarters into Oscar's space. Oscar picked up a handful of dirt and playfully flicked it at the horse. The horse scampered a few feet, then turned and looked back, then lowered his head and took a breath.

"A 'method'—*One…Two…Three*—is *human*. Americans want a step-by-step-by-step process because they have lost touch with nature and want to replace it with systematization. A method is exactly what horses do *not* do. Not only does a method take you farther away from feeling, it can do as much harm as good if you don't have a philosophy."

The horse stepped back toward Oscar, headfirst this time, and Oscar rubbed him on the neck.

"A hierarchy between us and horses exists, but we are responsible for their soul. As responsible as for our own soul. As responsible as for the soul of a child. Road to the Horse is 'kindergarten' for the horse. The main activity that should be happening is *play*. It should be about *relationship*, not training. America, it is too systematic; it's all the same. In ethology there is no system, no structure."

Oscar leaned his back against the horse's side. He put an arm over the withers and let the horse feel his weight. Oscar then took a long breath that went through his chest and stomach. His eyes were soft, gray-green with flecks of gold.

"Horses don't believe in romantic love. They believe in the herd. The herd is, for them, love. They get confidence from the herd." He blew air at the horse's neck, almost like a llama spitting. The horse took a step back. "In America, horses live in boxes. They eat grain. Combine all that with humans, and how humans think— it's not natural. There is stability in the herd," Oscar said. "There is a hierarchy." He pointed at the chickens. "Like them." And the kind of love humans *should* seek? In Spanish, he said something like, "If we *be, love* will be."

It was mild out, temperate, and the breeze rolled over the plains, over us, and towards the *Sierras*. Birds sang. Kittens meowed. Three dogs slept at our feet. A rooster pecked in the dust.

Oscar raised his hand and held out his index finger so we could clearly see it. Then he slowly brought his other index finger up and let the two fingers touch, like the finger of God giving life to Adam in the Sistine Chapel. Then he looked at us and spoke.

I nodded at his words but had no idea what he'd said. He held a secret that he was trying to share, but I couldn't quite grasp it. Maybe it was because I didn't speak Spanish. Or maybe I'd lived too much of my life in a city, or behind a screen. Or maybe I was too immature, or too *human*, or too goal-driven. There was a piece of me missing, like a skipped heartbeat, that left me anxious. He was that heartbeat... and I wanted it.

Oscar made his excuses in Spanish, climbed out of the pen, and hobbled back down the hill.

I turned to Sinead. "The dirt-toss and the llama-spit! *How* he spat! How much! For how long! In what direction! *How* he threw the dirt! How much! In what direction! It was as if he *was* a horse. He showed more timing and feel in twenty minutes than most people do in a lifetime. And it was all spontaneous."

"It's not re-creatable," Sinead said. "You can't teach people that."

"Which is regrettable."

"Or maybe not; maybe it's beautiful."

We sat down on a bench and waited for Cristo and the retreat group to wander up. I looked at the simple round pen before us, and I listened to the birds and the wind.

Wild horses scratch and kick and bite; they trudge on rocks; they push their way through branches that bite at their skin. The horse notices a single leaf that begins to flutter; he hears one quiet raindrop. A horse's sense of smell is compared to that of bloodhounds. A horse's skin is both thick and thin.

Oscar knew all that.

Humans are tall and slow. Clumsy. We preemptively, and fiercely, *categorize*. We call these categories "knowledge." Horses, on the other hand, know how things make them *feel*.

Oscar knew that as well.

"His timing was exquisite," I murmured.

"There is no method; he might never do the same thing twice."

Oscar's way with horses was so varied and creative that he would not be able to teach others to do it. But perhaps "teaching" was not the point. Picasso and Michelangelo were not "painting instructors," they were artists. They were born to inspire; to live and feel and invoke. They aimed for mastery. Someone could paint *Guernica* by number, and maybe do a great job, but the piece was important because Picasso did it at *that* moment. That moment in 1937 when Basque women, kids, cats, and cattle were bombed, then machine-gunned, and Europe was on the brink of war. The painting, eleven feet by twenty-five feet—taller and longer than a horse and cart—was finished in six weeks. It was the timing of it! Timing for an artist has the same importance as it does for a predator chasing prey—it is the difference between going hungry, or not. Living, or not.

Oscar was an artist. He and Cristo had not resorted to selling paint-by-numbers, but they were willing to share a space, share their environment, share their philosophy. *Do what you want with it,* they seemed to say.

The horse took two steps away from him.

"I'm too fast. I need to slow down."

Cristo reapproached. He had just explained how he could be unpredictable—quick, playful. But *within that* there should be a predictability. Just like with puppies playing, there were things that were out of bounds, and horses needed to learn not to cross those boundaries.

"My dad is braver than I am," Cristo said. "Or is it crazy? No, the word is something else. I'm not sure of the word. With the horse I am looking for *answers,* not *reactions.*"

The horse he was playing with that afternoon was a Thoroughbred the color of carrot soup and bred for polo. Cristo reapproached; the horse startled. He approached again, paused, then got a hand on the gelding and slipped a halter on.

"In America, they saw my dad with horses and said: *If people see this and try to do it, they will get hurt.* But I go slower. I don't go till the horse is ready."

Cristo bent his knee and touched his foot to the back of the horse's leg. He ran his leg up the horse's leg like he was his lover. Then with a cupped hand, he patted the barrel, then the rump. The horse flinched, not quite trusting this strange man.

Cristo explained that in this play he was getting to know the horse. Exploring his physical and mental barriers.

"It's as if I am scouting out a house, looking for a way in. I walk around, I look at the structure, the stories, the doors, and the windows. How am I getting in? A broken window? An unlocked door?" Cristo unclipped the rope from the halter. The horse stood still. Cristo jumped. He swung the rope. He skipped. He danced. "I want this horse to *answer the question*—not react," he said. Cristo came toward us and leaned on the round pen rail. The horse followed, and Cristo laid one arm over his withers again. He smiled with his eyes, and it was endearing and addictive. I smiled right back. I stood up to stretch.

I was ready for any opportunity to get in the ring, but it wasn't appearing.

Cristo took a deep breath. "Like in tennis, always come back to center. The center of the court is the center of emotions. The tension we feel is like a wave. Choppy at first, but getting smoother and shallower."

"That's what I liked about JR Robles at Road to the Horse last year," I said. "He was even keeled. Not a rogue wave in sight."

"Didn't he stop early?"

"Yes. He was winning after the first two days and stopped halfway through the obstacle course. I loved it. I don't know if people will remember that he didn't win. Everyone who was there will forever remember the standing ovation that he got. And what he did gave others permission to stop, too, if it felt like that was the right thing to do."

Cristo had been standing with the weight of his arm on the horse's back; he cupped his hand and gave the horse a thump, the way an athlete might encourage another player with a slap on the rump or shoulder. Then just as suddenly he backed off. The carrot soup horse lowered his head as Cristo took a step away and looked at him with questioning eyes.

"You know, even if he quit because he had to, that's not the point. It's what we learned from it."

Cristo was right. So many of the greatest stories are not about the perceived "winners"—Eddie the Eagle, the Jamaican National Bobsled Team, "Rudy," Terry Fox.

Sinead asked if he was going to get on.

"If your expectation is for me to ride," Cristo said, "it adds a weight to my shoulders about something I don't need to do."

I knew that weight well.

"Smile and breathe," he said. "Let it go. That's my recommendation."

"Who did you learn from, besides your dad?" Sinead followed up.

"No one," Cristo replied. He was focused on the horse beside him again.

"The horse is tense, anxious. It's like when I travel, Abril gets tense. She gets tense because she can sense how I'm feeling. I make her tense. So I go to her and I say, 'It's me. Not you. It's not personal.'" He rubbed the horse's leg with his leg again. The horse startled. Cristo brought his foot almost onto the horse's neck. From there he reached back and rubbed the hind legs.

"That's amazing," I whispered to Sinead.

"They never try to kick," Cristo said.

Never say never, I thought.

Cristo took another break and again came over beside us. Flor, his wife, poured some hot water from a thermos into a maté mug, and handed it to him.

"It is like having a child," he said. "Take our younger daughter, for example. I know I can make her happy if I do everything she wants. But maybe I can make her happier if sometimes I *don't* give her what she wants."

I asked myself the same question constantly. Not only for my horses and kids, but also for myself. *What will make me happier tonight after the kids are asleep? A few drinks and Ted Lasso? Or wrestling with writing a book and facing my demons?*

Cristo went to the far side of the round pen and separated a saddle from its nest in the dirt. He caught the horse again and hoisted the saddle on. The horse's eye was soft, but his neck was high. Then Cristo cinched the saddle up, and the horse stood still, but his eyes bulged. When Cristo asked him to set off, the gelding bucked twice, then trotted stiffly. The skin on his neck and shoulders was taut.

Less than thirty seconds later, his eye and skin softened a little, and Cristo turned his back to him. Cristo let the horse stand while he accepted another round of maté from his wife. He leaned against the fence and sipped. The horse watched him, still, but still alert.

"I laid him down a few days ago, I'm going to do it again if you are okay with that." He looked at each of us. We nodded.

"I am not in favor, usually, of laying down a green or wild horse. But this horse knows me now. He is still worried. By laying him down, I can let him know that I am not here for the wrong reasons."

Sinead asked when he might choose to lay a horse down.

"When I feel like—" he said, then thought a moment, struggling to find the English words. "When I feel like I will get old waiting."

Not many people teach the process of laying a horse down to the public because it is controversial. Some people swear by it, using it as a trick, or for bonding, or to build trust, or to help a horse that nothing else seems to be able to help. Others hate it, saying it is cruel and simply about showing man's quest for dominance, and that it is unnecessary.

What is known by many as "the lay down" can be taught slowly and smoothly, or it can be done primitively and aggressively. It can be encouraged with patience, or forced with fear and intimidation. I had once asked an old, pink-cheeked, paunch-bellied cowboy about teaching the lay down, and he replied gruffly that, depending on how you did it, it could be "like making love, having sex, or rape."

In his book *The Faraway Horses*, Buck Brannaman writes about a scene from the 1998 movie *The Horse Whisperer*, directed by and featuring Robert Redford, where the horse in the film is laid down by Robert Redford's character. Buck was the "Equine Technical Advisor" for the movie.

> *The scene became somewhat controversial because many people thought we were being unkind to the horse. Nothing could be further from the truth. Laying a horse down is a technique I learned from my teachers, and I've used it over the years with horses that are really troubled. Under the right circumstances, it can save a horse's life by helping him into a frame of mind where he can trust the human. In many cases, this will be the first time in his life that he's been able to do so....*
>
> *A really troubled or terrified horse is pretty much convinced that the human is a predator. He's pretty sure that when he finally does lie down, he's going to lose the one thing that means everything to him, and that's his life. This moment is the opportunity to go to your horse. As Tom Booker did with Pilgrim in the movie, you can sit with him, rub him, comfort him, and cuddle him. You can show him that even though you have every opportunity, you won't take advantage of him. You're there to be his friend, to be his partner.*

Buck then goes on to say:

> *When people ask me to lay a horse down the way they saw it done in the movie, I decline. Laying a horse down is not a*

circus sideshow act. It's a valuable tool for helping horses with troubled lives.

It would have been nice if there had been time in the movie to explain that laying Pilgrim down was done to save his life, but as I've said, The Horse Whisperer *wasn't about teaching people how to work with horses. It was a love story. My own story is about horses, and I guess it's a love story, too. I do the things I do when I work with horses because I just plain love them.*

In his little thatch covered round-pen, Cristo lay the carrot-soup-colored horse down with astonishing feel. It took just under four minutes. There was no commotion. The horse found his way to the ground just as rainfall winds its way around rocks and pebbles to the lowest point.

"This is the first time in his life that he is relaxed," Cristo said, as he ran his palms over the horse's back and neck, stretched out flat in the dirt. Then he got a brush and brushed the gelding. Then he got a hoof pick and picked the horse's feet. Cristo took the rope off, but the horse stayed down for eighteen minutes. His eye was soft. His breathing was regular.

When he was ready, the horse stood up. His nervousness came back, but less so, like part of a weight had been lifted. Cristo rubbed him, then put his arms around his neck.

"You want to hug him?" He looked at me. "To feel his energy?"

Darn right I do.

I threw my shoes off and leaped over the fence, full of enthusiasm. *Easy*, I told myself. I stopped short about eight feet from the horse's orange tail. I took a deep breath. I settled my shoulders, leveled my gaze, relaxed my chin. The horse turned to face me. I shut my eyes and took another breath. I glanced at Sinead, then I gave Cristo and the horse a small bow.

I eased over and wrapped my arms around the horse. The muscles along the crest of his neck were taut.

"I can feel it," I said. "It's almost electric."

At this point, perhaps, Cristo expected me to leave the round pen, but instead I seized my opportunity. I gently rubbed the horse's legs with my bare feet the way I had seen Oscar do. I floated around the horse like a native son of Argentina. Cristo, Flor, and Sinead faded from my view. Worries about our farm back home, and the kids, which had been circling in my mind, disappeared. On and off I played with that horse. It couldn't have been more than ten minutes, but it was the most present I had been in months. Maybe years.

That evening, as we cleaned up for dinner, Sinead said, "You looked more relaxed in the round pen today, more comfortable than usual. Did you feel that?"

I nodded, surprised that she had noticed what I thought was something I had just felt. "Part of it was just being here in Argentina, and part of it was having no shoes. It felt more natural. It's like all these things we have to protect us—boots, pants, hats—also create boundaries that separate us from *feeling* the horse. The separation that keeps us safe also creates a distance between us."

Sinead and I borrowed Cristo's car, a four-door, bronze-colored Ford EcoSport Storm, and drove to *San Luis*. The sun was high. Our spirits were high. We zipped through fields of corn. Feral sheep and horses grazed beside the road—sometimes meandering onto the road. A peloton of cyclists ascended a hill, going in the opposite direction of us as we cruised into town.

The city center was gray and busy, and I immediately missed Cristo's farm. We searched for parking, then started walking. Sinead offered me her hand and I took it, giving it a little squeeze.

"Butch Cassidy and the Sundance Kid robbed a bank here," I said. "Right here?"

"This city, I mean."

"How about their emphasis on philosophy over method?"

"Butch's?"

"Cristo's."

"I like it," I said.

"Both are so important," Sinead said. Then stopped. "How about there?"

I nodded and we entered a small restaurant whose tall windows overlooked the street. It was almost empty, which appealed to me. We were given seats near the window, but we ignored the passersby outside.

"You have great potential," Cristo greeted me the next morning. "You have power and conviction, but you must learn to dance."

"That's what I want. I want to learn to dance."

The three of us made our way up the dirt driveway to the guest kitchen. Dogs, chickens, and children scampered out of our way.

"Don't 'stop' him," Cristo told me. "*Guide* him. Let it *be*. Go with the horse. Be remembered as the one who danced with the horse. You can offer a small sample of power, but *guide*. Then when he stops, you both stop. Create a safe place for him. Then, later, when he is desperate, he will let himself be guided to a place of safety. Be a partner with him from that first day." Cristo paused and looked at Sinead. "That's why you two are married—that's what you are trying to do with the horse. Make him feel like he is with the right person. The right being."

The rest of the retreat group wandered toward the kitchen with us, and Cristo spoke louder to include them all. "That's why starting horses can be the easiest thing. They are untouched. *You* can make the difference. I train my brain to love every horse. I train my brain to do the same with people. With each one I say, *This is a creature that deserves the best of me.*"

In the house, food was held in wooden crates near the long table. The cups were tin or enamel, the ladles were wooden and chipped. Dried flowers and herbs hung above us from thick scratched wooden beams. Behind the sink was a window that looked out to the yard. Three kittens inhabited the outside sill. One was lying down. One was looking in at us. The third was swatting at a butterfly.

"Everything is energy. Look at that." Cristo pointed at a cabinet. "That was once a tree. It might have been three hundred years old. Before that it was something else. Because of that I try to be respectful."

Sinead and I stood, eating our breakfast near the stove. A group of six of us now surrounded Cristo as he spoke.

"When the horse is afraid, that is the best time to be there for him," he continued. "That fear needs to be there. so that *you* can be there for him. You say, 'That can happen, but not with me. I'm your friend.'" He paused, looking at each of us. The murmur of conversations in Spanish rose from behind us at the long table. "Real danger doesn't exist," he said. "It's an illusion. My mother always told me to be careful. She was worried about heights and snakes. But my father encouraged me to play. He taught me respect for these things. And then he was the one I trusted the most." Cristo ran his hand through his hair. "Horses would never do the things we ask them in the wild by themselves. They wouldn't jump five feet, they wouldn't run forty-five miles, they wouldn't play polo. But together, we create a fusion of souls so that horses can do more. It's like a general, leading troops into battle. *ARGGGH!*" he yelled suddenly, pretending to run across the kitchen, brandishing a sword. "As opposed to a horse that has learned to stop at a jump. That has lost confidence in us. Most of us have been disappointed by somebody—a friend, a parent, a partner. It is hard to regain their confidence. It was easy to lose it."

Sinead told a story about one of her horses at a competition in Florida. She was a young mare, and the warm-up arena had been chaotic. It was difficult for anyone to have relaxed, focused horses in such an environment. And it had been very difficult for this mare to trust Sinead that it would be okay.

"In Paso Robles," Cristo said, "I went to a show. That environment…it was aggressive to me."

Aggressive was the right word for some horse shows. Shopping in your face. Prize money. Television screens above the rings, more screens in the restaurants, screens in people's hands, as horses are dragged along behind them. All the emphasis on *outcome*—on taking, on getting, like visiting Vegas or playing Grand Theft Auto.

Then Cristo looked right at me and shared the only technical advice I'd learn in Argentina.

"Loosen the rope a little. *Let him go*. Make it even more like a dance. Let him lead a little, and go *with* him. Your energy…is it something he could get in sync with? It's not about having him be *happy*. Or you being *happy*. That's not quite the right word. There is something else…what's the word…*joy*." He paused, thoughtful. "*Joyful*. That's the right word."

I went for a run. No shirt, no hat. The sweat ran into my eyes. The pavement ended at the hills and my rhythm slowed as gravel slipped under my feet. My lungs burned, my calves ached. I gritted my teeth and doubled down. At the crest of the hill, I got my rhythm back, and then I turned a corner and saw a lake spread out before me.

I ran alongside the lake then veered off and picked my way along a gnarly trail. I crested another hill then came face-to-face with a fence. I vaulted it and pushed on. Running is about finding shortcuts, new paths, and stopping to say hi to locals. The best run is passing a local going the other direction, doing a one-eighty, catching up to him, making friends, running with him, and learning his favorite loop.

Running is about exploring.

The last half mile of trail was downhill, and I opened it up. My heart rate was high, and I could feel my pulse in my chest and temples. I was sweaty and red when I got back to the Scarpatis'. I stopped at the house, then changed my mind and ran down the short hill to the creek where I'd swum when we first arrived. I jumped in, clothes still on, and felt alive.

Sinead and I left early the next morning. Cristo drove us to the airport.

"Is that an eagle?" I pointed at a statue the size of a camel as we weaved through traffic.

"That's a condor. There are many condors here, in the *Sierras*," Cristo said.

We completed our first trip in reverse: hills, then green fields, then the town, then the airport. With our bags on the pavement, we all hugged. But I wasn't sad. Something in me knew I would see Cristo again.

32

"Tik," he said with an outstretched hand. "Nice to meet you in person."

"Pleasure to meet you," I said, slightly awed. The man before me was the Tom Brady of colt starting. That day he was on crutches, and after shaking my hand, he crutched off to start his clinic.

I went the other direction, to check in and pay admission. If I couldn't train with Chris, I could still show up and watch him work. The clinic he was teaching was in Lady Lake, an easy one-hour drive from Copperline. Agnes, a fellow horsemanship enthusiast, had come along.

Chris had gritty two-day-old stubble and a steely jaw. His black shirt and blue jeans fit his trim frame perfectly. On his head he wore a black cowboy hat, on his face black-rimmed rectangular glasses, and on his feet ocean-blue-and-yellow HOKA running shoes. He leaned on the aluminum crutches. I wondered why he needed them.

"I have a lot of people say," he began, "'I want to do this,' or 'I want to do that.' We are doing the things necessary to get to *do* that. Preparation is the key. We are doing the maneuvers that are necessary in order to do *that* thing. It's about preparation. It's your energy, your demeanor; it's a lot of different things. You have to learn how to be a little more patient in order to advance your horsemanship. The biggest mistake people make is to rush the preparation—they skip steps." Chris spoke like a professor. Or maybe a cross between a professor and a preacher. "Everybody wants to live on top of the mountain," he said. "People struggle, they climb, and when they get there, they are a little bit disappointed. Because they realize the struggle *was* the purpose."

He crutched a dozen steps down to look at the far end of the bleachers where Agnes and I sat.

"I have a herniated disc. I'm on crutches. I've had three back surgeries. I've got another coming up. Sixteen times I've had general anesthesia." Chris looked around and paused. It was dramatic, well-conceived. "Why are you here?" he asked simply. "You are here for a reason. Maybe you are on the verge of quitting. Maybe you are on the verge of getting hurt. The number one thing is *teaching horses to find relaxation*. The pressure is calculated. I start small. I build it so they learn to look for that release. One of the biggest mistakes I see in horsemanship or colt starting is that if you just 'get on and ride,' and you don't ever challenge the horse, and then help him negotiate that challenge, the environment eventually *will* challenge him. And then you *will* get hurt."

It felt like Chris was speaking directly to me. I wondered how many other people felt the same.

"Ride the horse, don't rely on the equipment. Engage your core. Every signal comes from here." Chris rubbed his flat stomach. "*This* controls your power, your energy, your balance." Then he looked up to the back of the bleachers where I sat. "We have Tik Maynard here with us," he said. "He will be competing at Road to the Horse 2024. He has done some good riding, written some good books. He wanted to start some horses with us. But I had to stop giving colt-starting clinics. 'Cause I'd have twenty-five horses show up, and then I'd have to start every single one, aside from a couple, because, you know why? Because people don't know how to ride their *broke* horses."

I wanted to smile. First, because he had looked up at me, said my name to the crowd. Second, because I had only written *one* book—so far. Third, because he'd given me the same lecture about colt-starting clinics over the phone. But I forced myself to keep a straight face.

"I've seen people ride for fifty years, and they still don't know how to ride correctly. If you 'hold on' you will *always* fall off. If you *ride* you will *never* fall off. Riding is offensive; holding on is defensive."

I noticed that he was wearing his Road to the Horse World Champion belt buckle. It glinted as he crutched back to the other end of the bleachers. "See that?" I pointed. "You can't buy those," I whispered to Agnes.

Chris paused and took a deep breath. "Awareness," he said. "Awareness of what our right hand is doing. What our left hand is doing. Also our breathing. My breathing is intentional. I'm in the zone. Here and now. And Tik—" He looked toward me in the stands again. "That's what happens at Road to the Horse. Trainers push, they rush, they skip steps. And the horse feels the pressure. You don't have to go on anyone else's timeline. To learn, you have to be relaxed. When you are tense, you aren't learning correctly. You don't have to get a yoga mat. You just have to slow things down. Be *here* and *now*. Be sensitive to a change in the horse. And when you are sensitive to that, your timing is better. Your horse is very forgiving, believe it or not. But it's not okay not to change. It's not okay to not get better. Don't be afraid to try. Be humble. I'm not a 'master horseman.' I'm not a 'professional.' I'm a *student of the horse*. That keeps my window of learning open. You never *master* horsemanship. You *never* master horsemanship. A horseman keeps learning."

Despite the crutches Chris gave the overwhelming presence of an athlete. The kind of man with determination; the kind of man you wouldn't want to go toe-to-toe with, even if you outweighed him by forty pounds. The kind of person you wanted with you if you were a pioneer on the American frontier.

The covered arena in which we sat was L Cross Equestrian Center, on Grays Airport Road, a few miles north and east of the Villages, about forty miles due south of Copperline. It was private property, but it had the sturdy industrial look of a place designed to constantly host the public. There were cattle in the fields next to the arena. All their bovine heads were lowered, munching the Bahia grass that is so common in central Florida. Around them grew live oaks that were hundreds of years old.

Chris came right up to the bleachers and leaned on them, inches from the crowd.

"With horses, you've got to train yourself to relax. Adrenaline is okay if you can learn to control it. Don't let it create anxiety. The day I quit training horses and started training myself was the day I became a horse trainer. I had a chip on my shoulder until I became peaceful and understood I don't have to prove anything. If you're at peace with yourself, it will go through to your horse. Horses read body language, and they can feel the energy off you. What is leadership? It's confidence, it's relaxation, it's knowledge—it's all those things. And horses feel that."

When Chris's introduction was over and the participating riders went to get their horses, I stole down to where he sat, and asked him about halters, bridles, and bits, for starting horses. He explained that he started horses with a halter and a rope just on one side. Then he switched to what he called a side-pull. He avoided bits.

"Teeth problems. Wolf teeth," he said, referencing the small teeth that usually erupted in the horse's first year and were removed later to prevent mouth issues. "You don't want to get into that."

"You have any of those side-pulls for sale here?" I asked.

"Nope. Sold out. But I can send you one," he offered.

"That would be great," I said, not really expecting him to remember.

The clinic recommenced, and I didn't speak to Chris again. But I did receive a side-pull in the mail two weeks later.

33

"Are you okay?"

"I'm fine," I lied.

"Are you sure you're okay?" Chelsea asked.

"Why don't you take her for a few minutes?" I whispered.

I held out the rope. Chelsea gave me a funny look, but took the rope attached to her little Mustang, Luna. I walked slowly out of the round pen, masking my limp.

Chelsea kept talking behind me, but her voice was a blur. I felt people watching me as I left the round pen. I took a breath, then another one, but they were shallow and I couldn't fill my lungs, as if I was pouring water into a glass with a crack in it, and the water kept leaking out.

I put a hand on the rail to steady myself. I swore at myself under my breath.

What would Natalie say? Probably something like, "Feel the fear... don't fight it." Something annoyingly cliche.

I looked at the ground. I took another, deeper breath. I felt the fear. I felt it in my gut and in my shoulders. I put one cowboy-booted-foot up on the lower rail of the round pen and stretched my hamstring. I shut my eyes and took another deep breath. Then I let it out slowly.

Chelsea walked up and said something.

I looked at her. I focused. "I don't think I tore it again. The pain is just flashes, not the electric shocks of a few months ago… it's more like a reminder. A flashback. What happened with Luna was the same thing that happened last time: the horse took off, I lost my stirrups, I had to cling on."

Chelsea asked one of her working students to take Luna back and untack her, and she and I sat underneath a big oak. Chelsea Candy and I were good friends now, after years of Sinead and me teaching at her beautiful farm in Maine. She'd brought the mare she was training for the 2024 Mustang Classic competition at the Kentucky Horse Park to Copperline so I could help her…and so I could get more experience starting horses.

As my panic eased and muscles relaxed, I told Chelsea about Ren Hurst and our phone conversation, about what Ren believed. It was difficult to talk to Chelsea about it. How do you tell someone that what she loves, someone else believes to be abuse?

"I don't know if I want to read her book," Chelsea said.

"I didn't know either."

"I don't know if I'm ready for it."

"I thought the same thing. Are we lying to ourselves? Maybe we just don't want to know the truth? Maybe it's too much out of our comfort zone? It requires too much change?"

"Maybe."

"What she says wouldn't hit a nerve in people if there wasn't some truth to it, right?"

I'd been gauging my response to *Riding on the Power of Others*. At first, I'd been defensive. But as I'd delved deeper, I started to understand Ren's view: how often humans use horses to "complete" themselves. Not only do we borrow their speed, we depend on them for happiness, we unload our shit on them, and we wrap our identity up with theirs.

I realized after reading the book it was not any horse's job to make me feel whole. It was mine.

If Ren had attacked me and my beliefs, or I had attacked her and hers, our phone conversation would never have happened. Instead, I was brimming over with awe that our two truths could coexist. Ren had deepened my understanding of human relationships with horses, and I felt richer because of it.

"I'll lend you the book," I told Chelsea.

"I'm glad you're okay," she said.

"This Road to the Horse thing is taking a lot out of me."

"Are you still glad you're doing it?"

I looked at the now empty round pen. I studied the hoofprints in the sand. I knew the fear and worry were stealing a part of me each and every day. But the fear also focused me, and each day that I pushed through it, I became a little stronger. Each day that a part of me was stolen, I became more *me*, like I was burning off unneeded layers.

"You know," I said, "in a weird way it feels like something I have been preparing my whole life for. It would be a shame to back out now."

"He is one of the handiest guys in the world," Ryan Rose said.

He was speaking about Nick Dowers. We were watching the 2019 Road to the Horse. It was my third or fourth time studying it—the head-to-head between Nick and Vicki Wilson.

I leaned back on the couch. Ryan, another horse trainer I respected who'd started a lot of colts, Jake, and I were crammed into a snug little TV room in Ryan's house. Ryan was from Wisconsin but had just bought a small farm in Reddick, near Orange Lake, nine miles from Copperline. There were two old couches and a creaky chair, none of which matched. Below the television was a boarded-up fireplace. Tyler, Ryan's lanky assistant, was there too. He wore an orange shirt that said *Madison Marathon*.

The television showed a closeup of Vicki. She was looking to get a hand on her horse. As she raised her hand, the colt smoothly turned away from her, like a leaf twirled by the breeze.

"Once they whirl, they keep whirling. They know what your agenda is," said Ryan.

"Don't stand in front of the colt and try to pat him," Jake warned.

While Vicki played approach and retreat in her black Antares helmet, Nick strode in, ready to rope.

"I wish I had time to learn to throw a rope," I said. "That would be helpful."

"Just practice a *toss*," advised Ryan. "Not a *throw*. To practice, just stand there, and *toss* the loop over a fence post."

I opened two boxes of pizza. Since Ryan was hosting, I had brought the pizza—two larges: one with tomato and mushroom, the other with garlic and jalapeños.

"See where Vicki is at?" Jake said. "She's rubbing the neck. That's better than being by the head. Her body is close…that's more important than touch."

"What about using a stick to bridge the gap?" I asked. "Just to get him used to being touched?"

"It can work. But it's also a whole other variable for him to get used to."

"See that scratching?" Jake pointed out.

"I see it."

"Don't do that! Rub, or gently push down."

I was becoming aware of so many nuances. How I rub, or pat, or scratch, or massage a horse really adds up. Scratching could help, but scratching a horse without an itch was like feeding a dog that wasn't hungry.

"As long as you are confident and consistent in what you do it will work," Jake noted. "What they are both doing is different from what I do. But it's working."

"Do you guys know what any of the others are doing to prepare?" I asked between bites.

"I heard John Baar is going to Circle Bar to start a bunch of colts for them," Jake said.

Nick Dowers' horse pulled back, and Nick went with him. Then after a pause he led the colt forward.

"I like that he tried to fix the pull-back when the horse wasn't trying to pull back," Ryan commented. "When the horse pulled back, he didn't pick *that* moment to try and fix it. He didn't pick the moment the horse was the most committed to doing the wrong thing. But he also didn't ignore it. He made a note, and he fixed it later."

"You're half teaching," Jake added in, "but also half trying to just get along with them."

"I gotta be honest," I admitted. "I'm nervous about the first ride."

"Hey, I'm nervous about first rides too," Ryan said. "If anybody says they aren't, they're lying to you."

Or lying to themselves, I thought. *Or they just don't know any better.* Either way, it made me feel better to hear Ryan say what I felt was normal. Even for cowboys.

"Some cowboys say, 'Don't grab leather, you'll look like a bitch,'" Ryan said. "But, hey, just do it."

"Just like we practiced," Jake agreed. "Hold on."

"And you gotta be in that saddle *a lot* before the competition," Ryan emphasized. "You gotta be *real* comfortable in that saddle! You don't want to be starting a horse and getting used to that saddle at the same time."

"What's the trick to getting my jeans not to rise up when I'm in the saddle?"

"Longer jeans," Tyler piped in.

"Have you ever done one of these?" I asked Ryan.

"I've done three colt-starting competitions. Before I get on, I have a routine pre-ride check. Just three or four things I do routinely before stepping into the stirrup. It's a nice check for you, and it presents an element of familiarity to the horse." He reached for another slice of pizza. "What about ground driving?"

I shrugged. I knew about as much about ground driving as I knew about plumbing or changing the oil on my truck. Which was to say, not much.

"When you have checked everything off, but something inside you is telling you not to get on yet, that's when ground driving will be useful."

"Also, it looks good. It's part of the colt-starting deal for a lot of people," Jake added.

"And it's a lot of exposure for the horse. Ropes beside him; ropes getting tangled around him; ropes touching him on the rump and the legs. You get the horse in binds, and then get him out of them."

On screen Vicki opened an umbrella. It was black, with her logo in white. Each trainer, I knew, was allowed to choose two props.

"The Pitchfork horses are going to be 'ranchier,'" Ryan said. Traditionally, the colts for Road to the Horse had come from the famous 6666 ("Four Sixes") Ranch, but this year, they were coming from the Pitchfork Ranch in Guthrie, Texas.

"'Ranchier'?" I repeated.

"More feral."

Vicki got on her horse bareback. I held my breath. "That's so brave."

"I don't know if I would do that," Jake said. "She is *committed*. If something happens, she is going to go flying."

"The thing is, with colt starting," said Ryan, "it's all educated guesses. You don't have enough rides to know how things are going to turn out."

I took a slice of pizza and leaned back on the couch. "Playing the odds."

"Exactly."

"Anyone want another drink?" I asked.

No one answered. Vicki was busy and active, on and off her horse, on and off, like a puppy jumping on a kid. Nick was smooth; there was not much wasted effort. He would set something up and wait for it.

I could see the value in each approach, and I hoped I would be able to take pieces from both their styles, but I knew I would end up being more like Vicki. Cowboys liked to conserve energy, be efficient, as they had a long day ahead of them. But I *liked* to move. I wanted to run around with my horses; I loved being able to bounce on and off, and to play with them.

I moved into the kitchen and mixed a whiskey and coke. I hustled back in time to see Nick dismount, then walk toward his horse's hind end.

"And *that*, that's a good thing," said Jake. "Step down and move the hindquarters.

"For this you want their feet 'sticky,' but not 'stuck.'"

"You sure don't see Nick smile much," I remarked. "He's all business."

"He is a super nice guy," said Ryan. "A good guy."

I didn't know if I would be able to smile much in the arena either. And I wasn't sure that was what I was aiming for anyway. Starting a horse should be fun, but it was also a situation that needed to be treated with thought and respect.

That was a tough balance to find.

The "hum."

The "frequency."

"Internal vibrations."

Jake kept trying to find different ways to tell me to chill out.

I couldn't get the four-year-old bay gelding to turn in and settle. Jake took the rope from me to demonstrate. I watched carefully. Part of it was the slightly different angle he used to ask the horse to turn. But a bigger part of it was my energy. It was off.

"You're humming here." Jake raised his hand to shoulder height. "You get the horse humming too." He lowered his hand to the height of his waist. "You need to lower the humming."

The hum he was talking about was my intention. It was my body language. My "internal frequency" was too high.

"Everybody has their natural state of energy," Jake said.

I thought of the hours of Road to the Horse videos I'd been watching.

"Wade's is low," I said. "Nick Dowers' is low. Vicki's is higher. Chris Cox isn't that low either."

"But Chris can change it," Jake said. "He can adjust!"

I started thinking about people I knew and their internal frequencies—their "hum." Nick, my pen wrangler, his hum was really low. Really soothing. My wife's could fluctuate. My dad's was lower, my mother's, higher.

"I'm pretty high," I said. "And I'm guessing at Road to the Horse, with those colts, I'll need to be pretty low."

"Yup, and that situation drives people's hum higher. Then you walk into the round pen with that too-high energy, and the colt

wants nothing to do with you. Half of Road to the Horse is the training, but half is creating the relationship."

Sometimes Sinead would say the same thing to me when I barged
too quickly into a room as she read a book or prepared a meal. "You're
at a 'here,'" she would say with her hand high. "I need you to come
down to here." And she'd move her hand down near the floor.

My internal hum whirred constantly, like the mixer that Cristo
used for the mayonnaise. It sat in my stomach and buzzed when I
was anxious. It also buzzed when I was exuberant or loving what I
was doing. If my buzz got too low, it made me feel uncomfortable,
even useless…guilty. With coffee or a cold plunge, I could bring it
back up and get back to work. But for the horses, I needed to turn it
down. Almost off—but not quite off. The great horsemen could find
that lower level when they needed it. I knew I had another level in
me as well. I needed to find it, quick.

Jake helped me for another hour, and I got better. But *not good
enough*, I knew. *Not good enough yet*. Before I left, I apologized for
not being able to make it the next day. I felt the same thing I had felt
when I worked with Glenn—that by not being there all day, I was
disrespecting what these men were giving me. I was leaving before
the lesson was done.

The problem was, the lesson was never done.

"Hey, man," Jake said. "You have a lot going on. Two kids. The
business. Horses in training. Horses to compete. You don't have to
explain anything to me. I get it! We just gotta keep doing the best we
can. Get the reps in. We gotta create our own *Rocky* montage."

The training montage in the 1976 hit film *Rocky*, starring Sylves-
ter Stallone, is considered by some to be the greatest movie montage
of all time. The viewer watches as, in a matter of minutes, Rocky
runs, boxes, does one-handed push-ups, gets punched in the stomach, does sit-ups, sprints along the waterfront, then takes the stairs

two or three at a time up the steps leading to the Philadelphia Museum of Art. At the top he raises his arms in the air in exaltation and in triumph over his own demons. The screen goes into slow motion, then zooms in on his face.

That could be me.

Maybe not exactly like that, but still—the general idea.

"Thanks, Jake." I gave him a hug. Jake was also a busy guy. He knew how to hustle. He worked out in the morning, then got his boy ready for school, then rode a dozen horses Monday to Thursday, and taught clinics most weekends. But I felt like that day, *he saw me*. It felt like we were developing into a team. And instead of taking his little speech as an excuse to train less, it made me want to train more. Train harder. Get better. Take the stairs, three at a time.

But the balance I had with Copperline, Sinead, and the kids was already near a breaking point. I had to be careful.

34

I stepped outside; the cold clamped down on me like a vise. Just as I was about to slip my boots on David Lichman texted me: *Your mailbox is full...give me a call...I have something that perhaps you can use.*

David's photo appeared above the message. He had a handlebar mustache that was graying under his nose, and he wore a gray country-tweed cap. Rimless, clear glasses gave his picture an air of thoughtfulness, and an almost invisible smirk gave him an air of mischief.

I thought David was one of the most talented, innovative, creative, fun horse trainers in the world. His interests included liberty training, trick training, and positive reinforcement training. I hadn't spoken to him in a couple years, so I took it as a sign to go back inside my warm house and call him.

Of course, I asked for his advice on Road to the Horse.

"Completely ignore the competition," David said. "Even if you do nothing, chances are, you will have done more for the horse than most. Everyone seems to get caught up in the competition. You look over in the next pen, you start thinking about what the other guys are doing, but the best winner is the one who does the least."

"Who is the best you've seen?" I asked David. I was sitting in my office looking out the window. It had rained the day before, and

Brooks and Goldfish, in jackets and boots, ran and splashed through the puddles in our arena.

They were going to get wet. They were going to be cold.

"Richard Winters," David replied. "He always has horses that are super soft and responsive, and yet calm. Whenever I've seen him teach, he would be sitting on a horse that was calm and elegant, with soft reins. It was really nice to watch, always."

I had watched Richard compete at Road to the Horse on video. I had never met him, but what I'd seen had impressed me.

"Win or lose," David told me quietly, "you can be a hero if you just focus on what the horse needs. I remember Richard said, 'I don't care if I get on this horse or not. How prepared will he be for the next citizen?' Anyways, I'm doing a massive clean-out. I have some pants I want to give you."

"Pants? Uh, okay."

"*Aanstadt Das* is the name of the company, owned by a fashion designer in upstate New York. Linda introduced me to her. They are very nice riding pants. Deerskin. She gave me two pairs when I was thinner. Each one is custom made. I want to give them to you. If they don't fit you, maybe you can find someone else."

I thanked him, a little unsure about the deerskin pants, and asked again for advice.

"I'll tell you one mistake I saw at Road to the Horse," he said. "I could see it right off. The trainer selected a horse that was super friendly. Then she skipped any kind of pressure with the horse, because the horse would follow her around. But then when the horse got worried, he didn't turn to her. She hadn't taught him to come to her when he was a little bit troubled."

I was doodling on a pad of paper at my desk as he spoke. But I put my pen down. I stared at the wall and envisioned what he was telling me. I tried to really *see* what he was describing.

"The horse looked wonderful, but he did not look to her when he got worried. You need that, and it's better for the horse too. They need to be able to find solace."

Whether we call it "solace," or "rest," or "peace"—that's what horses want, and that's what I would need to be able to offer him.

"Have you ever heard of someone using food at Road to the Horse?" I asked, knowing David's preference for positive reinforcement.

"If the colt will eat out of your hand, I would do it. You would be the first one to do it. I've never seen anyone do it. Oh, how was Chicken Camp?" he asked.

"Amazing," I said.

Brooks wore a crisp white shirt, forest green pants and vest, and an adorable bow tie. Rae, in her wedding dress, was radiant. She smiled and ran over. Brooks peeked out from behind my legs; his mouth was still, but his eyes gleamed with curiosity.

Rae crouched down. "Your suit is so cute."

"Why don't boys get to wear dresses?" Brooks asked.

"He is a little jealous of Goldfish's outfit," I whispered.

"Oh, Brooks. I love you," said Rae as she hugged him.

Soon Rae disappeared to prepare for the ceremony. Rae was a horse person and had been in our life since 2020. She was Brooks' favorite babysitter, and in a few minutes, Brooks would be the ring-bearer and shyly walk down the aisle. After the "I dos" and the kiss, we mingled with the other guests on a wooden patio. Sinead and I leaned on the railing and looked at the pond on the other side.

"That was special, wasn't it?"

"That was beautiful," said Sinead.

Soon our kids were giggling and chasing each other out one

door, around the patio, and in the other door. In and out, in and out, faster and faster. Music played, couples danced, and in and out of people's legs the kids wove.

I slipped out the side door and found the mechanical bull operator. Since the venue had a "farm-like" vibe to it, the happy couple had decided that a "bull" might provide some after-dinner entertainment for their guests. The operator wore a crumpled shirt, cowboy hat, and looked bored. Party lights hung over the headless robotic animal figure.

"Can I get a ride?" I asked.

"You gonna put that drink down?"

I took a swallow. "That's my courage," I said as I put the glass down.

The cowboy put out his cigarette and went to the controls. He nodded, so I climbed onto the inflatable mattress that surrounded the "bull." I climbed up. I took hold of the short rope that was attached to what would have been the "withers" of the bull.

As soon as I nodded, the bull started moving. It cut left, then up, then right, then down, then suddenly left again. After twenty seconds, my legs were burning, and I was launched off.

I rode the mechanical bull three times. The silent cowboy was the only audience, until Sinead wandered out.

She watched for a few seconds. "We should go before the kids crash."

"One more time?" I said, and she nodded.

I needed the practice, but I also hoped that by falling off the mechanical bull a few times, and landing on its inflatable mattress, I would lose some of my fear of being bucked off.

"This suit doesn't have much grip," I said when I'd been thrown once again.

Sinead gave an almost invisible smile and shook her head. "I've got *three* children," she murmured to the cowboy. The cowboy nodded and lit another cigarette.

I rolled off the mattress, stood up, and stretched my legs. The groin injury still niggled.

"Let's find the kids," I offered, picking up my drink and taking her hand.

I got up early to work on the computer. I was about to begin three days of a Martin Black clinic; Sinead was getting ready for three days of horse showing.

I was nervous for the clinic. *More than nervous,* I admitted to myself. *Afraid.*

"We all get nervous," a trainer once told me. "The difference between your butterflies and mine is that mine are flying in formation."

"Daddy?"

"Goldfish, are you awake?"

"Daddy!"

I went into her room and looked at her. She looked at me. She widened her arms, an invitation to pick her up, but she made no move to sit up. She waited for me to embrace her first.

"Okay, princess," I cooed. "Let's go dance."

I shuffled into the kitchen and swung her around as Sinead took the milk out of the fridge and the day officially began.

The clinic had only three participants, of which I would be one. There would also be a half-dozen auditors. Most of them knew Martin, which I didn't, although I'd read *Evidence-Based Horsemanship,* the book he'd cowritten with Dr. Stephen Peters.

I also knew he had competed in Road to the Horse in 2006; his son Wade had won in 2020.

Martin oozed quiet confidence. The first question he asked me was what kind of saddle I would be starting my colt in.

"You *could* start the horse in a jumping saddle," he said. "I did that a few times when I started horses for a jumper rider."

"I could," I said. "I *am* more comfortable in one. I'm not sure yet. I would like to get more comfortable in a Western saddle as well."

I had two horses that a neighbor had dropped off for me to work with. I hadn't met the neighbor and didn't know much about the horses. Martin helped me change that over the course of the clinic day.

Martin was able to talk, teach, tack up, rope, and ride for seven hours, without ever removing the toothpick from the corner of his mouth. He quietly pushed me to get better at groundwork with both horses. It was a full day, and it felt great to survive it, but when I got in the car to head home to Copperline and finally looked at my phone, I saw there were two missed calls from the kids' school.

Three missed calls from Sinead.

Violet was sick.

I'll be home as soon as I can, I texted, a different kind of worry and fear rising within me.

I hustled out of the driveway and south on 301.

As soon as I got to the farm and saw the exhaustion on Sinead's face, I realized how ill our daughter was. I carried her, crying, to the car, and strapped her in.

"I'm sorry," I said. She hated being strapped in.

I took Goldfish to Urgent Care, my thoughts consumed only by helping the little girl in the back seat feel better.

Home five hours later, after zigzagging across central Florida from the doctor's to pharmacies, the relief of knowing Violet would be okay allowing tiredness to take over, I lay in bed. One question kept circulated in my brain: *Why am I doing this?*

I forced myself to get up early the next day to write. But I was distracted by Facebook, Amazon reviews of my first book, and my own self-critical thoughts. And then the kids woke up. It meant no more writing would be completed, but seeing Goldfish with more pink in her cheeks raised my mood. She was still sick, and she would stay home from school, but she had enough energy to hug my neck when I picked her up.

Once the babysitter was settled with Violet, and Bernadette had taken Brooks to school, I got in my truck and turned the key. It started. But I didn't put it in gear right away.

I willed myself to head west on County Road 316, then north on 301, beginning the thirty-five-minute journey to the clinic. I slowed as I passed a woman, younger than me, trudging along the side of the road. Her head was down, covered in something that looked like a shower cap. She walked with a slow and steady rhythm. Her pace seemed set for the long haul.

I thought about Martin Black and the clinic, and considered the importance of arriving early to make a good impression. I also realized a white dude braking hard in a dirty black dually might be intimidating—even frightening—to a woman walking alone.

I hit the brake and pulled over. The lady reached the passenger-side window a few seconds later.

"I'm going another five miles down the road," I said to her. "I can give you a ride, if you want."

She opened the door, then reached high above her for the handhold, and clambered up. "Thanks," she said as she fastened her seatbelt.

"Where are you going?" I asked.

"Gainesville," she said, looking straight ahead.

"*Gainesville?*"

"Gainesville. I work at Paisano's."

"You're *walking* to *Gainesville*?" Gainesville was over twenty miles from where we were.

"It takes me six, seven hours."

"You don't have a car? Or someone that can give you a ride?"

She shook her head. "No, sir."

"You're walking six or seven hours to Gainesville to work at Paisano's. And then what?"

"Takes me six or seven hours to walk back."

"And you *live* all the way out here?"

We were not exactly in the middle of nowhere, but pretty close. There were no sidewalks, no buses. It was three miles to the nearest Dollar General, four miles to the nearest Winn Dixie, fifteen miles to the closest Starbucks. It would be a tough place to survive without a vehicle.

"Yes, sir," she said.

"You have family around here?" I asked.

"I'm from Jamaica. My family's all dead."

"I can't believe you're walking six hours."

"Takes me six, sometimes seven, hours."

"You ever get a ride?"

"I *had* a car," she offered after a slight hesitation. "It got repossessed. Just trying to make the money to get it back."

"That is rough…" I replied. "I'm so impressed that you walk twenty miles to work, though."

"What else can you do?" she said simply and without emotion.

After a few miles the road curved so we were heading west, which was where my destination was. Then we crossed over State Road 121, which headed north and south. Gainesville was north.

"I'll get out here," the woman said.

I pulled over. She climbed out.

"Wait…" I fumbled in my pocket for a twenty. I held it out. "I'd like to contribute to getting that car back," I said. She reached back in for the bill then turned north. "Good luck," I called.

I drove on, in my big dually, the radio playing Dolly Parton.

I'm a big turkey, I thought. *A jerk. A completely lucky, privileged, selfish son of a bitch.*

I hooked a left into a paved driveway, then veered left again onto a dirt track that meandered through the woods. I parked next to the big old wooden barn.

I was five minutes early. I went over to where one of the other clinic attendees, Cal, was practicing roping.

"Morning," I said.

"Mornin'," he replied, letting loose his loop, which flew smoothly and gracefully through the air before landing around the end of a bale of hay, tipped up toward the sky.

I picked up a coil and began practicing the swing that Jake had showed me months ago. I was on my fourth or fifth toss when I heard Martin's voice behind me.

"So you *do* know how to rope."

I turned and saw him standing in the shade of the barn.

"I want to give it a try," I said. I threw. I missed badly. I roped about as well as a chicken could fly.

Martin tilted his head a fraction of an inch, then headed to the barn. Cal and I put the ropes back and hustled after him. We joined the others, who sat in a half-circle around Martin. Pitchforks and brooms lined the wall behind him. Behind me was a stall, and the horse leaned over the half-door as if to be a part of the group.

After a thirty-minute discussion, Martin stood up and said, "Okay, let's meet out at the horses."

As the others dispersed, I hung back and got up the nerve to approach Martin where he stood beside his horse in the barn aisle.

"You okay if I tack up your horse for you?" I offered.

"You want to work your horse off my horse?" he asked, confused by my request.

"No…I was just wondering if I could saddle your horse for you, and you could watch, and tell me if you would do anything differently."

"Okay," he said. "Grab the saddle."

I grabbed the saddle from the rack near the cross-ties and heaved it up on the horse's back. I'd saddled thousands of horses since I was a kid, but the difference in pure bulk and shape of the Western saddle made the basic process feel foreign to me, unfamiliar. I wanted to get quicker, slicker, handier. I wanted to not have to think about it.

"Don't *throw* it up there. *Swing* it up." I took the saddle off, then swung it back up. "Smoother," he said. I swung it up again. "Smoother," he repeated. I swung it up again. "The outside stirrup needs to just barely fly over his back. You're bringing the whole thing too high, and then it plops down too hard."

I swung it up again. Then again. Martin's Western saddle was probably two or three times the weight of the English saddles I was accustomed to, and my arms were fatiguing. I kept going, determined not to show it. Martin shook his head. *Not quite right.*

When we could see the other clinic attendees were ready and waiting, I finally cinched up his saddle, put the horse's bridle on, and handed the gelding's reins to him.

"Thanks, Martin. I just need to do that about a thousand more times in the next five weeks."

He took his horse and led him out of the barn slowly and deliberately. "You'll get it," he said. The toothpick wiggled in his lips as he spoke.

Once I had one of the young horses I was working with caught, Martin coached me on his method for asking the horse to yield the hindquarters and to change direction. I couldn't get it. It was different than the way I had been doing it for years, and I was surprised how difficult it was to get just the right angle. Just like with swinging the saddle up, I felt like a complete beginner.

Martin texted me just before eight in the morning.

"We postponed the next group because of rain. If you'd like a roping lesson, we could work out something today."

I hesitated. I was busy and I was spent, but it would be a unique opportunity. And a helpful one. *If I could just learn to rope…* I called Bernadette and asked if she could babysit that afternoon—with her help, I could take Martin up on his offer.

I trudged downstairs and rode a few horses in the drizzle. Olivia was getting the horses ready; I asked her to hurry up. I checked my watch.

Take a deep breath, I told myself. *Let it go.*

The skies darkened and the rain pounded down on the windshield as I drove to Frank Barnett's place in Williston, just off Highway 27. Frank was a local legend, and Martin was crashing at his place while he was teaching his clinics down the road. *Frank and Martin…what I wouldn't give to be a fly on the wall while they talked horses!* Cal was there, as well, when I arrived. We gathered in Frank's covered arena. Cal lent me a rope. Martin carried over a carpenter's sawhorse with a plastic, rust-colored, cow-shaped head nailed to one end.

I stood to the side, ten feet away, and started swinging. Right off the bat, I hit three or four in a row.

"I'm feeling pretty good about this," I announced.

Martin laughed. "Frank," he called over his shoulder. "He says he's feeling pretty good about this."

Frank, who I had not met before, emerged from the shadows. Martin had known Frank for over twenty-five years. Frank, I guessed, was at least a decade older than Martin. He wore a black hat slightly askew, and seemed more apt to listen than to talk. I owned a copy of his book, a satire entitled *How To Succeed at Horse Training without Really Thinking*. In the closing paragraphs, Frank remarks, "I'd like to say that horse training can be a tough and dirty job. It can be full of long hot hours with little pay and few rewards. One of these days when you're sitting in the saddle with dust in your throat and sweat burning your eyes, watching the steam rise off your hot, exhausted horse I want you to remember this…somewhere out there is someone just like you with those same dreams and that same burning desire. Only they had the good sense to buy a boat."

Martin had me work on one shot for an hour: Approach the saw-horse from slightly behind the "balance point," imagine the horse moves forward, and throw the loop in front of him. He steps his head and neck into the loop. Simple.

The "balance point" Martin referenced was a similar idea to the bubble or flight zone, but also took into account which way the horse was going to travel. Step behind the horse's balance point and he would go forward. Step in front of it and he would go backward.

"It's the highest percentage shot," Martin said.

"What about when the horse stands still, facing me?" I asked.

"There are more variables," said Martin. "The horse can drop his head. He can raise his head. He can go left or right. How much time you have?"

I checked my watch and sighed inwardly. I should have been leaving then, and heading home. "Thirty minutes," I lied. I was going to owe Bernadette, big time.

Frank asked Cal to bring a dark-chocolate-colored gelding as

big as a moose into the arena. The horse trudged around in a circle, bored. I swung a loop at him and missed. I missed again. I missed again. And again. And again. And again.

"Too low."

"Too high."

"You threw too late."

"You rushed it."

"There was a twist in the rope."

The rain striking the metal roof provided a noisy backdrop for his straightforward critique. I tried to focus on Martin's specific instructions for how to stand, how to swing, how to bend my wrist, how to hold my elbow, and how to follow through. I made up my mind to follow his directions and stop worrying about if the rope landed where I intended or not. *Just execute the plan.*

I swung the rope in the air, twice quickly, then I released the loop slowly. I kept the right angle, then had my hand follow through softly.

The loop settled around the chocolate-colored horse's neck. *Yes!* I had done it.

I glanced at Cal. He smiled.

I looked at Martin. "That was the first time I didn't care if I roped him," I said, incredulously. "I was just trying to execute the movements correctly."

Martin laughed. "It's like golf. It can be so rewarding. It can be so frustrating. I can help you with the technique, but *you* have to figure out how to get your mind right. I can't help you with that."

"High involvement; low attachment," I murmured inaudibly.

"What's that?"

"'Ten minutes,'" I yelled over the rain. "I've got a few minutes left—let me try again."

I slipped the rope off the moose and let him walk off. I coiled the rope, then tried to repeat what I had just done right. I missed. I missed again. Missed again.

Focus on the task, don't worry if I catch him. Swing, throw. The rope landed around the gelding's neck.

A good spot to quit.

Reluctantly, I coiled the rope up and shook hands with Martin and Frank and Cal. "Thank you…" I said to each of them in turn.

"When's your birthday?" Cal asked.

"January."

"Keep the rope." He smiled. "Happy birthday."

By the time the kids dozed off that night—Goldfish with her head on my shoulder, Brooks turned and twisted so that his feet were by my head—Sinead was asleep as well, so I picked up a Lee Child thriller that I was partway through. *Personal*, the nineteenth book in the "Jack Reacher" series. A pen marked where I'd last left off, as I underline passages in most of my books.

I underlined:

"You're just a little bit unconventional. Which is the fourth of the four things you need to be. All of which you are. Which is

all we'll ever need. Smart people, working hard, paying atten-tion, thinking laterally."

I wrote in the margin: *I think this applies to RTTH.*
Then I read:

"Weird things are going to happen, and things are going to change, and the ground is going to move under our feet, but if we keep on thinking fast, we'll be okay."

I underlined that as well.

And then I fell asleep, and I allowed myself—one of the very, very, very few times that I allowed myself—to dream about winning.

35

"Rat, rattlesnake, or grubs?" Brooks asked.

"What's that?"

"What do you want for the picnic? Rat, rattlesnake, or grubs?" he asked again in a serious tone. He tugged my sleeve and led me toward the yellow two-person pup tent I had set up between the manure bin and the paddocks.

"Definitely grubs."

"Goldfish is feeling sick again," I said, switching her from my left hip to my right. "I'm going to take her for a walk to get the mail."

"Okay, I'll look for lunch," my son said.

In the era of "free delivery," packages had lost some of their status as rare and special, yet an unexpected gift in the mailbox still excited me. I grasped the packing envelope and ripped open the mustard-colored paper. I invited Violet to help. She ripped at it as best she could. A DVD popped out: *Roping Fundamentals with Martin Black*. Along the top of the cover it said: *From the Great Basin Tradition*.

In the Great Basin, rainwater doesn't flow into the ocean. It spans nearly all of Nevada, much of Utah, and parts of California, Idaho, Oregon and Wyoming, and there the water rests in lakes and swamps. Martin had been born in the Great Basin; it was where his heart was.

I carried the mail and the DVD back to the stairs that led to our apartment over the barn, and set them there, then went to search for Brooks. "*Coo-EEE*," I called, switching his sister to my other hip, then almost stumbling over his legs. He was sitting, silently inspecting a jar of grubs. Eight grayish-white, many-legged, squishy larvae.

"Can I eat one?" he asked.

"What did your mother say?"

"She said ask you."

"Yup. You can eat one."

He took a tentative bite, then wrinkled his nose.

"Slimy, yet satisfying?" I asked.

The kids passed out early that evening. Sinead had a cocktail party to attend, and so I poured myself a bourbon with one large ice cube and popped the DVD in. "Swinging a rope is one thing," said Martin on the screen. "Hitting a target is another thing. You can't teach experience. You have to have everything right before you let go of the rope: The angle of the swing. The position of hand and elbow. Then lots of cowboys can throw the rope, but they are still missing what's next: the horsemanship.... Some horsemen today, some of 'em might never of even coiled up an extension cord, much less been around a rope."

I laughed at that. He might, almost, have been speaking about me.

I continued watching, and for some reason, something clicked, and I began practicing roping three or four days a week. Just for ten or fifteen minutes at a time. Suddenly, I enjoyed it. It reminded me of being sixteen years old and shooting baskets during lunch hour.

"You like these?" I asked.

"They look baggy and long," Sinead said.

I was trying on Wranglers in Russell's Western Wear. I looked in the mirror.

"They *are* baggy, they're supposed to be looser so I can jump on and off. If they're all tight and bougie, I won't be as agile. Also, they are two inches longer than normal so that when I'm in a saddle they don't ride up above my boots."

"That's called 'stacking,'" a saleswoman in alligator-skin boots said.

Sinead was lifting belts one at a time and studying the designs. "I guess," she remarked absentmindedly. I kept the pants on, then I went looking for boots.

"How about these?"

"Do you need new boots?"

"The stitching is rotting on the boots I have. And they are too big. They're clunky when I run in them."

"Are you going to be running in your cowboy boots?"

"Definitely."

"Get them then."

I tried them on. I jumped and pulled my knees to my chest. I jogged on the spot. I kicked my heels to my bum. They felt snug and athletic.

Total cost for boots and pants was just under four hundred dollars. I handed over my debit card. It was rejected.

I looked at Sinead.

When I was a kid, I'd gone to a lot of horse shows with my parents. For years they'd made their living running a tack vendor booth and taking professional photos. They'd also both competed. They'd really hustled. They'd been on the same hamster wheel that Sinead and I were on: make a lot...spend even more...make a lot...spend even more. No savings or rainy-day money for us. It all went back into the horses or the farm. It didn't matter how much work it was, how much debt we went into, how many evenings we stayed up discussing how to pay for more horses, because horses were more than our careers—they were our passion, our pleasure.

Our addiction.

Sinead didn't hesitate. "Put it on the Mastercard," she said.

I handed the card to the lady with the alligator boots as I ripped the tag off my purchases.

"You going to wear them out?"

"I need to break 'em in quick," I said, pulling them back on.

In the parking lot I bounded ahead of Sinead. They felt good, but the costs of my preparation were adding up quickly. I was worried, but we were all-in. Not being all-in would have created a different kind of worry, one that scared me even more.

At the end of February, I finally decided that I was going to use a Western saddle at Road to the Horse, not a jump saddle. But I didn't own one, so I would have to borrow one.

"Why a Western saddle?" asked Juliette.

I had a few very specific reasons, but there was something else as well: Riding in a Western saddle was something that I didn't know how to do, and *I just wanted to know how to do it*. Learning how to carry it, swing it, cinch it up, and sit in it all added up to a sort of puzzle, and I liked puzzles.

I had learned more in the previous six months than I had in the previous six years. And it wasn't that I was a bigger person as a result. It wasn't that now I did *more*. Instead, I was leaner, thinner; I had learned to do *less*. Do less, do it better, do it rawer, and do it more authentically.

My goal going into March, the month of Road to the Horse, was to keep it simple. I didn't aim to do anything fancy or new. I wanted to be me. I wanted to do the same sorts of things other people had done, but I wanted to do those things *better*. I dreamed of having perfect timing. I saw myself start horses in my mind's eye night after night after night. I wanted to do it *my* way. I wanted to *be me* with the horse. And I hadn't felt totally myself in months because I had been learning so many other methods. I hoped that three weeks of doing it *my* way, with *my* team, would be enough time to get my confidence up.

"Why did you pick me?" Nick asked. He had driven down from Wisconsin. He and his wife and daughter were staying in their camper beside our barn while we prepared for Kentucky.

I put the kettle on the stove. "Coffee?" I asked.

"Just Red Bull."

"Nick." I shook my head. "It's nine in the morning…"

He shrugged his shoulders, so I passed him one of his energy drinks from the fridge.

"I wanted someone who knows me, and someone who knows horses," I said. Nick sat across the kitchen table from me. "I didn't want a coach; I didn't want a groom. I wanted someone who I could have honest conversations with. I wanted a friend and a peer."

What I didn't realize yet was there were two other traits that Nick had that made him the right choice. The first was his authenticity. Big black beard, big gold heart. He was Nick, and he wasn't trying to be anybody but Nick. I also didn't have to worry about him. I didn't have to worry about calling him too much, or too little. I didn't have to worry about him being rude. I didn't have to walk on eggshells around him. He was thoughtful in what he said, when he said it, and why he said it. Nick was an excellent team player.

He ruminated for less than a minute, then: "I know you can do it. You're capable of winning the whole thing."

I was trying so hard not to think about winning. Not only did so much depend on variables outside of my control, like the horse I drew, and the judging, but the idea of it being possible added pressure that I didn't need or want.

But I felt a thrill that Nick felt that way.

Ten days before Road to the Horse, Sam and I won the Advanced division at the Chatt Hills event in Georgia. Normally, such a victory would have been the highlight of the year, but it was immediately overshadowed by a long hike around the lake on the grounds with Brooks. His curiosity was contagious, and I found myself balancing on trees that had fallen over streams, poking around for frogs, picking up a turtle shell, holding a salamander, admiring a waterfall, studying animal scat, and scaling an abandoned deer stand.

It was a fifteen-minute walk around that lake, but that day, it took us an hour and a half. The last thirty, I carried Brooks on my shoulders. When we finished the lap, Sinead and Violet joined us.

"Dad!" Brooks shouted at me as he grabbed Sinead's hand. "You can go with Goldfish. I'll show Mom where to go."

Another two hours later, we all fell back into our camper, wet, dirty, and tired. After her bath Goldfish took her towel and disappeared. I turned around, and she was gone. I looked under the bed, on the bed and under the covers, under the table. Nothing. She was too young to open the door...

"*Gold*-fish!" I called, looking under the crib.

Nothing.

"Goldfish!" I said, turning over the duvet and pillows for the second time.

Nothing.

And then... "There you are, you little pickle!"

She was in the cabinet next to the bed. "Come look at your sister, Brooks. She is all folded up."

Violet crouched there, knees by her chin, looking out at us.

"It's so funny how she can do that and not give a peep," Sinead said.

"I used to do that," I said, "when I was in preschool."

"Hide?" Brooks asked.

"Hide for ages. Not making a sound. One time the teachers had to call Granny to come find me 'cause I was silent for hours. They thought I might have escaped! But I had just curled up in a ball, hidden away."

"Do you still feel like doing that, Dad?"

"All the time."

Nick and I took the dogs for a walk. Ferdinand ran ahead, while Walden, Nick's poodle, zoomed to the fence line and started sniffing along it. Walden was a working hunting dog.

"Caught the scent of something!"

"Raccoon?"

I slowed down. Normally I pushed the pace on these walks, but that evening I stopped and tilted my head to the left, then to the right.

"My *neck* is killing me," I said. The muscles in my shoulders and the back of my neck were taut and sore.

"My *back* is killing me," said Nick.

We plodded along, slowly, in silence. I thought about how both Nick and I were like old trucks now. We could still run and jump and lift, but our warm-up time was taking longer and longer.

Nick watched Walden stop to pee. Ferdinand came back for a rub behind the ears, then left again to explore. We were walking in the middle of the deserted road. The stars were out.

"What are you looking forward to?" Nick asked.

"What I'm hoping happens is I can find moments in that round pen where it's just you and me and that colt. And we are just training him, and everything else fades away for a few minutes."

Nick nodded. "Completely dialed in."

"Exactly. Sometimes I find that place effortlessly, sometimes it's impossible to find."

I imagined the opposite place, a place I had also been: frozen, moving with concrete feet, hearing every tick of the clock, feeling the stares of the crowd, my mouth dry, sweat pooling on my forehead.

The dogs were slowing down. Nick stopped and looked at the moon. "Why is your neck hurting?"

"From having kids on my shoulders for three hours yesterday as we traipsed through the forest."

"Being a dad is the best, though, isn't it?"

"It is, Nick. It really is."

"Daddy?" Brooks called.

"Yes," I said, walking back to his room. He lay in the top bunk, cheek on the edge, eyes liquid and looking down on me as I stood in the doorway.

"I'm scared," he said softly.

"What are you scared of?"

"Nightmares."

"I'll be right there," I said, pointing to the couch, where I was going to do some computer work. "If you have any bad dreams at all, just call me and I'll come get you, and you can sleep in my bed."

"My brain thinks about dinosaurs. I don't want it to, but it does."

"The thing about dinosaurs, Brooks, is that while they were real and they were once alive, they are extinct now. The closest thing you will see to a dinosaur these days might be a chicken. You know, there are things in life that scare me too. It's okay to be scared. Do you want me to read a few more pages to you?"

"Yes," he said, so I switched on the lights and opened *Danny, The Champion of the World*:

> I was glad my father was an eye-smiler. It meant he never gave me a fake smile, because it's impossible to make your eyes twinkle if you aren't feeling twinkly yourself. A mouth-smile is different. You can fake a mouth-smile any time you want, simply by moving your lips. I've also learned that a real mouth-smile always has an eye-smile to go with it, so watch out, I say, when someone smiles at you with his mouth but the eyes stay the same. It's sure to be bogus.

Brooks' eyes, meanwhile, had shut. I marked the page and put the book back on the shelf. I gave my son a kiss on the forehead and crept out of the room.

I sat on the couch. I opened my laptop. But I couldn't work. I thought about the past three days: We had simulated Road to the Horse at Yvonne Barteau's.

Yvonne was a Grand Prix dressage rider and trainer, based at

"The Oaks," an "Equestrian and Lifestyle Community" near Lake City, in North Florida. The subdivision had been designed by David and Karen O'Connor.

Besides Yvonne's dressage business, she also ran a nonprofit called Horses Without Humans (HWH), an organization dedicated to providing at-risk horses with the care and training to secure their forever home. She had two unstarted horses that she had offered us to use for the simulation. It was good practice for me, good training for the horses, and good marketing for her nonprofit.

I'd started both horses in front of a small crowd. Both horses were easy, and I was never really pushed. It was a unique chance to go through the timelines and the rules, and to work with Nick in the actual role of pen wrangler. On the last day of the simulation, someone had told me that one of the other competitors had "been doing a lot of these!"

I've only done one, I'd thought.

And these were easy horses.

36

It was a gloomy Sunday. Bernadette took Brooks and Goldfish on a walk. Sinead headed out to ride. Nick and I drove to Jake's.

I played with one of Jake's young horses while Nick and Jake watched. Jake pointed out a few times how the direction and intention with which I approached the horse could be improved. Playing with horses from the ground is similar to playing pool—so much of it is about understanding angles.

That morning I'd received a text from a woman I'd met a few months back. *I'll be wearing red and screaming at the computer. You can't see me, so I might even paint my face and act like a crazy soccer fan…*

That was nice. But then she'd texted: *You'll be back every year and break Chris Cox's record.*

I'd put my phone away. Hearing people say I *wasn't* good enough was easier to digest than hearing that she thought I was going to win.

What do I want to hear? I wondered. *What would help?*

"Those Pepto horses," said Jake, "you get your hands on those, and you are money."

He was referring to descendants of a famous Quarter Horse stallion named Peptoboonsmal. Of the Pitchfork horses we would get to choose from, five of them had "Pepto blood"—four of them as a grandparent, one of them as a great grandparent.

"You think everybody will be wanting the same horses?"

"Some people want a lot of horse. They want a lot of life in the horse they pick so they don't run out. But I don't think, the way you are going to be training the horse, that that's going to be a concern."

This is what helps, I thought. *The work, the preparation, the people that are involved in the process.*

"We have to pick which saddle we are going with," I said. "We have Jake's saddle, with the roping horn," I nodded at Jake in thanks for his offer to lend it for the event, "or Ryan's saddle with the reining horn."

"There are other pros and cons, beyond the horn," Nick pointed out. "The weight, the sturdiness, the look, how you feel in them…"

"What about the horn?"

"The instinct is to pull on it anyways, which is the worst."

We chose Jake's saddle. I was more comfortable with the amount I had ridden in it.

After nine months of preparation, we were leaving for Lexington, and the 2024 Road to the Horse the next day, and Sinead, Juliette, Nick, and Jake were helping me run through my final list of concerns. My mother was there too; my father and brother would meet us in Kentucky.

"Next item," I said. "I want our team to be the standard. I want everyone to look sharp. Be polite. I don't want anyone bad mouthing other teams. I want to be the kindest, most professional team there."

Everyone agreed.

"And no sneaking people in to the VIP area." I looked at my mom. "Would I do that?"

"Yes, you would. Not only would you do that, given half a chance, you would be corrupting your grandkids as well!"

My mother rolled her eyes at me. "I would never," she said.

I was trying to enjoy the last days at home with the team, but it was difficult. I was moving constantly, and it felt like if I stopped moving, I'd never be able to start again.

I took a sip of coffee and opened the door. Dark. Overcast. The smell of winter not ready to surrender. I recoiled from the bite of the cold wind. The breeze was traveling west to east, picking up steam over the Gulf of Mexico and then racing across the cattle lands of central Florida.

"It's colder than it's been in weeks," I whispered to Sinead, shutting the door again.

"Did you put the car seat back together?" she asked.

"I was just about to," I said, bracing myself, then hustling outside and down the stairs. The seat had been dismantled and hosed down because Goldfish had thrown up a bottle of milk in her lap on the way to school the day before. The seat still offered a tang of milk gone bad.

Nick and Jake had left the day before. We were trying to get to the Kentucky Horse Park in time to see the Pitchfork Ranch horses being unloaded. There would be fourteen geldings and five mares, all three-year-olds, arriving in three stock trailers. The geldings were for the "main event," and the fillies were for the "Wild Card" competitors. (The Wild Card competition had been added a few years prior and was run like a pre-game show, with the winner going on to compete in the main event. Having the fillies was a new idea, though, and an interesting one.) I wanted to follow

Vicki Wilson's advice: Watch the horses be unloaded. Observe. See which ones were curious, which ones kicked, which ones followed, and which ones led.

My mom drove as I sat in the passenger seat and catered to the whims of Brooks and Goldfish in the back. It was seven hundred and forty-five miles to the Kentucky Horse Park, almost all of it on Interstate 75.

"Mom, the speed limit is seventy, not sixty!" I objected. "It's an eleven-hour drive as it is!"

The deep voice of Luke Combs covering "Fast Car" by Tracy Chapman—one of my favorite songs—came on the radio. I closed my eyes for a few seconds and let the music fill me up. The pressure that felt almost overwhelming started to disappear. In its place came an itch. The same kind of itch I had felt at Cristobal's place in Argentina. It was an itch that said, *Let me in. Let me in that round pen! Let me get my hands on him. Let's see what we can do. Let's show the world!*

I itched. I craved. It was the itch of a child to not be left on the sidelines watching when it came time for the game. *Don't leave me off the team. I want to be a part of this. I want to play!*

And then Goldfish swung the lariat and hit me in the back of the head.

"I'm going to play an audiobook," I announced, opening my eyes. "Brooks, do you want *Charlie and the Chocolate Factory* or *Swallows and Amazons*?"

"*Swallows!*" Brooks shouted. Then, "I need to go potty," he cried.

We stopped for the fourth time between Macon and Valdosta, Georgia. I unstrapped both kids, took one to pee, changed the diaper on the other, filled the gas tank, and we hit the road again.

"You know, Brooks," I said, "Granny read this to me when I was your age."

"Shh."

Better drowned than duffers if not duffers won't drown, the audio-book proclaimed.

"That's the best line in English literature," my mum declared.

"What's it mean?" Brooks asked.

"I love this story," Mum said. "It's going to make me cry."

"Granny will explain it," I told Brooks.

Wednesday

"Want to meet for breakfast? Discuss strategy?" Jake asked. "It's been chaos. These kids are all over the place."

"You look stressed. Just let me know what I can do to help."

My brother Jordan, his wife Robin, and my niece Mera had come down from Canada and were staying in the Kentucky Horse Park campground in our camper. Jake and I ran Brooks and Goldfish over to where the rig was parked.

"They were a lot this morning," I said to Jordan. "The same way that juggling baby alligators might be a lot."

"We got this," Robin said.

"How are you feeling?" my brother asked.

"Hey," Jake interrupted. He had his phone out and was looking at it. "They just unloaded the horses."

"What?"

I wanted to scream. All this way, all this rush, and we had missed the horses unloading by an hour. The mist of tension that had been quietly circulating in my body, that I had been resisting, started to concentrate behind my eyes. I caught myself glaring at everyone. At my son. At my daughter.

But they didn't care what happened. They were happy, playing with their cousin.

I relaxed my jaw. I brought my shoulders back and down. I focused on my breathing.

"Hey, Stormy," I said. I shook his hand. I had met him the year before when I'd come to Road to the Horse with my dad, but I reintroduced myself, then introduced Nick and Jake.

Stormy's grip was firm, his eye contact to die for. He wore a cowboy hat. There were a few gray hairs in his lampshade mustache There was a warmth about him that made me want to move closer. Stormy was from Texas, as many people at Road to the Horse were.

"These are the fillies."

"Where are the geldings?"

"They aren't here yet."

I looked at Jake and Nick. Jake gave me a small smile. We hadn't missed them. Only the fillies had arrived and been unloaded.

"Stormy, what's your official role here?" I asked.

"Well, 'remuda manager'…'arena manager'…" He went on, but his voice was drowned out by a forklift unloading round pen panels. There were green panels, orangey-red panels, marine blue panels, gray panels, and black panels. Each competitor would be in a different-colored round pen. The tubular structure and new paint reminded me of being in a bike store as a kid and coveting a new mountain bike, all shiny and glistening and new.

"How long have you been helping at Road to the Horse?" I asked Stormy.

"I was here in 2007, 2010, and 2011 helping competitors. But I've been on payroll since 2013."

The five fillies were already settling in. One was munching hay, two were lying down, one was drinking, and the fifth had come over to the fence and was looking at us with knowing eyes.

I stared at them. "Which one would you pick?"

"Paper-wise there's nothing wrong with any of 'em," Stormy said, without looking at any of them. "They all look pretty good. I wouldn't pick the leader. And I wouldn't pick the one that's getting picked on a lot."

"Which one?" I pushed Stormy. But I knew it would be difficult to tell, as they had mostly settled into a resting state. The best time to view the young horses would be when they were moving into a new space. That's when we would be able to tell who was curious, who was scared, who was confident, and who was always at the back of the herd. But even then, there was a lot of luck involved in picking because the way a horse interacted with other horses wasn't necessarily the way the horse would interact with people.

The way horses are curious and confident is situational. They might be confident about going into a new space, but not confident when a person is approaching them. It's situational for people too—someone might be confident taking an exam, but not with public speaking.

Stormy walked over. He squinted. "Well," he said. He studied them. "Well…" he said, drawing it out.

And then from around the corner came Pat Parelli. He sauntered up in his usual solid-color long sleeve shirt, with the top two holes unbuttoned, and cream cowboy hat.

"What do *you* think?" I asked him.

"You pays your fees, you takes your chances." He smiled.

I knew I wasn't going to get a serious answer, so instead of asking him a serious question, I asked: "What's your favorite color? You got a favorite color?" To most horsemen, a horse's color is just a color; it's what's inside that counts.

"Fat," he said, and I couldn't help but laugh.

Pat wandered off as Mike Major appeared. At his throat was a scar from where a bull's horn had gone through the flesh and come out his mouth. I introduced myself.

"How ya doing?" he asked. I noticed a hearing aid behind his ear.

I didn't tell him the truth. That the day before I had been feeling pretty good, I'd had that itch, but that since the fourteen-hour—thirteen pit-stops!—drive north, since arriving and meeting all the men and women I looked up to, my confidence had once again plummeted. Instead, I said, "It will be a relief to get in that round pen."

Mike tipped his hat back. "Yeah, you don't even have to think. You just get in there and let the horse tell you what to do."

And that was it for me. *That's the quote of the weekend,* I thought. I realized, of course, that what he was suggesting was simple…but not easy. The idea only worked if I was experienced enough, and if I was present enough.

Technicians were setting up screens and checking mics. Floor performers practiced their routines in the arena. A wide, elevated rotunda circumnavigated the arena and stands, and on it, men and women, cowboys and cowgirls, hustled around like worker ants, setting up booths. Booths for beer, cowboy hats, jewelry, art, boots, and saddles. At my booth, I had books. As I'd imagined all those months before, it was set up with a bookshop theme: frayed red-and-gold carpets, two deep leather chairs, a dark wooden table with a lamp on it, and bookshelves, *crammed* with books.

"I love it," I said to the faithful crew putting it together and hung out for a few minutes. I picked up a flag, then a rope, then put them down again.

"I'm going to take a lap," I said. I couldn't sit still. I was vibrating. The itch to get going, and the fear to face it, left the usual question behind: *How will I handle the pressure?*

I went back downstairs for the first competitors' meeting, led by Tammy, the Director of Operations for Morris Media Network, the producer of Road to the Horse, and the person who had invited me to be there. But just as we were about to start, it was announced that the geldings were arriving any minute.

"I know it's important to you all to watch them be unloaded," Tammy said, "so let's go take a look. We will start this meeting right after."

Two stock trailers had backed right up to the loading bay. The whole setup—from the footing and lighting to the walls and fencing—was designed for horses, and the unloading was expected to go seamlessly. But just before the event staff opened the rear trailer doors, Mike called out: "Hey, Tammy, that gate might need to be opened a little more!"

And then I noticed it as well.

The horses would travel like a stream off the trailers, taking the path of least resistance. The way this particular gate was turned was a few inches offset, and a horse might easily see it as an invitation to head in the wrong direction. The rest of us were so focused on the colts about to emerge that we hadn't noticed the problem. Only Mike had been present enough to see it. *That* was a horseman: someone who knew horses well enough that he could almost predict the future.

I was going to have step up my game a bit.

Seven young geldings unloaded from the first trailer. They stepped off, a river of black, gray, chestnut, and roan. I listened to the cowboys around me referring to the chestnuts as "sorrels," which would take me a good couple days to get used to. A sorrel is to a chestnut like a cinch is to a girth. Or a fiddle is to a violin.

All the horses were a similar size and shape—after all, they were all three years old and at about the same stage in their physical development. I couldn't tell one "sorrel" from another. There it was again, my weakness. I could tell a big colt from a small colt, and a black from a gray. But *this*…this would take some focus.

There were about two dozen of us watching, sitting on the arena fences, boots hooked around the lower rails, like cowboys in a movie. The second trailer unloaded smoothly. Eventually, I counted *nine* sorrels. All about the same height, and all about the same color. The only difference was the white markings, or lack thereof, on their legs and faces. Socks or stockings? Star or snip? Blaze or stripe? Some of the markings on their faces were unusual, so I used my old memory tricks and made up words to describe them, like someone being asked to interpret ink blots: *Butterfly. Elephant. Bat.*

The differences on the outside, to my eye, were minimal, but the differences on the inside, I knew, could be huge.

"I just wanted to tell you how much I respect you for doing this," said Ken McNabb. "It's not a part of what you do. You must be really confident to step into this arena. I mean, heck, four of the five judges are wearing cowboy hats."

We were each mounted. He was on one of his ranch horses. I was on a leggy seven-year-old Thoroughbred that had raced twice and was now training to be an eventing horse. I had borrowed the gelding from a woman named Cathy Wieschoff, a talented trainer and rider. Her other passion was drumming. Every week, she got on

Facebook Live and played along to hit songs by Sarah McLachlan, Tina Turner, Dolly Parton, Rascal Flatts, the Bee Gees.

"Thanks, Ken," I said. I was trying to let Cathy's horse settle, so I was content to sit and chat a while. "That means a lot."

I looked around. There were a few other riders in the arena as well, but I was the only one in tight pants. Road to the Horse was primarily a Western event, but it was important to me to find the right balance between appreciating the cowboy culture while staying true to who I was and the way I did things. While I would be starting my horse in a Western saddle, I had decided I would do my educational demonstration on Saturday—something each of the competitors were invited to offer outside the competition—in an English one. For the competition itself, I would be wearing cowboy boots, but also a helmet. I didn't want anything to feel forced. I knew if I was going to do my thing, it would have to be just that—*my thing*.

I had spent my whole life, and especially the past year, learning from other people. I had put myself in situation after situation that was out of my comfort zone. And now, Ken was right, I *did* need to be really confident to step into the Road to the Horse arena.

Heck, I thought, *I need to own who I am.* There was no point in being somebody else at this point. No point in pretending or imitating.

Let's see if I can be all me.

Thursday

I woke up with Brooks' feet in my face. I tumbled out of bed and slipped into my recently purchased Wranglers and boots, both of which were just broken in enough to feel both new and comfortable. Sinead and I snuck out of the hotel room, and my mother, who was staying in the room next door, tiptoed in to stay with the kids. Brooks didn't wake up.

We met Nick, Jake, and Juliette at the still-dark Alltech Arena. It was the first time we were all together in person. There were a few other people there early as well, setting up booths, turning on lights.

"I was running late," Nick began, "putting my shirt on in the hall…tucking it in in the elevator. I was surprised when the elevator stopped and a young lady was standing there, ready to get on. My belt was undone, and I had my hands in my pants…I panicked!" We all laughed as Nick continued, a still-horrified look on his face. "'Sometimes you're in a hurry, and you just have to finish in the elevator,' I told her. She just tilted her head at me, and then I realized what I had just said. 'Let me just clarify,' I added. 'Finish *getting dressed.*' And she rode down in the elevator with me."

"Who was it?" I asked, still laughing. "I bet it was someone here. Who else would be up that early?"

"I don't know," Nick said despairingly.

"Here they come," Juliette said.

One of the Pitchfork Ranch crew, mounted on his saddle horse, trotted out, followed by the fourteen three-year-old geldings, followed by two more crew, also mounted.

"It's so great to see them so relaxed," said Sinead, nodding toward the colts.

Juliette leaned forward. The horses spread out. One of them lay down to roll. Then eight more followed suit.

Horses don't learn new skills through imitation as fast as people, but they are very susceptible to *social facilitation*, when an instinctive behavior by one horse releases the same behavior in others. That was like when someone near me yawned, causing me to yawn too. When one horse plays, another is more likely to play, when one horse urinates, another is more likely to, and when one horse rolls, others may soon follow.

"I've never tried so hard to remember a group of horses," I said. "I think I already know their markings better than I do our own horses at home."

"You probably do," Sinead said. She knew full well what my strengths and weaknesses were. "Thank goodness they've numbered them."

Each horse had been assigned a number between one and fourteen, and that number had been painted in white on their hindquarters, the digits about ten inches high.

My eye kept coming back to the gray horse—maybe because he was easy for me to remember.

"I like him too," Nick said.

"So, I've got the gray as our first pick. Then Thirteen, then Eleven. Then Ten, then Fourteen."

"You're not going to have to pick last," he said.

"There's a twenty-five percent chance," I replied.

"There's a twenty-five percent chance you'll get *first* pick," he countered.

I saw Stormy and called over to him: "Any troublemakers this year?"

"Nah," he said. He had a lopsided grin.

"That's good."

"I'm like a horse," Stormy said. "I have a short memory. I don't hold grudges. Maybe a dull horse, cause there's not much flight in me. Not much fight either."

I smiled.

"Not unless you really back me into a corner, anyways."

I nodded. "Noted."

Friday

I'm like Brooks. I enjoy sleeping in. Alarm clocks are right up there with Instagram and AI-narrated audiobooks—things I wish had never been thought of.

But the Friday of Road to the Horse, I didn't need an alarm clock. I woke early and stared at the ceiling for two hours. I went through my rail work pattern over and over again. *Walk, trot, canter, left. Walk, trot, canter, right. Stop, back, turn. Dismount, pick up the feet, lead, mount.*

At breakfast I ordered oatmeal. It wasn't my favorite, but I knew it would sit the best in my stomach during the long day ahead.

Nick, Juliette, Sinead, and Jake and I reviewed our order of pick for the horses, the plan for the day, and the plan for the competition. My list of principles—the ones I'd read to the team all those months ago—flickered through my mind as we talked.

- *The horse should not know I am trying to win.*
- *Be the best prepared.*
- *We are a team.*

To consider the principles again in some ways took the pressure off, but in other ways, it put the pressure on. It put the pressure on in a way that I could control, for I could not control who won. I could only control what I did. I could not control how the horse reacted, I could not control how the crowd or judges reacted. But I could control myself. And that's what I was determined to do.

More than anything I just want to be able to leave saying I did the right thing, and I tried my best, in that order. And that's a pretty sweet feeling, actually, win or lose, when that happens.

The sky was overcast as dawn broke.

I looked out the window as we drove along Newtown Pike. On our right was a black sign with gold lettering: FASIG-TIPTON. The farm entrance had manicured hedges, a tree-lined drive, and stone walls. Another sign was a fertile green, with gold lettering: COBRA FARM. The logo was a coiled snake, also gold, wearing a three-pointed crown.

"When I first visited Lexington, most of these fences were white," I noted.

"Why did they paint them black?"

"I think they switched in 2015. It was supposed to save them fifty thousand a year in maintenance."

"Crazy."

There was already a line at the main gate to the Kentucky Horse Park. We pointed at our pass on the dash and swung down the driveway. A sign proclaimed: "HORSES ALWAYS HAVE RIGHT OF WAY."

Finally, we turned left toward the Alltech Arena. Banners hung limply on the fences leading toward it. WESTERN HORSEMAN read one. IT'S COOL TO BE A COWBOY read another.

"Let's hustle," I said as we parked. "Equipment inspection is in ten minutes."

Nick got the saddle and pad. Jake grabbed the sticks and flags. I grabbed my three lariats: one that was mine, one that I had borrowed from Jake, and the one that Cal had given me, which was the color of rosewood and felt like callused skin.

Dan James passed me in the staging area. He glanced at the ropes and laughed. "Look at all those different colors."

I smiled weakly. *Does a real cowboy have all matching ropes?* I wondered.

After the Wild Card Competition with the fillies, which CD Wilcox won, the geldings were herded back into the main arena, this time in front of the crowd. There were now four competitors: Ken McNabb from Wyoming, Donal Hancock from a remote cattle station in Australia, CD Wilcox from New Mexico, and me. We stood on the stage and drew straws to see who would get first, second, third, and fourth pick of the colts.

I drew last pick.

Each of us had sixty seconds in which to walk down onto the arena floor with the herd, and in which to make our final decision.

Donal picked the gray that I had on my list as my first pick. CD and Ken picked horses that weren't in my top four. Then it was my turn.

I walked down the stairs off the stage. I aimed for the herd as if to walk right through the middle of it, but then thought better of that plan at the last second. I swerved left and walked along between the horses and the fence line. I had narrowed my pick down to two horses, thirteen and eleven, and now I was looking for a sign.

The horses milled around, walking, flicking their tails. Then number eleven was right there. I slowed down, I eased to a stop, then I held my hand out in a relaxed fist, palm down. Number eleven stretched his neck out, reaching his nostrils toward me as if to sniff me. I let him almost touch me, then I stepped away.

I turned around and walked back through the horses, then climbed the stairs back up to the stage.

Cristo hustled up. He gave me a hug, then held me at arm's length. He kept his hands on my shoulders.

"In a difficult moment," he said, "you know how to be. And this will be a very difficult moment for them. Maybe you don't know in your brain memory, but you know in your cell memory. He will be like your child, your baby; make him feel safe. Feel his body. Feel his legs. Get all over him. Feel your soul. Let him feel your soul."

My mouth was dry. I couldn't say anything. My body was tense, as if for battle. He was right, I was feeling more stress than I had ever felt before, but I had to not let the horse feel any of it.

I hugged Cristo right back, firm.

And then Nick, Jake, Juliette, Sinead, and I walked along the concourse together. We went down the stairs toward the arena, one at a time. Music played. I felt the love of the team. *The heart of the herd is in the horse, and the heart of the horse is the herd.*

I was right on the edge.

I was ready.

Nick and I stood in red shirts beside the red round pen while the horses were herded in by the three Pitchfork cowboys.

I noticed CD Wilcox was dressed in black in the black pen, Ken was in blue in the blue pen, and Donal was in green in the green pen.

And that was the last I saw of them for almost two hours.

That was the last I heard from them for almost two hours.

"Road to the Horse fans…are you ready?" yelled The Horseman's Host.

The crowd roared.

They counted us down from ten…and I stepped into the round pen.

I carried a twenty-two-foot rope. My plan was simple.

Number Eleven looked toward the in-gate. He called to the other horses. He wasn't paying attention to what was in the round pen—he certainly was not paying attention to me.

Number Eleven was Capera Catt, a sorrel with a star, a snip, and white on all four legs. He was sired by GOODLUCK CAT and from the dam BECACO CAPERA.

My first step was to see if he could pay more attention to what was *inside* the pen than what was *outside* the pen. Even if he sniffed the ground, that was better than whinnying to the other horses, since it was closer to me. I started by playing approach and retreat.

Two minutes in I changed my plan slightly. I put the rope back and Nick handed me a lariat—the rust-colored one that Cal had given me. I lifted my arm to swing and saw the young horse's ear flick toward me. It was about as tiny a thought toward me as I had ever noticed. I stopped swinging and took a break.

Thanks, Tom Pierson, I thought. I'd caught it that time.

Four minutes in the colt looked at me. Then he took a step toward me. Then thirty seconds later he did it again. *That was it!* That was the "first line," our first bit of communication. It was more than a look—it was a word. Our first word. I grinned inwardly.

There was a long way to go, but that was a very definite, very particular, very important moment. Once it happened once, it was just a matter of seeing if I could have it happen again and again. Seeing if we could communicate, *talk*.

Number Eleven stopped and looked out. I noticed his tail flick, his neck tense. His eye was round and dark and liquid and brimming with intelligence. He was taking everything in. I jogged back and forth, one side to the other. I was like a horse at that moment, infused with some joy and some stress..and I wanted to run.

I missed a few attempts to catch Eleven with the lariat, then switched back to the twenty-two-foot rope.

At 11:36, he stood and touched my hand. A small shiver ran up my arm into the back of my neck. If love was being present, I was all in. Smitten. It felt like love always feels to me. Like emerging from crisp, cold, clean water into the feeling of the sun on my skin. I continued to play approach and retreat with the colt. Back and forth, again and again. He became more curious each time. As he became more curious, he became more confident. I saw his neck relax a fraction of an inch.

Then he turned and left. *Let him go,* I told myself. *Don't make him feel trapped.*

Twelve minutes in I was the only one not to have a rope on my horse. But he had touched me, and I had touched him. He still walked out of confusion, he still left me out of nerves, but I could relate to both, and he was looking at me more and more. Soon he was looking *into* the round pen more than looking *out of it*. He touched the back of my hand with his muzzle, and I retreated. We were building on that earlier first step toward me, that first word. Now we had our first sentence.

I love first sentences.

Once we had one, I knew more sentences would follow. I wasn't sure how long it would take, but I knew it was going to happen. I was able to take a deep breath. And when I did, time slowed down even more.

It was just me and this colt.

At fifteen-and-a-half minutes, he pushed his nose against me, the first glimmer of *him* looking to build the relationship. *Maybe I was something he could scratch on?* I softened momentarily to let him.

Then I roped him. I allowed myself a brief smile. Not being able to catch him had been one of my major fears. But immediately I remembered the words of Bruce Logan, who I'd trained with in Texas fifteen years before: "Anybody can rope a horse. It's what comes *after* that's important."

I let the rope drift. *Don't let him feel caught. Just use it to give a hint…a soft feel now and then.*

There were two "bridges" to cross next: one was touch, and the other was the proximity of my body to his body. They might seem the same, and they were related, but to some horses they were as different as a glance and a glare. The goal was to introduce one new thing at a time.

I reminded myself to hold the rope with a soft hand. *Allow the drift! Don't be quick to stop him! Don't be quick to turn him! Don't be quick to pull him!* If I stopped him too much, turned him too much, or bent him too much before I had him thinking *forward* I risked shutting him down. Horses are naturally "forward thinking," but it's something we can take out of them.

I continued to let him touch the back of my hand, and then I would retreat. "If we only retreat when horses become frustrated or upset, we teach them to become upset," Elsa Sinclair had told me. "We must retreat *before* we hit resistance, *before* they are upset. We must train our timing!"

I had trained my timing. And I was in the zone; time kept slowing down. I kept retreating *before* I hit resistance—a difference in timing equivalent to a single flap of a hummingbird's wings. Almost impossible to get perfect. There was no tell. All horses have a tell, but I strived to back off before it even showed up.

Eleven carried his head with his poll slightly higher than his withers—a neutral height. He moved in a smooth rhythm. But he hadn't looked hard at me yet; I was still constantly in his soft vision. I moved in a rhythm as well. In and out. Both our heart rates were coming down. I could sense it in him. I wasn't thinking at all; I was only watching and listening and reacting.

About twenty-five minutes in, I was able to slip a rope halter around his muzzle and behind his ears, and take the lariat rope off. I threw the lariat to Nick.

At thirty minutes in, I took our first break.

In my mind, I had broken the hour and forty-five minute session on Friday into three thirty-minute sessions, with a ten-minute break between the first two, and a five-minute break between the last two. The second thirty minutes was all about getting the young horse comfortable with my body *next to* his, *near* his, *on* his. Basically, I was focused on *taming*—taming first, training second. *Taming* meant the colt would learn to feel safe around me, emotionally as well as physically. There should be no fear, and no pain.

Another word for that was trust.

What was trust to a horse? It was him knowing that no matter what situation I put him in, it was going to end okay or better. Maybe it could even end great.

How could I build trust with Eleven? Two main ways: The first was to put him in situations where he was comfortable and have them end well. The second was to put him in situations where he was *uncomfortable*, and have them end well. I wanted him thinking, "Geez, *that's* all you wanted? I can do that!" Most of the time I put the young horse in easy situations, but I also put him in a few difficult ones. These were short-lived, and I made sure I set them up so they ended well. I stood with him as he processed each one. I gave him time to let his adrenaline leave the situation, to let his heart rate come down and his eye to soften. This was the solace that David Lichman had reminded me to let him find. I knew a relationship could be deepened by doing hard things together.

I asked Nick to pass me the blue tarp that was part of my approved kit of props, and I laid it on the ground.

After I sent Eleven over the tarp, he started to trot. I was prepared to run with him. *Quick feet. Quick feet.* I remembered the quote from *Born to Run* by Christopher McDougall:

> *Imagine your kid is running into the street and you have to sprint after her in bare feet.... You'll automatically lock into perfect form—you'll be up on your forefeet, with your back erect, head steady, arms high, elbows driving, and feet touching down quickly on the forefoot...*

Then Eleven stood, and I began to lean over his body, to slide on bareback and quickly off the other side. *On. Off. On. Off.* As my feet switched from one side of his body to the other, I switched the angle of the rope from his halter under his neck. These were two tricks to staying safe: keeping my feet close together when off the ground so they could always land together, and keeping the rope on the same side of his body as my feet so when I came down, I could tip him toward me.

The third trick to staying safe when getting on and off colts? *Always read the horse.*

The sorrel colt's body was athletic, more compact than I was used to with my eventing horses, and tough and lean from living on the range in Texas. His coat was soft. He smelled of wild sage and cypress. But it was his eyes that I couldn't get enough of. Innocent. Wary. Curious.

I lay flat on his back, stomach down, feet on his bum, arms around his neck. I reached forward and scratched under his chin. I rubbed his neck. *Rub slower,* I told myself. It was so easy to rub at the rate of human progress, when what he wanted was a rub at the rate of Mother Nature. *Slow down.*

"I believe that's called 'The Canadian Cuddle,'" I heard The Horseman's Host announce.

Next I introduced the bareback pad. It was lightweight, supple as dried mango, and easy to get on and off. The idea was that if the colt got used to the pad, getting used to the Western saddle would not be such a big deal. The smaller the steps, the easier the learning! All along I continued to pepper in touching his legs. I got to know his legs well: his hind legs with white halfway to his hocks; his front left with a white sock; his front right with just a ring of white above the hoof. His legs were tight and clean, no scars, no swelling.

"Just sprinkle it in. Just sprinkle it in," Glenn Stewart had told me. I didn't want to try to pick up his feet until he could stand quietly as I rubbed my hands down those smooth, clean legs.

With twenty-eight minutes left in the day, I faced another of my fears and saddled the colt for the first time. I had practiced it dozens of times for real, and thousands of times in my head. I had practiced for *this moment.* I knew a lot could go wrong. I took a deep breath and smoothly tightened the cinch.

It was on.

I rubbed his head, then I led him off. Then I ran away from him.

I could feel him look at me as I left him. There is almost nothing as confidence-building for a horse as something retreating away from him. *I couldn't retreat enough.*

I took a short break, found the middle of the pen, then sent him forward. He walked off, smooth as a cat, rolling his shoulders like waves on the ocean. We took another break, then I sent him off in the trot. He trotted a circle, then something set him off. Maybe he felt the girth in a different way. Maybe his tension was just rising. He started to buck.

Ideally, I would have set up the saddle and the situation enough that he didn't buck. But he did. *What should I do?*

- Option 1: Leave the round pen and let him.

- Option 2: Send him forward. It would have been my first choice a year before. Now it was my second choice. Something I would, maybe, get to later. The risk with sending the colt forward was that I might either add more fear to the situation or I might build a pattern of bucking. Or both.

- Option 3: Drift with him.

- Option 4: Pull the rope and try to shut it down.

I drifted with Eleven, not letting the rope go tight. He bucked eight times, twelve times, fifteen times. Then he let up a little, and that's when I took a feel on the rope, like a firm handshake, and turned him toward me. He stopped and looked at me.

I asked for one more step toward me. *Click for action, treat for position,* Dianne Canafax had taught us at Chicken Camp. He took a breath, tired from his romp, thinking, then licked and chewed. Licking and chewing could be interpreted in a few ways: relaxed, relax*ing*, thinking, ruminating, coming down off tension…or simply a change in the autonomic nervous system. It was a good thing to see in that moment. I rubbed him on the shoulder and the neck, then eased back beside the saddle and tightened the cinch again, just enough that it wouldn't slip.

I moved him off again at the walk, trot, and finally the canter.

With fifteen minutes left on the clock, I started thinking about riding the sorrel colt for the first time.

Just like Joe and Emer had preached in Ireland, I wanted to protect his mouth. I was going to ride him in just the halter.

With eleven minutes left I mounted and sat in the saddle. He was still, but not frozen. He was aware, but not scared. If anything, my heart rate was higher than his. I took a deep breath. I rubbed him in front of the saddle; I rubbed him behind the saddle. I took the rope to one side and tried to turn him. Nothing, just a dull resistance. I asked again. He raised his head. He braced his neck. And I realized my first big mistake of the weekend: I had not prepared him well enough to turn.

"The only thing you might have done to better prepare that moment was to teach him to turn smoother from the ground first," Jake would say to me later. "Get him to 'unwind' himself with the rope around behind him."

I stuck with it. It got better, but not good enough. The colt tossed his head in frustration. I asked Nick to come in with the flag to help. I asked with the rope, then Nick raised the flag, and Eleven scooted off. Not what I had planned. We all tried again. *Better.* As soon as he followed the rope, I leaned back in the saddle and rubbed him on his hind end. Then I gave him a slower rub by the withers. But my rubs were still too fast. *Slow it down!* I told myself.

Soon I found a good moment to hop off. But I immediately remounted and dismounted from the other side. *Keep it even.* Then I took the rope over his head, and he shied away from me. I drifted with him, but I knew I had been too quick again. *Easy,* I reminded myself.

Don't be strong.
Don't hurry.
Be smooth.
Be soft.
I took a deep breath.

With seven minutes left in the day, Eleven was walking along the rail, licking and chewing as he went. He was also blinking. "Blinking is thinking" goes the saying. Really, he felt amazing. It all felt amazing. *Be ready*, I reminded myself. *It doesn't matter how good it feels, he is still green as an unpicked banana.* He trotted off, and I grabbed the back of the saddle. I let the rope-reins drape long, and I had little control. I "let him wander" like Eric Smiley's young Irish horses. Mainly I was observing him.

Then I dismounted, removed the saddle, ran my hands down his legs. I began looking for a place where he would stand. When he offered it, I hopped on bareback. I sat up, and as I rubbed him, I looked around the arena for the first time in almost two hours.

It felt good. *Really* good.

I slipped softly off, and with a minute left, I took the colt's halter off and tied it around his neck. I rubbed him again. I wanted to create a "gray area" where I could ease out of his space. Just as we ease into a dance, we ease out of it. I didn't want anything to feel abrupt to him.

Then I took the halter off all the way and I left the pen. Nick immediately gave me a hug. I was tired and still very aware of Eleven on the other side of the fence.

The five Road to the Horse judges submitted their score cards. The high score and the low score for each competitor were dropped, the other three were added together. Then the scores for that day were announced.

Eleven and I won Friday.

I opened the invitation. Printed on thick, glossy paper, like playing card stock, was:

TALL TOPS & TOGAS
A COWBOY TOGA PARTY
Friday, March 22
The Griffin Gate Ballroom
Best Dressed Awards

It was a chance for everyone to cut loose. I was proud of my team and my family, for showing up and showing spirit. My brother Jordan made a toga out of a sheet, borrowed a pair of my cowboy boots, and curled some willow branches, stripped from a tree outside the hotel, into a crown.

He was all in.

In the ballroom, our group sat down. I took a long breath. It didn't go all the way through me, but it was enough for now.

"What was the best part of your day?" Sinead asked me.

"The meeting this morning. It felt like we were all on the same page. On the same wavelength. I drew a lot of strength from that…" I looked at her. "Also…I caught my horse."

"You have been *obsessed* with being able to catch the horse," Sinead said.

As I thought about it, the realization dawned that there wasn't a best part of the day, because the day itself was one of the best days of my life. Right up there with my wedding day.

People danced, mingled, had a few drinks. I had one bourbon. I thought a lot about Eleven, my sorrel colt.

We left the party early, but it took me hours to fall asleep. I closed my eyes and went through my plan for the next day.

Now that I had gotten to know Eleven, I could start to predict how he would react to things that I did. If the embodiment of love was *being present*, I had been totally in love all day. I felt pretty sure that the colt had been too. He didn't understand me yet, but he was *in it*. In the game. Trying to figure me out.

There was a lot I was going to have to fit in the next day. The ceiling I was staring at was almost black, but I could see Number Eleven clearly. How he moved. How he thought. What would get him curious. What might encourage him to think. Scenario after scenario played out in my mind, and in that way, I was able to practice a little more before the morning.

Saturday

"TomCatt," someone said. "Let's call him TomCatt."

I looked around the table at Nick, Jake, Juliette, and Sinead. Noëlle Floyd was there too. Noëlle was a friend from Vancouver, and also the captain of a rapidly rising equestrian media company. The kids were still snoring. My mother was watching them again.

We discussed the previous day—what was good, what could be improved—and the coming day, our plan. We were drinking hot lattes. There were three orders of eggs on the table. One order of the yoghurt and granola. I had the oatmeal again. The white tablecloth was immaculate. I laid my notebook down on it.

"I like it," I said. "TomCatt. You like it?"

The others nodded.

"TomCatt it is."

Three Pitchfork Ranch employees, mounted, with pressed white shirts and cowboy hats, herded the horses in one at a time. Three sorrels and a gray.

Eleven, now "TomCatt," trotted back and forth. He called to the other horses. He stopped. He looked into the crowd. He sniffed the ground of the round pen. He trotted again. He found himself on the far side, away from the pen gate, and he broke to the canter, back to the near side of the pen. His wide eyes took a lot in, but he didn't investigate anything in particular. He was worried. He wasn't used to being alone.

Sounds, smells, sights filled my senses. I took a breath. I looked at my horse. *You won't be by yourself much longer*. I allowed that outer world to fade away as I heard The Horseman's Host announce: "Round Two will start in TEN, NINE, EIGHT, SEVEN..." like it was New Year's Eve in Times Square. "1:45:00" was on the Jumbotron screen, next to the logo for Pendleton Whisky, one of the sponsors of the event.

I walked up to my colt. I was able to give him a scratch immediately. He looked at me and I walked away. Just like in Round One, my goal was to walk away *before* he showed worry. I wanted to be able to approach him, anytime, anywhere, and have him not feel uncomfortable about me coming into his space. In order for that to happen, there had to be a lot of times where I would retreat if he didn't feel right about me coming into his space.

As I slipped the rope over his withers, and let it fall around his neck, I heard Dan James speak to the crowd: "So often we have an expectation that when we are working with horses we want them to stand still, but the way in which Tik is working with this horse here is allowing the horse to move his feet even as he is catching the horse."

Trying to make a horse stand still before he is ready is like yelling at someone to "RELAX!" It is far better to set up the scenario that invites the horse to stand still and wait for it to happen. So I let TomCatt trot. I jogged beside him. I hustled to keep up. Short strides, quick strides—that was the trick. After a lap or so, I took the rope toward his hindquarters and turned him to face me. He licked and chewed. I wanted to rub him between the eyes, but I thought he might turn his head away, so I waited. Then I retreated. (I cannot tell you how much I regret all the times in my past when I barged into a horse's space bubble before I knew enough to be more polite.)

I was asking TomCatt to trot off when he decided to sniff the flag I'd left leaning against the side of the pen. I screeched to a halt. I let him be curious. The voice of Vicki Wilson was in my head. "You can create bravery through curiosity," she had said to me. "Curiosity is the future."

Mostly I just played nice with him for the first part of the session. I didn't want the colt to think every time I came into the pen with him it meant "work," although I did move him around a little—to the left, to the right, over the tarp. TomCatt's internal hum was a little lower than the day before; mine was not.

It was a proper second date.

Before I knew it, thirty minutes was up, and I was due for my first break. It was tempting to keep going, but I stuck to my plan. I walked out of the round pen and looked up. Nick was there to greet me.

Then I walked back into the pen, and once more I walked up and let TomCatt sniff the back of my hand, and then retreated away from him. I picked up the rope connected to his halter. I was careful not to pull on it, but to be ready to drift with him. I sent him between two barrels we had positioned in the round pen. With a little over an hour left, I reintroduced him to the saddle pad in preparation to be saddled again. Then Nick passed in a wooden platform to practice walking over, and I placed it on the ground between the barrels.

I was doing a lot. Going from one thing to another. Like the way I clean the house. Maybe I was doing too much. While Friday (Round One) had felt smooth, like a stream flowing quietly, Saturday (Round Two) was taking more turns, like a "Choose Your Own Adventure" book. *Is this the direction I want to go? This way? Or this way?*

Round One had been about really just one thing: *connection.* But Round Two was about preparing the horse for Round Three, but without ruining that connection.

It's pretty easy to have a friendship when nothing is asked of you. It's a little tougher when we need to get a few things done. As trainer Josh Nichol had once told me, "Having a relationship where you can't ask for anything difficult isn't really a relationship."

I'm not a patient person. Instead, I've honed my observation skills. When Tom Pierson told me to watch the ear instead of waiting for the eye, it was a level of nuance that was deeper than my own. Now I watch for that ear. I try to find that subtlety in every aspect of a horse's behavior. What that allows me to do is constantly notice tiny improvements. And I get excited about each tiny improvement because I know, I've seen, how quickly they add up. And so, it can appear that I'm patient because someone thinks not much is happening, but for those noticing every change in the horse, something is constantly happening. It's exciting.

It feels to me like the *opposite* of patience.

When I'm with a horse and there is no improvement for even thirty seconds, I start to become impatient. So what do I do? I see if I can make a small, or sometimes big, change in the situation, so that the horse can make a tiny improvement. I don't like waiting around while nothing is happening any more than the next guy.

One percent improvement—that's enough. If I can notice a *point one* percent improvement, that's even better.

When I worked on the backup, TomCatt got stuck. Twice, three times I had to add in a big bump, and it was ugly.

This was a result of another big mistake: I had not "peppered" the backup in soon enough and smooth enough, and now I had found myself in a dead-end alley. I knew enough not to keep going. I took a break and went back to TomCatt's feet. *First, rub. Second, have him learn to shift his weight. Third, pick that foot up. Fourth, have him learn to rest his weight in my hand.* It took a lot of trust for a horse to give me his feet. Like the "trust fall" humans do when we shut our eyes and fall into someone's arms—we have to believe someone will catch us.

At just under an hour remaining in the day's session, I had TomCatt saddled, and I got on, stayed on for a few seconds, and then stepped off the other side. I led him forward, let him settle, and mounted again.

I "tipped him" to get him to walk off. I did it with the rope, as if I was leading him from the ground. No leg. I wasn't expecting him to buck, but I was sure ready if he did. I remembered what Chris Cox had said: "If you hold on, you will always fall off. If you *ride*, you will never fall off. Riding is *offensive*; holding on is *defensive*." Inwardly, my heart raced. Adrenaline coursed through me, but I didn't want him to notice. I controlled my breathing. I softened my seat and leg. I was still, but I was careful not to freeze. I wanted him to carry a live weight, not a frozen one.

TomCatt was not turning left, though. *Should I get off? Is there a better way? A smoother way? Something I have not thought of?* I stuck with it. A snap decision. This round had seemed full of decisions I had to make quickly. I held the left rope-rein that I had attached to the halter. I waited for him to follow the feel of it. TomCatt's head was up, then left, then right. Finally, he followed it. I breathed out. I gave him a rub. At first his neck was high, then he took a breath, and it lowered an inch. I reached forward to see if I could rub him around the ears or the eyes. He looked back at me and I saw his eye. *Hello there*, I thought.

After a break, I asked him to back up again. He shook his head. Because I had not implemented the backup gradually enough, he had learned to toss his head. I was upset with myself. *Stupid!* But I needed to learn from it and continue. I finally got one good try, and I moved on. *Don't get caught direct-line thinking.*

At forty-six minutes left, while mounted, I got a canter both directions. I felt I could ask because TomCatt's shoulders were loose, his back was soft and strong, and he was thinking forward. He was thinking about me, and I was thinking about him. It was an optimal moment to try the gait, but the steering was still not good enough. When I tried to go left, he tried to go right. When I asked him to go right, he wanted to go left. In other words, he was going *against* the pressure of the rope, rather than following it.

So when I finally got a nice turn, I stepped off. I settled my arm over his neck, and I followed Cristo's advice: "Just hug him. Just be with him."

It felt good.

Then I took the saddle off, leaving it on the ground of the pen, and stepped out for our second break. *Five minutes.* I stretched. I looked around.

TomCatt stood in the middle of our red round pen. He sniffed the saddle. He lowered his neck and took a deep breath. Seeing him do that felt great.

With thirty-five minutes left, I was back in the pen. I was slightly ahead of schedule. Everything was still feeling good…maybe *too* good. TomCatt didn't have many foibles, but he was worried about having the Horseman's Stick—a four foot stick, with a five foot string attached, that served as an extension of a trainer's arm—touch his bum, so I just let it lie there so he could learn to "wear it." When he moved, I jogged with him. I had to hustle to keep up. I wanted him to know I wasn't going to shut him down too quickly.

When there was twenty-nine minutes left, I rode TomCatt out of the round pen and into the main arena. Nick opened the gate and held it for me, like a doorman at a hotel. TomCatt started trotting. Just like on the ground, I flowed with him. Elsa Sinclair had told me two things that help a stressed horse: *leadership* and *movement*. Now was the time to let him move. I kept the reins long. I compromised a lot, both on speed and on direction. I allowed him to choose a path to follow. Then I let him stop to sniff the ground.

"First you go with the horse. Then the horse goes with you. Then you go together." A great quote from one of the founding fathers of natural horsemanship, Tom Dorrance.

After a few minutes, I gradually added in turns.

Then I gradually added in gentle accelerations.

He was feeling *so* smooth, like we were a couple of leaves drifting on a breeze in the September sun. I leaned back and rubbed him behind the saddle. I let him stop by the crowd. I looked into the audience and smiled. *This was about as good as it could feel!*

Then at twenty-five minutes, TomCatt started to trot. Then he started to canter. I went with him. Then he sped up. *Uh-oh.* He started to buck. *Damn it!* He bucked again. *Here I go!*

I was catapulted off.

I had been caught not present enough.

I wasn't quick enough to grab the horn or the cantle. *It was my own fault!* I needed to be both ready *and* relaxed, at all times. And I had chosen the wrong moment to be *only* relaxed. My neck and shoulder hit the dirt first. *They will be sore later,* I thought. TomCatt continued to buck, two, three, four more times as I pushed myself off the ground. I got up quick. I checked myself. *Nothing broken.* I took a deep breath. *No tension.*

TomCatt stopped, but it was more of a freeze than him choosing to relax. His nostrils quivered slightly. He looked at me. His eyes seemed bigger, rounder. I eased back up to him, slowing or stopping each time I reached the edge of one of his space bubbles.

A minute later, I got back on. I "tipped" TomCatt off to the left. He allowed himself to be tipped. I tipped him off to the right. He followed the feel. It was a quick recovery, but I didn't risk cantering him again outside the round pen. I don't know if that was a decision I made for him, to give him more time, or if it was a decision I made for me, because I was scared I was going to get bucked off again.

Maybe it was a little bit of both.

TomCatt stopped and I rubbed his neck. I took a breath. I mentally went through the buck one more time to see if I could learn something from it. If I had been ready to grab the horn…if I had been ready to turn…if I had been ready to grab the cantle…if I had been ready to do any of those things I could have stayed on. But I hadn't been ready. And no matter how good things had felt, I should have remembered our relationship was not even three hours old. He was still prone to nerves, still subject to fear.

"There is a lot that needs to be let go in the name of the relationship," Honza Bláha had told me. TomCatt had been scared. He'd bucked. I'd fallen off. There was no need to give it more energy than that. Like Janet Jones said, "Never punish fear."

Might as well kick a dog that finally comes home.

I rode back into the round pen. Nick had set up the obstacle called the "car wash"—a frame archway with strips of plastic that hung down from the top of the frame. It was a similar question to the "Noodle Wall" we would face in the obstacle course. The goal was to teach TomCatt to walk through it. I wanted to see what I had. I thought I had built up enough trust to see what happened when I pushed the colt, but I had to be very careful that I didn't take too much out of him. Mostly, I was trying to put confidence *into* him.

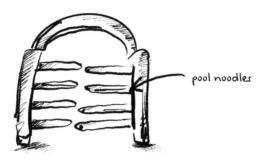

pool noodles

Then he stopped at the car wash. I closed my leg and asked again. He stopped again. I needed to offer him a higher ROR or he would get discouraged. Nick came in and pulled apart the strips of plastic to make the obstacle seem less "solid" and easier to see through. The colt and I made it through. *Good.* Then I went to turn again, and again TomCatt was confused. He felt the halter and he braced his neck and jaw against me. I held the rope-rein with my left hand and waited for him to follow it to the left. Two seconds, three seconds passed, then he followed it, and I released. It was a good place to take a break.

The young horse's reaction was an easy thing to understand. If I was playing outside and someone I didn't know tied a rope around me and pulled, my first instinct might be to brace against it as well. I'd be tempted to stand my ground. I might say, *The hell with you!*

"Only fifteen minutes remain in Round Two," the host announced. "All four competitors have now taken their first ride."

I dismounted but left the saddle on.

I sent TomCatt around at the trot, then stepped in at an angle toward his hindquarters and lifted the rope. It was the most fluid way I knew to have him turn and follow that rope without a brace. He followed the feel, smooth as cream. In a rare moment, a voice from the stands caught my ear. It was the sound of Jake's voice. Afterward,

I couldn't remember what he said—maybe it was "Yes," or "Atta'way," or "Good"—but it was a little hint that I was going in the right direction. I tipped one of the blue plastic barrels in our red round pen on its side and sat down. TomCatt raised his head. He rocked back on his heels. *This is different!* he might have been thinking. *What is this person doing?* I relaxed my shoulders. I waited.

The colt took a breath. Not the enormous dramatic one I was hoping for—the one that goes through the horse's shoulders and barrel, and is usually followed by a more relaxed neck, and licking and chewing, and blinking and thinking—but still. I'd take it. I stood back up. I wasn't quick to get in his space. I eased back in.

What next? I wondered. We had checked a lot of boxes in this session. TomCatt was tiring. Tiring mentally, tiring physically, tiring emotionally. I was too. I looked at him. His weight was balanced evenly, casually, like an outfielder waiting for the next pitch. His eye was still alert, but less wary. There were some patches of sweat on his shoulder. He looked like a young athlete. At home I would have ended our session there, but I thought maybe I could spend a few minutes working on something easy, something confidence-building, something that didn't take much physical or mental effort on his part.

What could I do that was easy? I ran my hands down his sorrel coat from his neck, over his left shoulder, and along his left front leg. I had a clear plan for the legs, and it was proceeding in a textbook manner. This was something I could do while he rested.

I stepped back on, settled softly in the saddle, and picked up the lariat. I wanted to let TomCatt see it, feel it, hear it as we wandered around the pen. I introduced it to his body and peripheral view slowly and rhythmically. Quietly. I kept it coiled. Then he eased to a halt, and I let a loop form. I swung it on one side, then swung it on the other side. *So far, so good.* At some point the next day, in Round Three, we would need to drag something. Each competitor had been given a rope tied to a stuffed animal to use in practice. (Mine was a unicorn, white with a rainbow mane and tail.) I had little experience with a lariat, and I had almost no experience with dragging things from horseback. But I knew enough to know it could all go wrong pretty quickly.

With under three minutes remaining TomCatt perked up. I hadn't planned on asking for the canter again, but he felt ready to offer it. His walk was smooth, and his trot was lively. I weighed the pros and cons quickly.

- *Cons:* We were both tired. He might buck.
- *Pros:* He felt ready to offer it, and I didn't want to ignore that.

I decided to face my fear and ask for the canter. I knew that if I got it today, there was a chance it would help me tomorrow. If it went well, TomCatt would remember it as something positive, maybe even fun. And if it went well, *I* would remember it as something positive, and maybe even fun. We both needed it.

And if it didn't go well.... If he did buck.... Well, it was high risk, high reward. The decision was probably the biggest risk I would take all weekend.

Sometimes you have to take a chance. An educated chance, anyways.

He sped up. He trotted faster. And then he was cantering. Normally, I would have tried in both directions, to keep it even, but instead, I just hopped off, rubbed him, and removed the saddle.

With one minute left, I lay across the colt's back. Then I swung a leg over and sat on him bareback. I slid off, undid the halter, and let it and the rope slide off, but stayed next to him. I rubbed his withers. At that moment he took the big sigh I had been waiting for earlier. He lowered his head and licked and chewed. His eye softened. I wished I could have stayed in the pen with him longer. Just to spend some undemanding time together. Just to hang out, like two horses resting near each other, flicking our tails at flies, peaceful. Instead, I glanced at the clock. Then I left TomCatt and stepped out of the round pen with six seconds left.

TomCatt and I won Saturday.

"Best and worst," said Sinead.

We went around the table. I was last.

"The team was my best…. You guys. Thank you." I looked at Nick, Jake, Juliette, and my wife. "The worst…was feeling a little lost about halfway through."

I tried to explain what I meant. On Friday I had been in the zone one hundred percent, and I had never questioned what was next. But that day, Saturday, I had run into a few places where I'd had to think. *Do I do this or that? Work on the tarp or the backup? Canter or rest?* I had still been in the zone, but it hadn't been as playful or as smooth as the first day. It had felt more like the play of an adult and a horse than the play of a kid and a pony.

That evening most of the team went to a party, but Sinead and I went to get Brooks and Violet from Jordan and Robin, and then we planned to have an early night.

At the campground, we found Robin watching the three kids while Jordan was manning the grill. I hugged them both. "Thank you *so* much."

My brother flipped a burger. "A bunch of people congratulated me on their way back here after the competition," he said. "They thought I was you."

I laughed.

"You were really good today," he said.

I hugged him.

On the car ride back to the hotel, Sinead and I listened as our kids told us all about the campground. My brother had taught them both how to climb a tree and had taught Brooks how to use a knife.

I glanced at Sinead, wondering how she was taking this admission. She widened her eyes at me. I smiled and shrugged.

Back at the hotel, with the kids in pajamas, Sinead offered a trade: "I'll watch the kids if you go downstairs and grab us a couple drinks."

"Deal."

I ordered a Kentucky Bourbon Barrel Ale for myself, and vodka soda for Sinead. While I waited, I looked around the bar. Lots of drinking. Some food. About ninety percent of the patrons looked like they had just come from the Horse Park. I saw Pitchfork Ranch vests, Road to the Horse t-shirts, and quite a few cowboy hats.

A few people waved or came up and shook my hand. There were two or three calls of, "Congratulations!" from a rowdy crowd of middle-aged women. I breathed it all in.

Then I paid for my drinks and went upstairs to my family.

Sunday

I woke at three in the morning.

Thirty minutes later, I rolled over. "Sinead," I whispered. "Are you awake?"

"I am now."

"I can't sleep."

"Think about your breathing," she said.

"Thanks," I said. *I am so far past the point where thinking about my breathing is going to help,* I thought.

"Or read a book," she whispered. "Just don't keep going through the skills, the techniques." She rolled away from me.

A dim glow from the lights in the parking lot allowed me to see the shadow of the bed next to ours. I could just make out the silhouettes of the kids.

Goldfish was near the edge of the bed, closest to Sinead. Before Road to the Horse, our daughter had never slept in a regular bed before—always a crib with sides. Brooks slept next to her, also a first. I could just make out the shape of his head, his delicate cheeks, his cute nose.

At seven, my mother again snuck in to watch the kids, and Sinead and I went downstairs for breakfast. Just like the previous two days, Nick, Juliette, Jake, and Noëlle joined us. The tone alternated between technical and serious, and joking and light. It felt like their presence created a shield that enveloped and protected me… and TomCatt.

As we headed to the car, Nick gave me a purple, pocket-size spiral notebook.

"Read this when you're in the waiting room," he said.

I put it in my back pocket. I looked him in the eyes. "Thanks, Nick. You have been amazing. I could not have asked for more from you."

It was Sunday, so we began with a prayer. Matt West, The Horseman's Host, removed his hat. For the first time I noticed he was balding slightly. Not as much as me, but enough that I felt a kinship with him.

"Our Gracious and Heavenly Father," Matt began. His voice was deep and rich. I bowed my head. "We come to you today, thankful for so many blessings you've given us. But thankful first and foremost for the life that you created for all of us. Today, Father, we ask that you put your hand of protection over this arena. We pray that you continue to be with these incredible horses, these horsemen, and all the folks that have traveled to be here with us this week."

Most of the men and women in the audience looked down. Some of them sat. Many removed their hats and held them against their chests. I stood with my arms at my sides, listening. Present. Thankful.

I wondered if our faith determined how we worked with horses. Were horses created *for* us? Did they have a God-given role to play for us? Do we have a responsibility to look after them? Or did they end up the way they are, and we end up the way we are, simply through millions of years of evolution and coincidences?

Fate or chance? Or something in between?

Next were the national anthems: the Australian, followed by the Canadian, and then the American.

The four competitors were invited onstage and introduced. The scores were read. I had a lead, but not an insurmountable one.

"Anything can happen in this final performance," said Matt to the crowd.

"We've seen that time and time again," agreed Dan James.

Then the officials, judges, and competitors all walked the final course. The rail work was first: Walk, trot, and canter both ways. Stop. Back up. Turn both directions. Dismount. Pick up the feet. Lead forty feet. Then re-mount.After that, we were to navigate the obstacles:

1. Serpentine Poles
2. Raised Walk (Zigzag)
3. Pinwheel
4. Tarp
5. Ground Poles and Jumps
6. Noodle Wall
7. Rope Swing
8. Rope Drag
9. Gate and Box
10. Mystery Obstacle
11. Bonus Mystery Obstacle
12. Freestyle

Competitors would get a score between "0" and "5" for each component of the rail work and each obstacle. We also got overall scores on things like: "Forward Motion," and "Clarity of the Message," and "Clinician's Demeanor." We were allowed to ask questions about the obstacles and how they would be judged, but for the most part we were all quiet. We were all nervous.

While for the first two days, we had all been competing at the same time, in the same arena, next to each other, on this final day, Sunday, we would compete one at a time in front of the audience, while the others waited backstage.

And in reverse order of go.

Which meant TomCatt and I would go last.

So the Wildcard competitor, CD Wilcox, stayed above ground, while Ken McNabb, Donal Hancock, and I were led to a windowless room backstage. No phones were allowed. There was a "zero communication with the outside" rule. If we had to go to the bathroom, we had to ask permission from one of the two "guards" who was then tasked with escorting us there and back.

In that room the three of us sat. We said a few things to each other, told a couple stories, but mainly, we just waited our turn. We could hear the crowd now and then when they clapped and cheered.

After an hour or so they came and got Ken. An hour after that, they fetched Donal. And then, an hour later, I was led up the ramp and let loose into the arena.

TomCatt stood in the round pen. I studied him. I looked at the set of his head, the rhythm of his walk, his eye. I knew him better than I knew most horses after a month. We had been through more together already than I'd experienced with most horses in my lifetime.

I was introduced. I waved to the crowd, and then everything outside the round pen became a blur.

It was just TomCatt and me.

I walked up to him. I held out my hand; he touched it gently with his muzzle. I backed away, retreated, then I approached again. He touched my hand a second time. I heard the rhythm of his breathing.

I approached a third time and haltered him. He moved, but I was ready, and I drifted with him. Within ninety seconds I could lie on him. I brought out the flag. First, I let him follow it. Then I moved him around with it. TomCatt jumped ahead. He turned left. He was looking to me even more than yesterday, but he was also more anxious than yesterday.

Why?

I checked myself. Was my energy bringing it out in him? No, I didn't think so.

Maybe it was because he was the only horse in the arena for the first time?

I needed to ask myself: *How will that affect things? How can I help him? How can I make sure he looks to me?* With more anxiety he would have more energy, more movement, which wasn't so bad. But I would have to keep looking for relaxation. I would have to work hard to keep his trust.

I let him stand. I rubbed his legs.

I took the rope around him, then unwound him with it. I let him stop and think and process. I fetched the Western saddle and pad that Nick had placed within reach before the round began. I slipped them on the colt's back. As I snugged the cinch, I felt his body tighten. This told me the TomCatt was still worried about the saddle. I would have to find that razor-thin line between getting him going forward and letting him relax and stand still.

We were in the zone, but still, time flew by. It was like water on hot cement, evaporating before my eyes.

TomCatt's eyes were gradually softening. He started to glance at me more, not past me or through me. Then his eyes developed a soft glow as he really looked *at* me. He blinked; he licked and chewed.

I knew he was trusting me, but would it be enough? Would it be enough *in time*?

The first two days had been about time management, but Sunday was time management on steroids. I had to make decisions every few seconds about where to spend time and how long to spend there.

With five of my twenty minutes of round pen time left, I mounted. I had left it a little late, but I kept moving. I held my hands high and wide. I stayed back in the saddle and asked for the trot, then the canter. I wanted him to experience it inside the round pen before we moved to the main arena for the rail work.

I got the canter both directions, then with just over three minutes to go, I hopped off. I was battling the clock, and I knew it.

I didn't want him to know it.

I stepped back into the saddle, then stepped down again. Tom-Catt was still moving a lot, which was the only thing that was a little unexpected. It didn't feel like a huge issue, but I noted it. Once I had the canter in both directions, I went ahead and left the round pen with one minute still left on the clock.

For the next thirty-five minutes, I knew I would be trying to find the balance between the ethical considerations of going at the speed of my colt, and trying to win. It was an awareness that I had with every horse I rode; it was a consideration that Sinead and I talked about at the end of each day on our farm. The question existed in tiny moments every day, for every person who handled a horse: *I'm late for work, but he needs to cross this puddle to get to his stall—how fast do I go? She doesn't want to stand still right now, but I need to groom her—do I make her? He won't get on the trailer and we need to leave—do I increase the pressure?*

The biggest difference between Road to the Horse and the questions I asked myself every day was that now I was facing them in front of a live audience.

We stopped at the far end, away from the in-gate. TomCatt licked and chewed again. My body was tense. My heart rate was high. Neither were good on the back of a green horse. I took a breath. I thought about the process. I thought about my team. I reminded myself that this part of the weekend was where I had the most experience, and I was prepared. I relaxed my muscles. My heart rate came down.

I remember no sense of enjoying myself in that arena or not; no sense of being scared, or not. I was just focused. That was it. I was constantly reading TomCatt and adjusting my plan in thousands of small ways. I was completely present in that space with just him.

I asked TomCatt for the canter as we headed toward the in-gate. We got it. But then we got a little stuck at the end of the arena. I closed my leg, brought my energy up, clucked, tapped, clucked, tapped, using a short stick on his hindquarters, quietly, predictably; I didn't want to catch him by surprise. We made it back to the opposite end, and I gave him a break: I let him stand, I gave him a rub. By letting him rest away from the in-gate, I hoped to "even out" the arena, getting rid of his draw to the gate and making his world more neutral.

Then I started declaring. When I was ready for a required movement to be judged, I announced to the judges that we were about to perform it. For example, "I declare my left trot." As I rode my shirt came untucked, and my jeans rode up above my boots, but I didn't notice right then. What I did notice was that TomCatt was freeing up in his "sticky" places, like the in-gate. He looked ahead more and more. He was becoming more and more comfortable with me on his back. What we had going was the start (just the start!) of a *partnership*. I caught glimpses of it. Glimpses of us doing things *together*.

I dismounted and picked up all four of his feet. One at time. It went smoothly. It might have been the skill I had prepared the best. I was proud of both of us. I tucked my shirt in and then said, "I'd like to declare my mount," before stepping back into the saddle.

Then we headed to the obstacles.

The first three went smoothly. Almost perfectly. Then we came to the large blue tarp branded by "Platinum" in white letters and laid out flat in the dirt for us to walk over. TomCatt stopped. I turned away. We came back and he stopped again. We turned away from it a second time. He flew to his right. Then he became anxious and started to trot, so I changed my plan on the fly. I left the obstacles totally, and we trotted and cantered around the whole arena. One of my biggest worries was losing his willingness to go forward, and I knew I had just lost some of what I had put into the colt's Forward Bank Account, probably a little from his Trust Bank Account too. I needed to top those accounts back up. Give him something easy to do, something he could do well. Trot and canter!

Then we went to the jumps.

At the jumps he hesitated, but I was ready, and I let his neck go long. This was the obstacle I was most practiced at. I knew that a long neck would give him balance and confidence and draw him forward. I had been teaching horses to jump for thirty years.

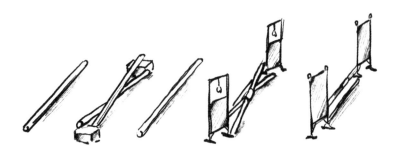

At the "Noodle Wall," TomCatt stopped immediately. The obstacle was similar to the "Car Wash" I had set up for him the day before. Both asked the same question: Can you push through this when your rider asks and emerge on the other side? But they were different enough that he wasn't connecting what he had learned on Saturday with what he was seeing on Sunday. We walked around the Noodle Wall, then returned to the front and stopped, facing it head-on. He touched it with his nose, but showed no signs of understanding it was something he could go through. He touched it again. I rubbed him.

The crowd was silent. I tried one more time even though my gut told me no, because his eye was soft. He moved forward through the Noodle Wall a couple inches. I then broke one of my own rules and pushed when he was trying his hardest. He backed up.

I regretted what I had done immediately.

I left the obstacle and went to the next one. I needed to get the ROR up again, give him some confidence. So I picked up the lariat. I swung it, and he was quiet. No tension. I replaced it where it hung. *Good. Check.*

Next, we were to drag a chariot the size of an average garden wheelbarrow by a rope. A stuffed unicorn like the one we had practiced with was strapped to the front of the chariot. TomCatt was worried. I quickly dropped the rope.

"Five minutes remaining," the host announced.

He didn't want to go near the next obstacle—the gate. Then he started to buck. I stayed on. I took a breath. *Easy,* I told myself. *I need to get him thinking forward again,* I thought. So we went for a trot, and he felt better. Then I took him back to the gate. He was more curious about the gate the second time. But I wasn't willing to push any harder there. With three minutes left I dismounted and led him through the gate. He was nervous, but he was trying. He was trusting me.

"Two minutes," I heard over the loudspeaker as I closed the gate. I could have left it there. I *should* have left it there.

Instead, I got on TomCatt one last time.

There were five rings to move from one hook to another: yellow, green, black, blue, and red. With fifty seconds left, we headed to hang them…and TomCatt started to buck.

I held on. He stopped bucking. I gave him a rub. I closed my legs gently, asking him to go forward again, and he bucked again. Then again. Then again. The crowd held its breath.

"Time has expired," echoed through the arena as TomCatt bucked one more time.

I stayed on and the crowd stood up and cheered.

But it was not the way I wanted to finish the weekend. Not at all.

Someone took TomCatt from me; I don't remember who. Stormy probably, with his quiet demeanor and lampshade mustache. Without TomCatt, without a purpose, I began to let go. I was steered backstage, and I immediately crumbled onto the dirt and leaned against a wall. People and horses milled around. No one spoke to me. I didn't know how the others had done. I didn't know how *I* had done. I didn't know how the judges had scored any of us. All I knew was that a wave of utter exhaustion, nine and a half months in the making, swept over me.

Sinead spotted me from a doorway, rushed over and crouched next to me. She put a hand on my shoulder. "You look white," she said.

"White?"

She sat down in the dirt next to me. "Are you okay?"

"I don't know."

Ken, Donal, CD, and I rode into the main arena. For this ceremony I was on a gray Quarter Horse that I had borrowed from Dan James, as Cathy's Thoroughbred had been returned to her.

The scores were announced.

TomCatt and I had won the third day as well.

Which meant no math was needed. We had won the whole thing.

I had won the World Championship of Colt Starting.

There was a victory gallop, and as I cantered around the arena, I took my helmet off for a few strides and waved to the crowd. I beamed at my parents. I saw Sinead and Brooks and Goldfish, and I felt so happy I felt sad. I saw Nick, and Jake, and Juliette clapping. I waved to them.

I dismounted and walked up on stage. Hands appeared in front of me to shake. Another giant check was presented to me.

When it was my turn to speak, I thanked everyone I could think of. Then I paused.

"I think probably the biggest thanks goes to…my horse and, um, hold on…" Tears had gathered in the corners of my eyes. Wet drops slid down my cheeks. I was overwhelmed.

What I felt for TomCatt was a sharp love, biting, like a teenage affair during summer vacation. The two lovers meet, they spend every waking moment together; at night they lie awake dreaming about the other. Then all too soon vacation is over. Back to school, back to work. Their young minds had not planned for the end.

I held my hand to my face. I took a breath. "This horse owes me nothing…" I said as best as I could. "There is nothing that he owes me. If he didn't do something, it's because I didn't teach him, or I didn't train him, or I didn't earn his respect, or I didn't earn his trust. He gave me everything he had, and I just want to thank him the most."

Then Brooks, Goldfish, and Sinead came up on stage. Brooks carried his green snake stuffy. Goldfish stared with big eyes. Sinead wore a white Team Canada shirt. She looked so good. Then Nick, and Jake, and Juliette came up. Then my parents. Then the crew who helped with my booth.

Matt West, the Road to the Horse Horseman's Host for 2024, had one last thing to say:

"Let's celebrate our newest World Champion, *Tik Maynard!*"

We had been under a spell, but I knew it couldn't last forever. We had a flight to catch.

I gave Nick a hug goodbye.

"Did you read the note?" he asked.

Oh my god. My hand reached for my pocket. I had forgotten.

I opened the purple notebook on the plane.

It's the homestretch. I thought you might want some company in your solitude. I want to remind you to breathe, to take little moments to appreciate and revel in the experience you are having and the one you are about to have in the arena shortly. If you are nervous, embrace it. Breathe it in, soak in it, and breathe it out.

Let it out and breathe in the amazing moments we've all had. Remember to go slow when you want to go fast. Remember to be grateful to TomCatt, he will be there for you. If he is worried, it is not a fear of consequence or of you, it is simply the fear of the unknown—and in that you and he are brethren.

I am so. Incredibly. Proud of you. Proud to be a part of the team, and so grateful for not just this experience, but for ev-

erything you have given me. Curiosity. Strength. Knowledge. Courage. Thank you, Tik. Go, Tik. Go and do what you do best and inspire.

Love, Nick

The note was written all in capital letters, and Nick's penmanship was deliberate and gentle.

The fourth page held an equipment list for the round pen:

- *Bareback pad.*
- *Saddle.*
- *Up one hole on back.*
- *5' flag, 4' flag, flag with baggie.*
- *Horseman's stick.*
- *Dressage whip.*
- *Rope halter with 12' rope and 22' rope.*
- *Rope with ring.*

The rest of the notebook was empty.

After

Tuesday, we hit the ground running. Back to school for the kids, broken fences, paperwork, lessons.

"Are you going to do it again?" one of my students asked.

"Don't ask him that," another student said. "That's like asking a woman who just gave birth if she is going to have a second kid."

"Well, I don't know if it's like *that*," I countered, looked down, "but it *was* the most emotionally exhausting experience of my life."

I had no real time to reflect or talk about what had happened in Kentucky until I called Nick on my evening walk. I was in jeans and bare feet. The wind blew at my t-shirt. Ferdinand ran ahead. I lit a cigar.

"So many feelings," I said. "I'm proud of the job I did. I really prepared for this. But the support I received from so many—I feel undeserving of that. I feel not good enough. But it makes me want to be better. To be deserving. I guess I want to be better at everything: better competitor, better horseman, better person."

I walked to the end of the road, touched the gate, turned for home.

"I could have used a week to just hang out and unpack the experience," Nick said. "And then I get home and there is such a stark contrast between my passion for training animals, and what I'm doing."

I winced. I wished he had come back to Florida with me to train horses, instead of Wisconsin to renovate decks and bathrooms. But Nick had a young family, and he was making decisions that had repercussions beyond just him now. He was a good horseman; he was a great person.

I again pondered the question I'd asked myself when I'd begun my Road to the Horse journey: could someone be a *good horseman* without being a *good person*? Of course, would have been my answer before this year. Horses don't care how we treat other humans; they care how we make *them* feel. But now I wondered, maybe being a good horseman *encompassed* being a good person. It all depended on how I defined the word. Could I just make up my own definition?

I could. I did.

Nick was Exhibit A.

I had an email from Martin Black. "After watching all the horses and the other guys," he said, "it's pretty obvious to me why you won. It's not easy to take the time to save time. Especially in a competition with a clock. Wyatt Earp proved a cool head and steady hand was more important than being quick. I think of that often with livestock. You had way more break time and got way more done.... I could see your little horse coming out tomorrow and in a short amount of time advancing to a nice useful horse at whatever level. They can't all win first place, but the training shouldn't determine the loser."

I was incredibly proud to have Martin's approval…and to be compared to Wyatt Earp. But mainly life just carried on, as it does.

I took Sam to the Kentucky Three-Day, where I was in the moment for dressage, and then in cross-country I went out too fast and had a run out. I made the same mistake I had always struggled with: a part of me was looking more at the scoreboard than at my horse.

I had regressed. *How many times do I need to be given a lesson before I learn it?*

Then Sam and I went to Tryon, and there we did much better than we had at Kentucky. I stayed more in the moment, more focused on the process. I stopped thinking about winning and started thinking about getting better, getting my horses better.

It had all come together for me.

Why? Was it the preparation? The love? The being present? The high involvement, low attachment?

It was, of course, a combination of things.

I think, in the end, it was most of all about one question: Could I just be me, *totally me*, for one weekend? Could I be the best version of myself for three straight days in a row?

My performance at Road to the Horse had been far from perfect. There were things I would do differently, knowing what I know now. But I had prepared with my whole heart, and I was present the whole time. To give anything less than that would have been unfair. Unfair to myself, unfair to the people who had invited me, unfair to the people that came to watch, and most of all, by far, unfair to TomCatt.

To give less than my best would have been to snub my nose at an immense opportunity, a great gift.

On the third of July, 2024, Road to the Horse announced I would be returning in 2025 to defend my title.

On the ninth of July, I was trail running on the Sunshine Coast in British Columbia, flying down the hill, jumping over rocks and wooden steps, when I caught my left toe and hit the ground with a heavy thud.

I broke my left arm in three places near the elbow. *Bloody hell*, I thought. *Here we go again.*

But the question was now presented: Would I be able to repeat the mindset that I'd had at Road to the Horse in 2024? History is rife with examples of athletes, authors, singers, and actors who have pulled off a superb performance in one game, or at one event, and then never been able to repeat it. In many ways, finding the right mindset is simpler for an "underdog"—there is something raw, gritty, and pure about his state of being.

"It's tougher to defend a title than to win one," goes the old saying.

I decided that if I accepted the challenge, if I went back, then I would try to ignore expectations and approach the competition with the same principles, presence, and humility as the first time. I needed to prepare as thoroughly as I had the year before. But mostly, I needed to *not* try to defend a title. The idea of a "title" would loom over my preparation like a dark cloud. I needed to not look up at the cloud, just to focus on the horses in front of me. That was the almost impossible mission of "high involvement, low attachment." I must care deeply about the process and not at all about the outcome.

There are many parts of starting horses that don't come easily to me. Many of the fears I began the journey with I still have. The only part that doesn't intimidate me is the work. I'm looking forward to the work. Most horse people are like that. We wish there were more hours in the day to slog away.

I love beginnings. First words. First sentences. Middle ones are good too—they have all the substance and laughter. Last sentences, though—endings—can be so sad. The end is so difficult to get right.

After Road to the Horse, I purchased TomCatt from the Pitch-fork Ranch. He is living with Sinead's retired horse Tate, my retired horse Sapphire, and my mother-in-law's retired horse Margaret. The four of them have about six acres of grass to roam. I take TomCatt out to play in the round pen a few times a month. I have only ridden him three times since Road to the Horse.

We're not in a hurry.

Acknowledgments

Thank you:

Sinead for being a better wife and mother than I imagined was possible when we married. Raising Brooks and Goldfish with you has been, and continues to be, the best experience of my life. That we are managing to do it while we keep all these other balls in the air is in large part a testament to your strength, and to the community you have gathered around us. You are a relentless seeker. You push me to be a better person. I'm so impressed with, and proud of, your talents as a rider, competitor, coach, mentor, writer, podcaster, commentator, selector...

> *You're scared of heights and oceans*
> *and the end of time.*
> *You don't surf the waves*
> *or ski the hills*
> *or solo climb.*
> *But you chase your dreams,*
> *And you're willing to change.*
> *I've never met a fearful person*
> *so brave.*
> *I just can't get enough of you.*

You are the rainbow after the rain. You... (I know, I know, you stopped listening five minutes ago. Okay, let's keep going...)

Brooks and Goldfish for just being you. *Entirely you.* That's enough, and it will always be enough. I love you.

Telf, Tash, Justin, Callie for supporting from afar. Telf for proofreading and for sharing a cigar with me now and then. Tash for inspiring me with your Ironman performance. Justin and Callie for being just awesome! I'll see you at RTTH in 2025.

Jordan, Robin, Mera—Jordan for running and asking the right questions. Robin for all the child support, and being a great supporter of my brother. Mera for playing with Brooks and Goldfish.

Mum. What can I say to my mother that hasn't been said before? (Because what has been said before probably isn't appropriate to print here.) You have unconditional love for your children, and if I have learned one thing from you that I want to bring to my family, that is it.

Dad for going with me to RTTH in 2023, then for thoughtfully saying I shouldn't compete there myself, and then supporting me totally when I did anyways. I still think about all the lessons you gave me, and the number of times you let me ride and compete on your horses when your career would have been better served if you had ridden them. I'm curious to see if I will be as selfless as you if my kids get into horses.

David O'Connor, also for thoughtfully saying I shouldn't compete at RTTH, and then showing up as a judge. There are two ways to create change in the horse world, judging from the outside, or toiling thanklessly away from the inside. David, like a lot of characters in this book, has chosen the latter. So let me give him at least one thank you: *Thanks, DOC!*

Bernadette, my mother-in-law, but not *just* a mother-in-law. And Jim, supporter, friend, visionary.

Greg, Niki, Teddy, Sidna, Holt, Sybil, Talula. Also in-laws, but not just in-laws. *Family*!

To everyone who discussed and practiced colt starting with me, or who inspired me on the road to Road to the Horse: Glenn Stewart, Jake Biernbaum, Dan James, Ryan Rose, Jonathan Field, Kathy Baar, Monty Roberts, Buck Brannaman, Martin Black, Joe, Emer, Elsa Sinclair, Honza Bláha, Ren Hurst, Eric Smiley, Mary Kitzmiller, David Lichman, Linda Parelli, Chris Cox, Pete Rodda, Stacey Westfall, JR Robles, Vicki Wilson, Josh Nichol, Shawna Karrasch, Pat Parelli, Janet Jones, Warwick Schiller, Linda Boggs, and all those I have unintentionally forgotten. While I learned a lot from all these men and women, any mistakes I made were mine alone.

To Westfälisches Pferdestammbuch for hosting us one afternoon.

To everyone who came to Chicken Camp and our fearless leader Dianne Canafax.

Cristo, Oscar, Flor, Abril, and the kids. Thanks for being the most welcoming hosts I can imagine. Argentina was simply wonderful.

Amanda, for watching RTTH with my Dad and me in 2023, and continually offering encouragement since then.

Cal, for the rope.

Natalie, for being present, and for a smile that I could hear on the phone.

Rachel, for using that dull stainless-steel blade on my groin. Burt, as well, for the dry needling. *It hurt.*

Noëlle, for believing in me, for helping me learn to pivot, and for not just talking the talk, but walking the walk, putting your money where your mouth is.

Talk *is* cheap, to everyone that gets out there and takes a chance.

Abisaí, Lucia, Zury, Betsua, Danna—for your help. I hope one day to be able to visit your coffee shop in Costa Rica.

Allisson, the kids love you. Please visit again soon.

Rae, for being so present with the kids—they love you. (And the wedding photos are amazing!)

Matt, for flying over to visit, *twice. (*And thanks, Hanna, for allowing him.) When's the wedding?

While I was getting ready for Road to the Horse, and writing, our team of riders, students, staff, and supporters kept everything going. Thank you, Nate, Erica, Jace, Cat, Kelsey, Olivia, Kayleen, LeeAnn. Thanks to Lindsey, the most loyal help we have ever had. You're part of the family now too. Lauren, how could we do any of this without your assistance from Wisconsin? You are all amazing!

Our syndicate members and supporters: Brenda Jarrell, Paula Shook, Debbie Smicka, Dr. Angie Yates, Betsy Goodwin, Kathy Happ, Sarah Jaycocks, Kate and Art Schaeffer, Dean and Brigitte Flint, Mary Beth Gordon, Julia Strawbridge, Alison and Justin Osborne, Rebecca and Brian Hamaoui, Bryan Baldwin, Bernadette, and Mandy Pope.

To Mary Beth for acquiring three horses for me to start. And to Donna for hosting a clinic with Glenn Stewart and supporting in many other ways as well. (Glenn, those ten days were just what I needed!)

To Yvonne Barteau and her Horses Without Humans Rescue, for hosting a simulation with two of the organization's rescue horses.

To everyone who took wonderful photos of the week at RTTH. Haley— for the sizzle real and the cover photos.

Erik Schmidt (Offshore Artwork), for the wonderful drawings you see in this book.

Mary Alice Monroe for the words of encouragement, her books, and for recommending I read Pat Conroy.

To everyone who chipped in to buy me a cowboy hat, I love it and appreciate you all.

My Road to the Horse team: Nick, pen wrangler, animal trainer, friend. I look forward to many more projects and ski trips with you. Jake, it would be easy to take such a world class coach for granted when you live just down the road. I don't. Juliette, you are always there when we need help. Smart and witty. I can't wait to see what's next for you. Sinead, a woman who can read both horses and husbands.

Tammy and Stormy and Dan and Matt and the whole Road to the Horse crew, volunteers, and organizing committee. You put on one hell of a show. Thank you.

To the sponsors of Road to the Horse, and to the Pitchfork Land and Cattle Company. You breed some nice horses.

To my "Booth Team": Chelsea, Donna, Morgan, and Maddie in 2024. In 2025, Kelsey, Chelsea, Sarah, Mary Hurston, and Bonnie. Thanks!

To the Trafalgar Square Books team: Martha, for believing in this book and seeing it through. Rebecca, for the editing, the layout, and dozens of other details…also for asking the tough questions—you are brilliant. I look forward to working with you again.

Making time to write felt impossible. It was Sinead's idea, in May 2023, for me to raise money in order to take the hours away from the business to work on a book. But who was actually going to write a check for me to *write*? Well, these people did: Jon Boldt, Lisa Hartzband, Lesley Elston, Martha Wolfe, Art Davidson, and Zib Thieriot—thank you from the bottom of my heart.

ACKNOWLEDGMENTS

In July 2023, Sinead and I flew to Boston with Debbie Smika, had lunch on the patio at ReelHouse, overlooking the harbor, then drove to Lake Pearl in the scenic town of Wrentham for a sunset fundraising gala. Thank you to the Lorusso family for hosting. Thank you to Casey Smith and Helena Harris for organizing. Thank you to everyone who dressed up and came on out to support us. That was a fun evening!

Later, Kathy Happ, who, as if sent by heaven, more than matched what everyone else had come up with. Her support kept me going. It allowed me to travel to Chicken Camp and to Argentina to study, but it was greater than that... it was like...like she believed in me. And that's what *really* kept me going. That is one of Kathy's great gifts: to believe in people. Kathy is currently undergoing chemotherapy—please consider donating to the Lynn Sage Breast Cancer Foundation in Chicago.

Judy Miller, thanks for hosting a Wednesday evening get-together when we arrived in Lexington. Your home is beautiful. What a way to start the week!

Cathye Bouis, thank you for helping me purchase TomCatt. It's also because of you that I can continue this journey with him. Liberty, reining, ropin', ranchin', working equitation, competitive trail—we are going to do it all. Thanks, Cathye. You are an amazing horsewoman and an amazing person.

Lastly, last, last, but far from least, thank you, TomCatt. Just like the thank you to my kids, thank you for nothing else other than being you.

Entirely you.